Marketing Strategies

PEARSON
Education

We work with leading authors to develop the strongest educational materials in marketing, bringing cutting-edge thinking and best learning practice to a global market.

Under a range of well-known imprints, including Financial Times Prentice Hall, we craft high quality print and electronic publications which help readers to understand and apply their content, whether studying or at work.

To find out more about the complete range of our publishing, please visit us on the World Wide Web at: www.pearsoned.co.uk

Marketing Strategies

A Twenty-first Century Approach

Ashok Ranchhod

**With contributions
from Julie Tinson
and Claire Gauzente**

 **Prentice Hall**
FINANCIAL TIMES

An imprint of **Pearson Education**
Harlow, England • London • New York • Boston • San Francisco • Toronto • Sydney • Singapore • Hong Kong
Tokyo • Seoul • Taipei • New Delhi • Cape Town • Madrid • Mexico City • Amsterdam • Munich • Paris • Milan

Pearson Education Limited

Edinburgh Gate
Harlow
Essex CM20 2JE
England

and Associated Companies throughout the world

Visit us on the World Wide Web at:
www.pearsoned.co.uk

First published 2004

ISBN 0 273 65192 7

British Library Cataloguing-in-Publication Data
A catalogue record for this book can be obtained from the British Library.

Library of Congress Cataloging-in-Publication Data

Ranchhod, Ashok.
    Marketing strategies : a 21st century approach / Ashok Ranchhod, Claire Gauzente, Julie Tinson.
        p. cm.
    Includes bibliographical references and index.
    ISBN 0-273-65192-7 (pbk. : alk. paper)
      1. Marketing. 2. Marketing- -Case studies. 3. Marketing research. I. Gauzente, Claire.
    II. Tinson, Julie. III. Title.

    HF5415.R3217 2004
    658.8'101- -dc22

10 9 8 7 6 5 4 3 2 1
09 08 07 06 05 04

Typeset in Stone Serif 9.5/13pt by 30
Produced by Pearson Education Malaysia Sdn Bhd,
Printed in Malaysia

The publisher's policy is to use paper manufactured from sustainable forests.

Contents

10 New perspectives in developing marketing strategies   194

Preface

Marketing Strategies: A Twenty-first Century Approach addresses the changing nature of marketing. Now that we are in the twenty-first century many of the tenets of marketing that have served businesses so well until now need revisiting and updating. Social norms have changed. Technology is making greater inroads into the marketing process and has been instrumental in speeding up the process of globalisation. There are several textbooks on marketing strategy and many of these do an admirable job of explaining marketing strategy in a methodical and linear fashion. These books serve their purpose very well. However, as most marketers realise, the practice of marketing can be quite nebulous and difficult to define.

In order to understand the chaotic nature of marketing, this book does not follow a linear format. Each chapter considers some of the major issues that impact on marketing strategy development, and they can therefore be read in any order. The book also attempts to close the gap that exists in the understanding of cultural issues by offering case studies drawn from various parts of the world. It looks at marketing from different angles, in order to create a broader understanding of the discipline. It also provides a balanced mix of both practical and theoretical issues. Exercises in many chapters can be used practically by readers to assess their companies' marketing stances.

The book takes a largely European perspective. Rather than the conventional North American view, the underlying theme addresses issues such as sustainability and ethics. The book also tries to explain the holistic and rather organic nature of marketing. In fact, in line with the way in which marketing is evolving and the growing interest in market orientation, there is little discussion of the 4Ps, because strategies are often company specific. Rather, the book is radical because it brings together five of the main contemporary factors affecting marketing in the twenty-first century: sustainability, ethics, market orientation, the impact of technology and globalisation. There is an emphasis on understanding the role of branding and the development of customer relationships. This book helps marketers to 'think outside the box' and develop their marketing skills. In order to do this, it is important for marketers to ask many provocative questions before developing and implementing marketing strategies. This book indicates the types of questions that marketing managers and students should consider. The philosophy of marketing is as important as its application and implementation. This book helps you to understand this.

Structure of the book

The book is divided into 10 chapters, each with distinctive themes which interlink and support each other. Chapter 1 considers the key impacts on strategy making and how a range of key factors should be considered when developing a marketing strategy. The impact of new factors is also taken into account. Chapter 2 is partly conventional, but it questions the way in which markets are analysed and segmented. Chapter 3 is mainly concerned with the role that stakeholders play in the development of strategies. The difference between the Anglo-Saxon model and the European model of corporate governance is taken into consideration. Ethical and moral dimensions are also emphasised.

Chapter 4 largely follows on from Chapter 3 and develops the theme of sustainability and ways in which marketing could and should contribute to the development of sustainable strategies. The chapter ends with a practical example of how to formulate ethical and sustainable strategies given the changing nature of the consumer profile. Chapter 5 develops the theme of relationship marketing given the fragmenting nature of markets and looks at how brand strategies should be developed.

Chapter 6 looks at how marketing strategies can be implemented in this technological age. It also discusses the interplay between technology and people when implementing marketing strategies. Chapters 7 and 8 consider how organisations should be organised for marketing and how they can learn from implementing marketing strategies. Chapters 6, 7 and 8 therefore offer a new perspective on implementation. Marketing texts often shy away from the organisational perspective that is so important in developing and implementing marketing strategies.

Chapter 9 looks at the increasing importance of marketing metrics. Marketers are under pressure to justify their positions within companies. Developing useful metrics, which take into account both financial and marketing aspects, is important for monitoring business success. This chapter also considers ecological and ethical measures. Finally, Chapter 10 considers new perspectives in developing strategies. Many new ideas on becoming customer-centric, understanding the future impact of technology and the growing importance of rural marketing are considered. As marketing enters the twenty-first century, the consumer base is evolving, the world of consumption is changing and marketers need to become more ethical and accountable in their approach to business.

Key features

The text offers both a philosophical and a practical approach to marketing and has the following key features:

■ Discussion of the changing nature of marketing and the impact of technology.
■ Analysis of the fragmentation of markets and new strategies for working within this new marketplace.

- Insights into the stakeholder perspective.
- Comprehensive study of how analysis and segmentation is practised and some of the associated pitfalls.
- The arguments for sustainability and ethics are developed and practical ways of implementing these types of marketing strategies are explained.
- Numerous examples of different strategies.
- A range of case studies that illustrate the arguments posed.
- Global examples.
- Emphasis of the holistic nature of marketing.
- Highlights the need to understand cultural dynamics when implementing marketing strategies.
- Consideration of how branding relationships are changing.

When developing strategies, it is important that marketers take the range of issues considered in this book into account and keep an eye on how marketing is likely to change in the future. This book provides guide posts, not solutions.

Figure P.1 illustrates the key chapters and how they interrelate.

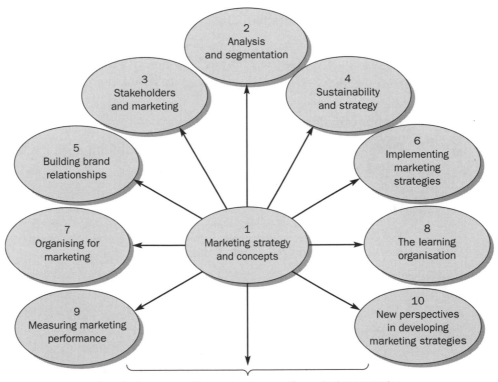

Figure P. 1 Key chapters and how they interrelate in the book

Student and instructor resources

A comprehensive package of supplements is available to assist students and instructors in using this book. To access the following supplements go to www.booksites.net/ranchhod:

Instructor and student resources

Teaching tips

Written by Ashok Ranchhod, this manual provides useful suggestions on how to use this book.

Cases

In addition to the cases that are in the book, these cases, along with discussion points, can be used to enrich and enhance lectures and tutorial sessions.

To obtain a password to access this site, please contact your local Pearson Education sales representative.

PowerPoint presentation

Created by Ashok Ranchhod, these slides provide you with a slide show ready for classroom use! Use the slides as they are, or edit them to meet your classroom needs. Students can access these slides to reinforce the lectures.

Author updates

Provided twice a year, these updates keep you informed on the latest issues in marketing strategy.

Links to other sites

With the changing nature of marketing and business, navigate the plethora of marketing related sites to help enhance your learning.

Ashok Ranchhod
Spring 2003

Acknowledgements

I am grateful to the two contributors, Dr Julie Tinson of the University of the West of England and Dr Claire Gauzente of the University of Angers for Chapters 5, 7 and 8. I also appreciate the administrative and research help given by Fan Zhou, Dai Yun and Binh Le. Without the help of Dr Calin Gurau, this book could not have been completed. He acted as a guide and gave considerable help in constructing Chapter 6. I would also like to thank the following reviewers for their constructive and insightful comments:

F.P. Broere, Vrije Universiteit, Amsterdam; Andrew Crane, University of Cardiff; Scott Dacko, University of Warwick; Keri Davies, Stirling University; Kjell Grøhaug, Norges Handelshøyskole; Dale Littler, University of Manchester Institute of Technology (UMIST); Robert Morgan, University of Wales, Aberystwyth, and Eric Waarts, Erasmus Universiteit, Rotterdam.

Finally, this book is dedicated to my wife Nilanta and my children, Jaimini, Chintan and Reshma. I am particularly grateful for their patience and ability to ignore various piles of papers around the house.

Publisher's acknowledgements

We are grateful to all copyright owners whose material appears in this book, in particular the following:

Figure 1.1 from Marketing through information technology: from potential to virtual reality, MEG 97, *Academy of Marketing*, Vol. 1, Newcastle Business School, University of Northumbria (Ranchhod, A. & Hackney, R.A. 1997); Figure 1.2 from Measuring market orientation: a multi-factor, multi-item approach, *Journal of Marketing Management*, Vol. 10, Westburn Publishers Ltd. (Deng, S. & Dart, J. 1994); Figure 1.4 from *Exploring Corporate Strategy: Text and Cases*, Pearson Education (Johnson, G. & Scholes, K. 2002); Figure 1.6 from Creating a sense of mission, *Long Range Planning*, Vol. 24, pp. 10–20 (Campbell, A. & Yeung, S. 1991), with permission from Elsevier; Figure 2.5 from The directional policy matrix-tools for strategic planning, *Long Range Planning*, June (Robinson, S.J.Q., Hitchen, R.E. & Wade, D.P. 1978), with permission from Elsevier; Figure 2.8 from *Contemporary Strategy Analysis: Concepts, Techniques, Applications*, 4th edition, Blackwell Publishing Inc., USA (Grant, R. M. 2002); Figure 4.1 from *Environmental Marketing Management*, Pearson Education (Peattie, K. 1995); Figures 4.2, 4.3 and 4.4 from *World Watch*, Vol. 13, No. 2, March/April 2000, © 2002 Worldwatch Institute, www.worldwatch .org; Table 4.4 from www.naturalbusiness.com/market.html, Conscious Media Inc. (2000); Figure 5.1 from Cultivating service brand equity, *Academy of Marketing Science Journal*, Vol. 28, No. 1, pp. 128–137 (Berry, L.L. 2002), copyright © 2002 by Sage Publications, Inc., reproduced with permission; Table 6.1 from The strategic market planning implementation interface in small and midsized industrial firms: an exploratory study, *Journal of Marketing*, Summer, pp. 77–92, American Marketing Association (Sashittal, H.C. & Tankersely, C. 1997); Table 6.2 from Prioritising marketing targets, *Marketing Intelligence and Planning*, Vol. 16, No. 7, MCB UP Limited (Simpkin, L.P. & Dibb, S. 1998); Figure 6.4 from www.dc.com/obx, with permission from Deloitte Consulting; Table 6.3 from *Information Masters: Secrets of the Customer Race* (McKean, J. 1999), © John Wiley & Sons Inc., reproduced with permission; Table 6.4 from www.oecd.org/daf/governance/principles.htm, *Principles of Corporate Governance*, p. 23, © 1999 OECD; Figure 7.5 from *Franchise et Culture Manageriale*, Franchise Research Committee, French Franchise Federation (Dubost, N., Gauzente, C., Guilloux, V., Roussel, P. & Kalika, M. 2000); Figure 7.10 from www.sagem.com with permission from SAGEM; Figure 7.11 from *Organizational Culture and Leadership*, 2nd edition (Schein, E.H. 1992), © John Wiley & Sons, Inc., reproduced with permission; Table 7.1 from Measuring organisational cultures: a qualitative and quantitative study across twenty cases, *Administrative Science Quarterly*, Vol. 35, No. 2 (Hofstede, G., Neuijen, B., Ohayv, D. & Sanders, G. 1990), © *Administrative Science Quarterly*, Johnson Graduate School of Management, Cornell University; Table 9.1 from *Promotion des ventes et action commerciale*, Librarie Vuibert (Ingold, P. 1995); Table 9.2 from Selecting environmental performance indicators, *Greener Management International*, Vol. 33, Spring, pp. 97–114, Greenleaf Publishing Limited (Scherpereel, C., Koppen, V. & Heering, G.B.F. 2001); Table 9.3 from *WBCSD Project on Eco-efficiency Metrics and Reporting: State of Play Report*, World Business Council for Sustainable Development (Lehni, M. 1998); Figure 10.1 from The antecedents and consequences of customer-centric marketing, *Journal of the Academy of Marketing Science*, Vol. 28, No. 1, pp. 55–56 (Sheth, J.N., Sisodia, R. S. & Sharma, A. 2000), copyright © 2000 by Sage Publications, Inc., reproduced with permission; Figure 10.3 from *Marketing Management*, Vol. 4, No. 2, pp. 8–23, American Marketing Association (Sheth, J. & Sisodia, R.S. 1995); Figure 10.4 from Strategic marketing models for a dynamic competitive environment, *Journal of General Management*, Vol. 24, No. 4, The Braybrooke Press (Karin I. & Preiss, K. 2002), reproduced with permission from the publisher and authors; Figures 10.5, 10.6, 10.7 and 10.8 from *Innovation, Social Capital, and the New Economy: New Federal Policies to Support Collaborative Research*, PPi Briefing, July, Progressive Policy Institute (PPi) (Fountain, J.E. & Atkinson, R.D. 1998); Figures 10.11 and 10.12 from Ethical marketing for competitive advantage on the Internet, *Academy of Marketing Science Review*, Vol. 10, The Academy of Marketing Science, University of Miami (Gauzente, C. & Ranchhod, A. 2001), © The Academy of Marketing Science; Table 10.2 from Marketing social marketing in the social change marketplace, *Journal of Public Policy and Marketing*, Vol. 21, No. 1, American Marketing Association (Andreasen, A.R. 2002); Figure 10.13 from www.census.gov/prod/3/98pubs/p23-194.pdf, *Population Profile of the United States: 1997*.

Eminem CD sales impressive despite music sharing from http://www.usatoday.com/tech/news/2002/05/31/eminem.htm, 31 May 2002, © The Associated Press;

Playstation: going for old by Carl Radcliffe, TBWA London Ltd; INSIDE TRACK: Image in the balance by Andrew Pharaoh from *The Financial Times Limited*, 16 September 2002, © Andrew Pharaoh; Calpol™ – growing the brand by Nick Burgoyne, Warner Lambert Consumer Health Products Company; Life and death of a brand by Mark Lawson from *The Guardian*, 1 July 2002, © Mark Lawson/The Guardian; Setting of a chain reaction by Bharat Kumar from *Business Line – India*, 2 October 2002; Adapt or die by Pravir Malik from *Business Line – India*, 3 October 2002; Needle-free business has no point for Powderject by Simon Bowers from *The Guardian*, 4 July 2001, © The Guardian; Diet industry will be the winner of the battle of the bulge by John Carvel from *The Guardian*, 31 May 2002, © The Guardian.

We are grateful to the Financial Times Limited for permission to reprint the following material:

Internet banking: quick to adapt to technology, © *Financial Times*, 20 December 2000; Metro, a short sharp read from FT Creative Business, © *Financial Times*, 19 December 2000; Sweet ambitions to tempt more takers, © *Financial Times*, 16 July 2002.

Every effort has been made by the publisher to obtain permission from the appropriate source to reproduce material which appears in this book. In some instances we have been unable to trace the owners of copyright material, and we would appreciate any information that would enable us to do so.

1 Marketing strategy and concepts

Introduction: From structure to chaos?

Marketing as a subject is continually evolving and the recent impacts of ideas and technology need to be assessed carefully as the new century dawns. This book attempts to give some insights into the way in which marketing is evolving and progressing. The basic premise of marketing revolves around matching an organisation's offerings with consumers' needs. Whilst this basic premise is constant, the means by which an organisation's offering can be matched to customer needs are in a continual state of flux. With advancing technologies such as the Internet and mobile communications, several paradoxical situations arise. Although customers may be given a faster, more cohesive service, it can become depersonalised. Customers can become 'spoilt' and demand a one-to-one relationship, even though organisations may not have the resources to cope with this.

Strategy in marketing involves harnessing an organisation's resources to meet customers' needs through market analysis, an understanding of competitor actions, government actions and globalisation, together with consideration of technological and other environmental changes. The management of these complex interrelationships needs a more lateral approach rather than the linear approach often applied in conventional strategic marketing thinking.

This book attempts to unravel the difficulties associated with changes in marketing, juxtaposing new approaches with some of the more conventional approaches. The book therefore presents many of the latest marketing theories and uses a range of case studies to help readers to improve their marketing thinking and skills development. As ever, it is the author's view that good marketers need both practical experience and a good knowledge of academic approaches to solving marketing problems.

Technological advances

Marketing has evolved over the last two centuries as the systems of production and consumption have changed due to the unprecedented rate of development of technology. This rate of development in technology has seen the advent of mass manufacturing, near instantaneous communication systems and the development of rapid transport systems. It is clear that marketing, in this context, initially moved from fragmentation to mass marketing to segmentation marketing (Tedlow 1993). There is now another technological drive resulting from powerful computing techniques (Patron 1996). The increasing globalisation of communication for the average person (Cronin 1996) and the development of technologies for flexible manufacturing (Yasumuro 1993) is leading marketers to consider the absolute dislocation of time and space in undertaking marketing transactions. The Internet, in turn, offers a virtual, 24-hour shopping experience in any market sector to any person in the world able to access it. At the same time, traditional retailers such as Tesco are offering a 24-hour shopping experience without the Internet.

Figure 1.1 shows the development of these phases and also alludes to the possibility that markets may yet again be fragmenting (Ranchhod and Hackney 1997) because of the ease of communication. Paradoxically, in the early part of the nineteenth century, markets were fragmented as a result of poor communications and transport systems. Fragmentation is occurring now as market segments cannot be clearly defined, with consumers continually rearranging their preferences as a result of greater product choices. Allied to this, rapid and continuous communication allows consumers infinite choices of products in scattered markets which can be accessed globally. Certainly much of the literature on postmodernism seems to point towards fragmentation. The fragmentation of society, made possible and fostered by the developments of industry and commerce, is among the most visible consequences of postmodern individualism (Cova 1996). This fragmentation is

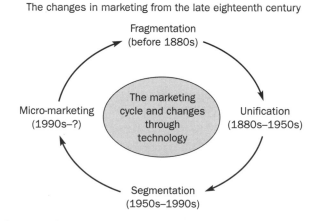

Figure 1.1 The impact of technology on marketing
Source: Ranchhod and Hackney (1997)

encouraged by the ability of individuals to maintain 'virtual' contact with the world, electronically, freeing them from social interaction but at the same time increasing their concentration on the ego by demanding 'tailored' products and services in the marketplace. There are indications that some of the demographic and lifestyle changes in society are just beginning to offer such a scenario.

The marketing concept

The marketing concept has been discussed at great length by a range of authors (Kotler 2000). The main premise of the concept is linking production and consumption. An organisation must be able to meet the needs of the customer, both in terms of organisational ability and the resources available. Meeting customer needs is a multifaceted activity that uses the full range of a company's resources, ranging from sales activities to final delivery and after-sales service. In service industries, although the range of activities will differ, their success will still depend on satisfying the customer. Charities too have begun to embrace the marketing concept, though for such organisations defining customer satisfaction is more nebulous and complex. Satisfaction in charities often resides with the recipient of food, money or training (World Wildlife Fund 2002). In all cases, the marketing concept relies on the creation of value for consumers. The connection between value creation and marketing is not new. The marketing concept has been defined as 'a process of achieving organisational goals through determining the needs and wants of target markets and delivering the desired satisfactions more effectively and efficiently than competitors do' (Kotler 1998). This suggests that organisations most likely to succeed in the increasingly dynamic and competitive markets are those that take into account the expectations of their customers and gear themselves to satisfying these expectations better than their rivals. It recognises that the process of marketing consists of understanding, learning and the realisation of values through marketing activities. Similar ideas can also be recognised through the definition of marketing given by the American Marketing Association (AMA) in *Marketing News*, 1 March 1985, which holds that marketing is 'the process of planning and executing activities to create exchanges that satisfy individual and organisational objectives'. However, in line with modern thinking, the marketing concept ought to take a much broader view and the definition should include the satisfaction of a range of stakeholders. Therefore, it is defined here as:

Marketing is the process of planning and executing activities that satisfy individual, ecological and social needs ethically and sincerely while also satisfying organisational objectives.

Within this definition, it is clear that marketing objectives are not always financial in nature and ecological and social needs are becoming increasingly important when developing marketing strategies. Marketing strategies are defined by the overall corporate vision of an organisation and constitute the actions taken to satisfy customers and their needs. In doing this, it is important that an organisation understands the competitive environment, the general environment and its role and obligations within these environments when developing and executing marketing strategies. Out of this understanding, an organisation can develop segmentation and performance criteria by choosing to follow particular options that may present themselves. These issues will be explored in detail in later chapters.

Marketing as a business process

That marketing should be thought of as the design and management of all the business processes necessary to define, develop and deliver value to target customers has often been the cornerstone of marketing thinking (Webster 1997). He suggests that marketing should include the following:

- *Value-defining processes*: processes that enable an organisation to better understand the environment in which it operates, to understand its own resources and capabilities more clearly, to determine its own position in the overall value chain and to assess the value it creates through analysis of target customers.
- *Value-developing processes*: processes that create value throughout the value chain, such as procurement strategy, new product and service development, design of distribution channels, strategic partnerships with service providers and, ultimately, the development of the value proposition for customers.
- *Value-delivering processes*: processes that enable the delivery of value to customers including service delivery, customer relationship management, distribution and logistic management, marketing communications management (such as advertising and sales promotion), product and service enhancement, and customer support services.

The role of market orientation

As a result of the discussions directly or indirectly associated with the marketing concept, pioneering work undertaken by Narver and Slater (1990) attempted to bring together the various elements which make up the marketing concept. These elements were put together as the market orientation scale, which could be empirically tested and provided organisations with degrees of market orientation against which they could test corporate performance (see Figure 1.2).

Different authors have developed different market orientation scales: Narver and Slater (1990), Jaworski and Kohli (1993), Ruekert (1992) and Deng and Dart (1994). However, the essence of all the arguments is as follows:

- *Information generation*. This is the generation of customer, market and competitor-related information as a result of an organisation's intelligence-gathering activities. The information is obtained either from internal or external sources.
- *Information dissemination*. Having obtained the necessary information, an organisation needs to disseminate this information effectively to all the individuals operating within its confines. If information dissemination is poor, it can be

Figure 1.2 Components of market orientation
Source: After Deng and Dart (1994)

difficult for an organisation to develop the correct strategy for a given market or set of customers.

■ *Implementation in response to the information received.* An organisation needs to act on the information received and it needs to act in a clear and precise manner. Therefore the *type* of information gathered and the *speed* with which it is disseminated within an organisation play important roles in determining marketing strategies and the implementation of those strategies.

Figure 1.2 encapsulates the key components of market orientation and how they affect the success of an organisation in the marketplace. In general, there are three main themes which relate to the marketing concept: **customer focus** – information generation pertaining to customers; **competitor focus**; and **responsiveness** – dissemination of the information obtained pertaining to customers across the functional departments, with a view to meeting customer needs as quickly as possible by having good inter-functional coordination within the departments.

Loyalty

For some organisations, loyal customers are of paramount importance for their existence (Davis *et al.* 1991). Retaining customers can have a significant positive impact on the profitability of organisations. Studies have shown that retaining an additional 2 per cent to 5 per cent of customers can improve profits by the same amount as can cutting costs by 10 per cent (Reichheld and Sasser 1990, Power *et al.* 1992). Large organisations such as Procter & Gamble are studying how and why customers contribute to profitability. Most researchers and practitioners (Wilkie 1990, Oliver and Swan 1989) agree that satisfaction occurs when purchase expectations are met and even exceeded, i.e. the attributes associated with products are the ones desired by customers. This implies that organisations should, in addition to being customer and competitor oriented, be satisfaction oriented in order to meet purchase expectations. Dissatisfaction is the result of unfulfilled expectations. Herein also lies a problem for marketers as it is not always easy to ascertain precisely what customer expectations are. Marketers who understand the impact of customer satisfaction on business performance will want to secure future sales on the basis of the recommendations of currently satisfied end users of the products because what happens in the current buying decision will affect future purchase decisions (Tanner 1996).

Given all the factors that enlarge and elaborate the notion of the marketing concept, over the years, marketers have devoted considerable time and effort to developing marketing planning.

Strategic planning to deliver the marketing concept

Countless authors have written about strategic planning in the marketplace (McDonald 1993, Grant 2002, Johnson and Scholes 2000, Ackoff 1981) and many organisations spend a considerable amount of time and energy developing and executing strategic plans. All these plans largely contain marketing stances and positioning strategies designed to place an organisation in a winning position vis-à-vis its competitors. A definition of strategic marketing planning, therefore, could be as follows:

> *Strategic marketing planning involves careful analysis of an organisation's environment, its competitors and its internal strengths in order to develop a sustainable plan of action which will develop the organisation's competitive advantage and maximise it within given resource availability.*

These planning systems are often systematic and are designed to help organisations to work through a strategic plan step by step. These steps guide an organisation towards a deliberate strategy (Mintzberg 1987). This process is often driven from the top of the organisation and based on complex deliberations between different functions within the organisation. Much of marketing literature is preoccupied by this linear, rational approach to strategic planning. Mintzberg (1994) calls this the **rationalist** approach. A proponent of this type of deliberate planning is McDonald (1993) who discusses the marketing planning process in detail. The essential steps involved in this process are outlined in Figure 1.3.

The analytical part of such plans often begins with a SWOT (strengths, weaknesses, opportunities and threats) analysis. The SWOT analysis informs the assumptions which have to be made. The model also needs an audit of the current activities of the organisation. The audit and SWOT analysis are nearly always incomplete because all the information required to make perfect strategies is often hidden or not available. As a result, informed assumptions based on the available data have to be made. Following this exercise, the objectives are set as measurable outcomes. The feedback loops are designed to create an iterative process of planning. Mintzberg (1987) argues that in a planned strategy:

> *Leaders at the centre of authority formulate their intentions as precisely as possible and then strive for their implementation – their translation into collective action – with a minimum of distortion, 'surprise free'. To ensure this, the leaders must first articulate their intentions in the form of a plan in as much detail as possible, to minimise confusion, and then elaborate this plan in as much detail as possible, in the form of budgets, schedules and so on, to pre-empt discretion that might impede its realisation. Those outside the planning*

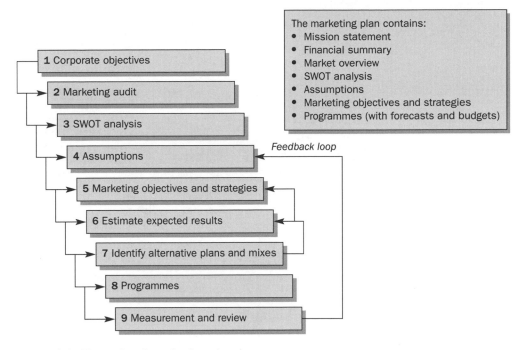

Figure 1.3 The rational marketing planning process

Source: Adapted from McDonald (1993)

process may act, but to the extent possible they are not allowed to decide. Programmes that guide their behaviour are built into the plan, and formal controls are instituted to ensure pursuit of the plan and the programmes.

Other models take a more overall strategic point of view, where many of the human and cultural issues are taken into account. Johnson and Scholes' (2000) model is much more comprehensive and is based on **analysis**, **choice** and **implementation** (see Figure 1.4). Within this comprehensive framework, marketing strategies are developed from comprehensive portfolio analyses.

Many forms of strategy are possible. If one takes the view that the environment is uncontrollable, then it is probable that an organisation will have to adapt to the environment. However, a definition of the 'environment' is not straightforward. For some, the environment means the physical environment, encompassing weather, politics and war. For others, the environment means the 'near' environment, encompassing competitors and the general market environment. Organisations are rarely immune from environmental pressures and therefore environmental turbulence has to be taken into account.

Environmental factors

Studies into market orientation often utilise an environmental turbulence scale to understand the effect of the environment on the level of market orientation adopted by organisations. However, this environmental turbulence scale only measures the

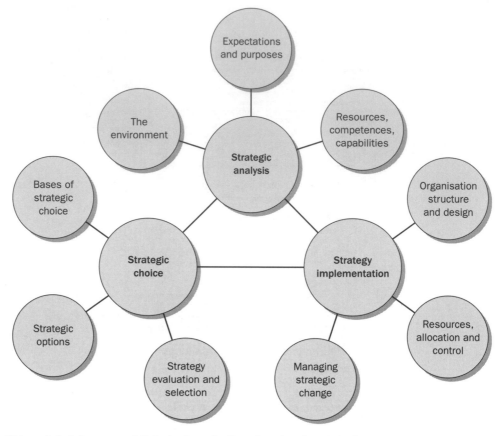

Figure 1.4 Johnson and Scholes' marketing planning framework
Source: Johnson and Scholes (2002)

impact of technology and competitors within a given market. For a greater understanding, organisations need to begin to understand the role played by the general environment, including global climate and political issues, as shown in Figure 1.5.

Within this environment, organisations may follow a range of strategies which are planned, entrepreneurial, ideological, umbrella type, process driven, unconnected (different strategies in different areas of an organisation), consensus driven or imposed (Mintzberg 1987).

Hamel and Prahalad (1989) argue that strategy has to be developed in a way that stretches and leverages an organisation. Market analysis and then strategy formulation as practised by many marketers is not enough to position an organisation for sustainable growth and to enable it to gain competitive advantage over its rivals. An organisation needs to understand and leverage its core competences to the full. For example, Hamel and Prahalad feel that many organisations are competent at diagnostics but not at actually breaking down managerial mindsets. To quote from their paper:

Driven by the need to understand the dynamics of battles (GM vs Toyota, CGS vs CNN, Pan Am vs British Airways, RCA vs Sony), we have turned competitiveness into a growth industry. Companies and industries have been analysed in mind-numbing detail, autopsies

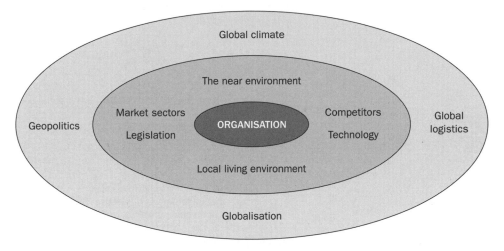

Figure 1.5 Environmental factors affecting strategy

performed, and verdicts rendered. Yet when it comes to understanding where competitiveness comes from and where it goes, we are like doctors who have diagnosed a problem – and have found ways to treat some of its symptoms – but who still don't know how to keep from getting sick in the first place.

Thus the views of Hamel and Prahalad open the door for a greater analysis of the underlying managerial issues when analysing markets and competition.

Creating a sense of identity

Creating a sense of mission within the organisation is important for many organisations (Campbell and Yeung 1991). Many marketers would contend that a marketing plan is incomplete without reference to an organisation's mission. The proposed Ashridge model (see Figure 1.6) takes into account the purpose, values and behaviour standards of an organisation. The purpose of an organisation often determines the markets that it will enter. For example, the Co-operative Bank, based in the UK, only believes in ethical investments. This creates a particular type of market opportunity, which determines the types of segments that will be interested in its products. The values of the organisation drive the purpose and strategy, with behaviour being actionable and measurable (such as customer satisfaction and service quality). The distinctive competences of an organisation may be constrained or enhanced by the resources available to it. The resource-based theory of strategy is concerned with how these distinctive competences can be leveraged and enhanced.

It is argued that a well-crafted mission statement can provide the following advantages to an organisation (Bart and Baetz 1998):

■ ensure unanimity of purpose;
■ arouse positive feelings about a firm;

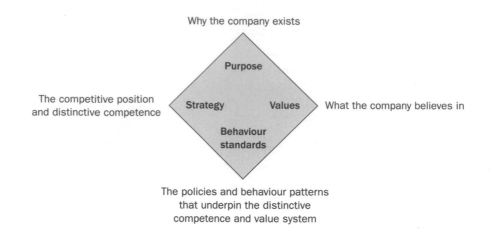

Figure 1.6 The Ashridge mission model
Source: Campbell and Yeung (1991)

■ provide direction;
■ provide a basis for objectives and strategies;
■ serve as a focal point;
■ resolve divergent views among managers.

Pearce and David (1987) suggest that a well-crafted mission statement should address the following nine elements:

1 Customers (the target market).
2 Products/services (offerings and value provided to customers).
3 Geographic markets (where the organisation seeks customers).
4 Technology (the technology used to produce and market products).
5 Concern for survival, growth and profits (the organisation's concern that it be financially sound).
6 Philosophy (the organisation's values, ethics, beliefs).
7 Public image (contributions the organisation makes to communities).
8 Employees (the importance of managers and employees).
9 Distinctive competence (how the organisation is better than, or different from, its competitors).

In a recent study (David and David 2003) it was found that many organisations fail to include six of these nine recommended components in their mission statements – these being: market, technology, concern for survival/growth/profits, philosophy, public image and employees. This is interesting and disturbing as it indicates that stakeholders are given scant consideration and technology is not given the prominence it deserves given the dramatic changes wrought by the Internet and database systems. Clearly mission statements therefore have an important part to play in helping to frame marketing strategies. However, there may be limitations.

Limitations

There are problems with tightly defined mission statements. For example, as markets are constantly evolving even more rapidly, how rigid can an organisation's mission statement be? The Dixon Group is essentially an electrical and electronics-based retailer. In 1999 it launched Freeserve, an Internet service. Although this was a diversification from its normal business, Dixons saw the opportunity offered by the growth of the Internet and began to broaden its served market, not becoming myopic in its approach as discussed by Levitt (1960). The company broadened the target market but at the same it developed the capabilities for meeting customer requirements. The resources were leveraged accordingly.

Doing this is not necessarily straightforward, as profits also have to be earned in the new market. Grant (2002) maintains that organisations ought to look at the resources that they can leverage before thinking about positioning in the marketplace. The identification of these resources can then be utilised to position the core competences accordingly in order to exploit market opportunities. An organisation's resources may be made up of brands, financial muscle, key personnel, research and development (R&D) and distribution systems, among others. He contends that organisations are in the business of maximising returns from these resources over time. Resource-based strategy is based on assessing how an individual organisation's strengths and weaknesses in terms of resources can be leveraged in a unique way to exploit the competences that it possesses. The effective utilisation of these resources enables an organisation to meet its customers' needs more efficiently and speedily than competitors (Barney 1996).

The varied discussion above illustrates the complexities involved in developing marketing strategy. Strategy development, by its very nature, involves peering into the future. Strategies are created and executed within given time periods. Thus, in addition to the many points made above, time, fragmentation and technological developments need to be addressed before developing a new guide to planning.

Time as an issue in planning

Time is an important aspect of planning. Many organisations succeed or fail, depending on:

- the speed of entry into a market with a new product;
- the length of time a particular organisation has been operating within a particular market, which may endow it with market knowledge and distribution strengths;
- the length of time that an organisation has been operating within a market, which may also prevent it from taking advantage of new opportunities in new markets;
- the speed with which an organisation can harness its resources to meet competitive challenges;
- the time and place of the formation of an organisation.

Some management authors indicate that the moment when an organisation is founded impacts on its structure and strategy (Stinchcombe 1965), hence the age of the organisation constitutes a determining variable in its strategic choices and ability to change. In the strategic management field, Boeker (1989) demonstrates that both the age of the organisation and its history constrain the available strategic spectrum. He also shows that, when organisations have one specific dominant strategy, they are not likely to change it, even if poor performance is encountered. This type of analysis matches the notion of organisational inertia as identified by Hannan and Freeman (1984). Schein (1992) also discusses the predominant role of the founder in developing an organisation's culture and strategy; he or she may also be a product of a particular age and time.

CASE STUDY

FT

Internet banking: quick to adapt to technology

Bradesco's embrace of IT puts it among the world's leading online institutions and earns high plaudits

A couple of years ago, Jean Phillipe Leroy was met by disbelief when he told international fund managers about how Bradesco, Brazil's biggest bank, was taking advantage of the Internet.

'They know now. But it was a big shock for them at first to see us among the biggest internet banks in the world,' says Mr. Leroy, who is head of corporate relations at Bradesco's Sao Paolo headquarters. A study published earlier this year by Cluster Consulting of Barcelona that rated Bradesco as the third biggest internet bank in the world – behind Bank of America and Wells Fargo – has been extensively reported. Last year, Bradesco gained an honorary mention in Bill Gates' best selling *Business at the Speed of Thought*. In a chapter called 'Get to markets first', Mr. Gates writes that 'almost since its inception, this (bank) has made "time to market" practically a mantra'. Last December, Bradesco's first free internet service led to a sharp rise in the share price and was widely noted. Growth this year has been impressive. By October, Bradesco had 1,530,000 clients for its internet banking service, more than twice as many as in the same month of the previous year. A total of 9.2m transactions were conducted online during the same month, and of the 486,000 Brazilians who opened new accounts with Bradesco during the third quarter, more than half of the new customers – 51 per cent – were

banking by internet. Bradesco – and other big Brazilian banks such as Itau, Unibanco and Banco de Brasil – have been quick to adapt technology for a range of reasons. The Brazilian government's industrial policy is one. Until the late 1980s, Brazil protected its domestic computer industry by making it prohibitively expensive to import the machines. One of the by-products was that many companies researched and developed their own in-house technology.

Bradesco was particularly quick off the mark, being the first Brazilian bank to introduce computers. 'It has always been a bank that has been on top of the technology,' says Luiz Carlos Trabuco Cappi, the executive vice-president who is responsible for internet banking. At the same time, during the 1970s and 1980s Brazilian banks developed their systems to a much greater degree than elsewhere in Latin America in order to accommodate the effect of permanent levels of very high inflation. Because a bank needs to conduct financial transactions quickly if it is to make money in an environment where monetary values are rapidly eroded, systems to clear cheques within 24 hours were introduced, for example. In his book, Mr. Gates describes how Bradesco developed a cash-management software application to assist with payables and receivables, which it then sold to about 4,100 businesses. For another customer Bradesco developed a salary card that enabled employees to be paid directly from ATM machines without being required to have a bank account. Again, the system was quickly generalised. 'The bank focuses on short development cycles – weeks and months, no longer,' writes Mr. Gates.

Its management accustomed to innovation, Bradesco was able to react quickly to the opportunity of the internet. Initially it developed a system that depended on customers using a CD-Rom on which they entered details before transmitting by a modem. Subsequently a full online service has been introduced. Bradesco has been clever about introducing innovation to allow customers to personalise their access to the site, in order to defeat hackers and reduce the risk of fraud. The hours during which the site is open can be restricted, for example, says Mr. Cappi. The big advantage is efficiency. Mr. Cappi says that the average cost of an internet transaction is just 11 centavos, compared with 54 centavos for a

transaction conducted over the telephone and R1.20 for one conducted at a branch. But unlike many of its counterparts in the developed world, Bradesco is not seeking to replace its network of 2,500 branches with a cyber network.

Fearing that such a course might make it less easy to grow among the sector of the market which is just beginning to open bank accounts, Bradesco is developing a strategy which is designed to increase the efficiency of the network. At least one internet terminal has been placed inside each branch and a series of incentives offered to make both its customers and its staff more computer friendly.

Special lines of credit have been made available to allow its staff to buy computers. More than 17,000 of its workers have taken advantage in the last four months or so. Bradesco has also begun to install computers inside shopping centres and supermarkets, allowing even wider internet banking access.

Source: Hooper (2000)

Time as history: past, present and future

As an organisation ages, history is created. This history enables the organisation to draw on its previous successes and failures. The question of entry into a market may sometimes be linked to the history of the organisation. The case study on Bradesco illustrates both issues of time well. Bradesco was quick to grasp the opportunity offered by the Internet. The history of the company showed that it possessed good information systems, which helped with the foray into the Internet. Several authors have studied the impact that the order of entry into a market has on market share and business performance (Szymanski *et al.* 1995). First movers are supposed to have competitive advantage with regards to mastering technology, developing distribution systems and creating a brand image (Tellis and Golder 1996). However, late entry to the market might foster better market orientation. This is because the competitive intensity is likely to become stronger over time as newcomers are bound to demonstrate higher market orientation levels in order to reach a profitable place in the market (Porter 1985). Hence from a competitive point of view, time could reinforce the necessity of strong market orientation for young organisations or organisations entering new markets. In other words, the historical period in which an organisation is founded (and enters a new market) may produce different pressures of market orientation.

Ethics as a marketing issue

Many organisations are now becoming acutely aware that their marketing strategies are either hampered or enhanced by their ethical stances. For example, Nike found to its cost that many consumers were not only refusing to buy its products but were also ready to campaign actively against its activities because of the poor conditions and wages offered to workers in its factories in Indonesia. Nike is primarily a design and marketing company that subcontracts much of the manufacturing to smaller outfits. In 1998 the company was associated with offering unfair wages and poor working conditions to employees. The company has gone to great lengths to try to improve the situation, but the stigma still remains which means that the company will have to deal with the long-term effects and consequences for years to come. Prolonged bad publicity can have a critical impact on the brand. Other companies are taking a more proactive stance and are creating ethical alliances (Andreasen and Drumwright 2001) with non-profitmaking enterprises. These ethical alliances initially begin with a donorship but then extend to cause-related marketing, event sponsorship, employee exchange and the provision of services. Reebok, for example, is actively involved with Amnesty International, and Visa, the credit card company, is associated with literacy programmes in developing countries. Markets are now less localised and more globalised as products traverse the world. Such cause-related marketing strategies may become the means by which organisations distinguish themselves in the marketplace.

Towards a new strategic marketing planning model

The previous sections have highlighted and discussed the various factors that are dynamic in nature and that impinge on marketing planning. It is obvious that the more linear and iterative processes of marketing, although useful, may be too restrictive and not dynamic enough when organisations need to consider the various internal and external factors which must be taken into account when developing a strategic marketing stance. Organisations need to consider how best to leverage their resources and to understand their level of market orientation. It is necessary to rethink in terms of planning as a new interactive model is required, rather than the previous linear approach. For example, when planning, many organisations follow tried and tested models with the requisite audits and SWOT analyses. However, rarely do they analyse or understand their level of market orientation, resource activity levels and the requisite time horizons, which may be quite short or relatively long.

The previous case study illustrates the speed with which Bradesco exploited a window of opportunity. These strategic windows are not always available indefinitely (Abell 1978), yet Bradesco successfully manoeuvred its resources and knowledge within a short time span to build a better and cheaper customer service.

FT

A short, sharp read

Metro, launched under two years ago, is the largest free newspaper in the world. Now there are plans to extend the brand beyond the print.

For hundreds and thousands of people every morning, it has become a habit to pick up a free copy of the *Metro* newspaper on the way to work. But what if they then got off the train at their destination and bought a Metro expresso at a Metro internet café, as they walked to their offices past a Metro-branded billboard? Might that also become part of their daily routine? To listen to the sales pitch of Mike Anderson, managing director of *Metro*, the free newspaper owned by Daily Mail & General Trust, the answer is, of course it could. 'There will be other Metro moments,' he asserts, slipping easily into alliterative marketing speak. 'Within 12 months, Metro will physically be another product. That could be TV, internet, radio, a magazine or outdoor media. The question is where do we want to go from here?'

'Here' is less than two years since DMGT, publisher of traditional paid-for newspapers the *Daily Mail*, *The Mail on Sunday* and the *Evening Standard*, as well as a stable of regional titles, started giving away copies of a stitched tabloid to commuters on the London Underground. At the time, many people didn't think it would work. Who, they argued, would read a flimsy paper, filled with rewritten wire copy and soft, syndicated features? But DMGT has proved its critics wrong and now has bigger ambitions for the brand. Still, the short-term aim must be to roll out *Metro* to more cities round the country and achieve profitability within the next three years. The London *Metro* broke even after 11 months of operation, but new edition launches in Manchester, Birmingham, Edinburgh, Newcastle, plus another planned for Leeds in January, have resulted in losses for the parent company. DGMT declines to detail the exact losses, nor will it say how much has been invested in *Metro* since its launch in March 1999. However, Anderson will say that the London edition is highly profitable, and he is supremely confident about the rest of the business to make money. In the current financial year, he expects the *Metro* division to generate nearly £40m in revenues, compared with

£24m last year. 'It's the world's largest free newspaper, the sixth largest paper in the UK and the 14th largest in the world,' he boasts, referring to the circulation figures. 'From a standing start, that's pretty good.'

The *Metro* story actually began in Stockholm, where the late Lord Rothermere and his son, Jonathan Harmsworth, spotted a media phenomenon. Hundreds of thousands of people in the Swedish capital were reading *Metro*, a free paper published by Modern Times Group, and the pair decided to import the concept to the UK. A distribution deal with London Underground was the first step. Anderson, who joined *Metro* after it had been running for three months, says there were two occasions when he knew it would be a big success. The first was standing in Waterloo Station, watching people stream off trains and pick up the first available copies. 'I said to myself, we have a moment here when we own these people like nobody else does in the morning. Our great weapon was that we could take advertisers down there and ask them: "Do you want to reach this audience?" That's massively powerful.'

The second was when a newsagent in Wimbledon station complained because he was 250 copies down on his daily sales of national newspapers after *Metro* was stocked outside his shop. 'A huge percentage of people are not regular consumers of newspapers. *Metro* – a short, sharp 20-minute read – has captured the imagination of the lost children of the newspaper business.'

Metro charges advertisers two-and-a-half times more per thousand readers than the Daily Express. It offers advertisers access to what it calls an affluent, 'urbanite' readership, claiming there are a potential 3.5m people who fit into the niche; 88 per cent of its readers are in work and 77 per cent are under the age of 44. However it has not been plain sailing for the title. DMGT has run into trouble in Manchester, where the Guardian Media Group already had a weekly supplement to the *Manchester*

▶

Evening News, also called *Metro*, While the Modern Times Group – the originator of the idea – has launched its own free morning title in Newcastle. There are also issues ahead. Newsprint prices are set to rise next year. Competition in the regions is growing. *Metro* is as exposed as other metropolitan titles to concerns about a softening of the advertising market in 2001.

Nevertheless, the rapid success of *Metro*, which has occurred at a time of declining newspaper circulations, is a vote of confidence for DMGT and the print industry. It has also been a feather in the cap of the young Lord Rothermere, now chairman, who many observers doubted could begin to live up to the reputation of his father. In pride of place in a glass case in the *Metro* headquarters there is a model of a screw steamer named *Rothermere*. If DMGT can sustain the success of *Metro*, and build it into a multi-million pound franchise beyond print, Lord Rothermere's ship may well have come in.

Source: O'Connor (2000)

Figure 1.7 illustrates the key issues that an organisation should take into account when developing marketing strategies. Instead of a linear approach, a more dynamic approach needs to be undertaken and an importance level should be attached to each of the factors. This level of importance could then be utilised to ascertain the speed with which the strategy should be undertaken and the level of resource leveraging that is required, within given constraints. Eventually the values, purposes and ethical stances of the organisation should be fairly explicit. Some organisations enshrine these within a mission statement, whereas others do not have such a written statement.

The case study on *Metro* is a fine example of resource leveraging that has created a wide range of opportunities for this particular organisation. The idea of stretch-

Figure 1.7 Strategic planning factors

ing the brand may lead to greater opportunities or greater headaches, depending on the resource base of DMGT. If the company measures up in terms of its performance levels and offers the advertisers a good deal, then the diversification strategy may work. However, the company will be entering new markets and industry sectors, which will present a new set of problems as well as opportunities.

Summary

The above discussion and examples illustrate the view that marketing strategy is closely related to corporate strategy. The process of developing a plan is not always straightforward. A model for considering the key points of developing a marketing strategy is shown in Figure 1.8.

Organisations must consider a wide range of issues before they develop particular strategies. There are many schools of thought on how strategy develops and how it should develop. In this chapter, some of the complexities involved are illustrated and the major issues that need to be taken into account are highlighted. With the advent of new technology, the shape and nature of markets are changing. The old maxims are no longer true. One could argue that almost every product, media and location offer marketing possibilities. The markets are becoming both global and local. The new technologies and the Internet are continually helping to fragment markets into smaller pieces. The idea of satisfying a customer is no longer a linear process. A customer has to be satisfied on several dimensions all at the same time. These dimensions could include, among others, service, quality, speed of communication, quality of communication, product quality and brand image.

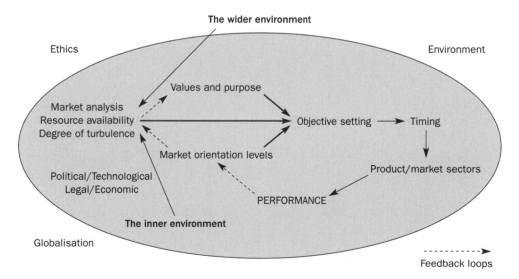

Figure 1.8 Key components for strategic marketing planning

The challenge for marketing strategists is to be able to blend some of the old ideas with new thinking and to be able to forge coherent marketing strategies that can work effectively in the twenty-first century.

Chapter questions

1 Discuss why developing marketing strategy is a complex task.

2 What role does time play in the development of strategies?

3 How can a strong market orientation help an organisation develop an effective marketing strategy?

2 | Analysis and segmentation

Introduction

This chapter has been titled 'Analysis and segmentation' as markets need to be analysed before any real segmentation can take place. The marketing concept is directly linked to the marketplace. For an organisation to succeed, it needs to understand the marketplace and its role within the marketplace. Moreover, it needs to match its corporate and marketing capabilities to the opportunities or threats that exist within the marketplace. This marketplace is becoming increasingly complex as new industry sectors emerge and old ones change shape. At the same time, much of marketing literature defines segmentation as some sort of division or clustering of customers according to defined criteria, such as lifestyles and behaviour patterns (Kotler 2001, Dibb 1998). In the first chapter we argued that markets, after passing through various eras of segmentation, are now fragmenting. This argument will also be explored later in this chapter.

Analytical tools and their limitations

SWOT analysis

Most marketers are aware of the need to understand an organisation's strengths and weaknesses and to match them to the opportunities and threats present in the marketplace. This is achieved using a tool commonly known as SWOT (strengths/weaknesses and opportunities/threats) analysis, which is used by many organisations to audit their activities. It is a simple but effective method by which organisations can ascertain their current position and then develop strategies to take effective action.

Strengths and weaknesses

SWOT analysis considers the key strengths and weaknesses that an organisation possesses in terms of products or services, distribution channels or brand image. The list can be endless, but it is often useful to link the strengths and weaknesses to specific areas within an organisation, such as human resources, finance, marketing or operations.

Opportunities and threats

Typically, events that take place in the environment and the potential impact these may have on an organisation determine the opportunities and threats. For example, many organisations may be taking advantage of the opportunities offered by the Internet and globalisation; those that compete on price may see threats from lower-cost producers in other countries.

SWOT analysis provides a very basic premise for organisations to understand their own capabilities within the marketplace. At the same time, through analysing the opportunities available, it offers a chance to consider potential segments in the market that the organisation may have overlooked. There are weaknesses with this approach as individuals undertaking the exercise may only make a superficial assessment of an organisation's capabilities. Sometimes strengths and weaknesses lie within certain sectors of an organisation and this may not always be clear from an open-ended SWOT analysis. A truly strong analysis needs to be accompanied by an organisational audit as well as market research on both customers and competitors. However, for initial analysis of an organisation's position, this is a simple tool and is relatively effective. Used in conjunction with Porter's (1985) industry analysis, it helps to develop a better understanding of the forces acting on an organisation and the potential options available to it.

Competitive strategy and positioning

In his seminal work, Porter considers how key forces shape competition and determine the level of profitability that an organisation may be able to achieve within particular industry sectors. The premise is that attractive industry sectors offer higher levels of profitability. This means that market *sectors* rather than market *segments* determine the profitability of an organisation. An example of this may be the textile industry in the UK, which faces a great deal of competition and within which companies jockey for position. The return on investment is low, with many manufacturers shifting production to countries where costs are lower. In the IT services sector, however, the market is largely fragmented, offering opportunities for small and medium-sized organisations to do well. So what are the key forces determining the shape of a sector? According to Porter, the key forces are as shown in Figure 2.1 and considered below.

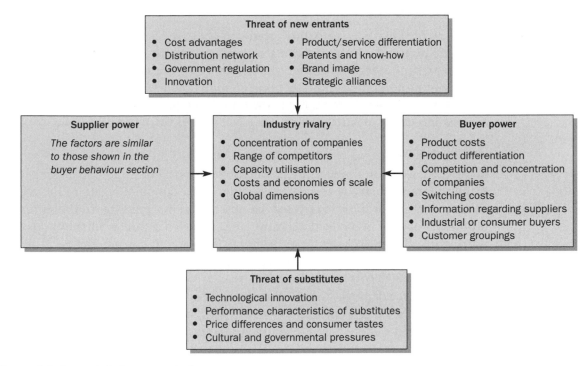

Figure 2.1 Porter's industry analysis

Source: Adapted from Porter (1985)

The threat of new entrants

If a sector is attractive, it will attract new players into the marketplace. For example, the computer games sector is currently very attractive to software games writers and to console manufacturers. The growth exhibited by the games industry has been extraordinary, and the sector now rivals Hollywood in size of revenue and turnover. It is therefore not too surprising that it has attracted a major new entrant into the marketplace – Microsoft with its Xbox. Organisations can deter potential new entrants by creating considerable barriers to entry, such as:

Brand image

The strong brand image of an organisation within a sector can be a major deterrent to organisations wishing to enter the sector. For example, Coca-Cola presents a formidable barrier to entry for many cola makers as it has a strong worldwide brand image. The brand also creates a differentiated image for Coca-Cola; this will be further developed in Chapter 5.

Distribution

Organisations that develop and maintain their distribution channels effectively present another barrier to entry for potential new entrants. The example of Coca-Cola is also relevant here in that its aim is to be able to provide Coke within 100 yards of every consumer. This type of statement shows that the company has strong distribution channels that are very difficult for new entrants to emulate.

Patents or know-how

For many organisations, patenting creates an effective barrier to entry. Many of the large pharmaceutical organisations rely on patents to protect their new drugs. Patents prevent others from entering the market for certain periods of time. When the patent protection elapses, other organisations can enter the market. For organisations such as Cisco Systems, the know-how developed with regard to maintaining IT networks acts as a barrier to entry for other players wishing to enter the market.

Cost advantages

Being the lowest-cost producer in a particular sector may deter potential competitors if they cannot match the costs of production. For example, Colgate-Palmolive can produce toothpaste at the lowest possible cost due to its experience in the sector and economies of scale in production. This type of experience can be difficult to develop overnight and presents a significant barrier to entry for other organisations.

Government regulations

Government regulations, such as those for drug approval, may be time-consuming and very costly for new entrants to comply with, deterring new organisations from challenging older, more established organisations.

Given these barriers to entry, organisations often have to consider whether or not it is possible for them to enter markets through specific segmentation strategies.

Industry rivalry

Competition within a sector can determine the level of profitability an organisation achieves. Some sectors of industry are intensely competitive, driving prices below industry cost levels, making the entire industry unprofitable (perhaps on a global basis). An example of this is the global airline industry, which has seen spectacular collapses such as that of Swiss-Air. However, organisations such as Ryanair and easyJet have shown remarkable growth as low-cost airlines. These airlines have cut costs by using more remote airports and no-frills services on the flights. Some of the main factors determining competition (Grant 2002) are:

- industry concentration;
- range and diversity of competitors;
- product differentiation;
- capacity utilisation and exit barriers;
- cost advantages or disadvantages.

Industry concentration

One or two major players dominate some industry sectors. For example, the software industry is dominated by Microsoft, giving it considerable power in its pricing decisions for the range of Windows products. However, when the company entered the new games console market previously dominated by Sony, Sega and

Nintendo, it faced price competition and had to drop the price of its Xbox. Coca-Cola and Pepsi Cola generally set the prices in the cola market and there are few challengers to this strategy. The revenue earned is used for advertising (building further barriers to entry) and new product development. In the airline industry, where the competition is global and there are many carriers, the price competition increases dramatically, with substantial variations within the different segments such as economy, premium, business class and first class.

Range and diversity of competitors

Organisations can often do well in certain sectors if they can agree on industry-wide pricing strategies. Where the sector determines to operate on a closed-shop basis, such as OPEC (Organisation of Petroleum Exporting Countries), this can be beneficial to all concerned, though experience shows that such cartels are now becoming difficult to operate, with one or two players often breaking agreed parameters (such as Russia, willing to expand its oil production).

However, it has been argued that many organisations are now confronted by a bewildering array of competitors who may or may not be from within their traditional industry sector. An example of this is the recent growth of digital music offered on the Internet. Traditionally record organisations competed against each other in a well-defined sector. Recently artists have realised that they can reach a global audience through webcasts, which was not possible a few years ago. Thus the computer-mediated environment through the Internet has created a different form of competition. In many instances, industry sectors are blurring; for example, television broadcasting is now accessed not only through TV sets, but also via computers and digital phones. The case study on Eminem shows the way in which traditional industry sectors are being challenged by the new broadcast media and how traditional sector-based thinking needs to change.

Product differentiation

Organisations often use product differentiation to create a distinctive image for their products. Often this is based on branding and pricing. In commodity markets, product differentiation is difficult. However, in luxury goods markets such as perfumes or designer clothes, differentiation offers certain segments of consumers a specific image and they are then unwilling to purchase different products even if the price differential is slightly higher or lower.

Capacity utilisation and exit barriers

In some industries there may be overcapacity in terms of production of particular goods. This is true of the automobile industry and the personal computer market. When this occurs, prices tend to drop. In large industry sectors, such as the automobile industry, it is difficult for organisations to exit the sector as the exit costs are prohibitive. Under these conditions, mergers and acquisitions often ensue.

CASE STUDY

Eminem CD sales impressive despite music sharing

LOS ANGELES (AP) – Eminem's record label was so nervous about music pirates cannibalizing sales of the rapper's latest CD that it released *The Eminem Show* nine days early, disrupting well-laid marketing plans.

But when the CD hit stores Memorial Day weekend, it still managed to debut at No. 1 in record time. Some industry observers say the CD's success in the face of widespread bootlegging proves that online music swapping doesn't crush legitimate retail sales and can actually generate better buzz for a new release.

'The jury is still out on how significantly file sharing actually effects record label revenues,' said Michael Goodman, a senior music analyst with Forrester Research in Boston.'But to a certain extent, file sharing can actually prime the pump for sales.'

SoundScan, which gathers sales data from more than 17,000 retailers across the United States, said 284,534 copies of *The Eminem Show* were sold nationally during the long weekend. 'We've never had a record debut at No. 1 on the SoundScan chart that hasn't had the benefit of a full six days of sales behind it,' said Mike Shalett, chief executive of SoundScan.

But Interscope Geffen A&M, the label behind Eminem, insists that illegal copies, made from one of three closely guarded master copies sent to manufacturers, hurt the release. 'I absolutely believe that the bootlegs and downloads have a huge negative effect on sales,' said Steve Berman, head of sales and marketing at Interscope, a division of Universal Music Group.

Individual songs from the CD became widely available online in mid-May, and bootlegged copies of the entire CD began appearing on street corners around the same time. It's impossible to calculate how many sales were lost in the process, Berman said. Interscope took a number of steps to counter the impact of the downloads, beyond moving up the release date.

Two million of the 3 million copies of *The Eminem Show* were shipped with a complimentary DVD that featured interviews and live footage of Eminem. The record label also pursued Web sites posting the CD, persuading some of them to remove it, Berman said. But some analysts said the music industry continues to take the wrong approach to counter online downloads.

Web surfers downloading music files are the same people who go out and buy the CDs, and music organisations need to treat them like customers, not criminals, said Sean Baenen, managing director of Odyssey, a market research firm in San Francisco. 'It's not a group of pirates looking to steal,' Baenen said. 'It's a group of people who want more choice and control over the music they receive.'

The early success of *The Eminem Show* in the wake of widespread file sharing and bootlegging provides some understanding to an industry trying to come to terms with a new marketplace.

'What's happened to Eminem is going to be a real learning point for the industry and artists," said Michael Bracy, a Washington lobbyist with the Future of Music Coalition, which represents artists' interests. 'Part of the puzzle is offering consumers some entertainment value that they're not going to get through file sharing,' he said.

Source: usatoday.com (2002)

Cost advantages or disadvantages

Some of the PIMS (Profit Impact of Marketing Strategies) studies show that organisations that have high market share often show better rates of return. In part, this may be because they achieve cost advantages through high production levels and thus have better economies of scale than their competitors. However, in other areas, excess capacity may mean that organisations are forced to sell at cost to cover overheads.

Buyer power

Porter regards the bargaining power of buyers as an important factor in determining the attractiveness of an industry sector. Buyers come in all shapes and sizes. Sometimes they are powerful; at other times they are weak. The relative strength or weakness depends on the desirability of the product and/or its utility to the buyer. Buyers can be classified as either industrial or consumer.

Industrial buyers

Industrial buyers tend to differ according to the sectors in which they are operating. The forces acting on them may also vary. In fact, the whole area can be extremely complex and it is impossible to illustrate all possibilities. However, listed below are examples of the forces that act on industrial buyers:

- Car manufacturers rely on tyre manufacturers for building cars. There are many tyre manufacturers and there is overcapacity. This gives car manufacturers strong buying power and the ability to switch suppliers if they wish. The tyre manufacturers are *mutually* dependent on the car industry. If sales of cars go up, so do tyre sales. If intense competition exists among buyers, as in the electric cable industry, they in turn will put pressure on suppliers such as Pirelli.
- The need for specialist products or services puts pressure on industrial buyers. In the computer industry, processors and their quality is of vital importance to computer manufacturers. These manufacturers therefore have less bargaining power with suppliers as they rely on specialist devices and quality. In the biotechnology industry, certain companies, such as Biocatalyst, provide specialist enzymes for producing olive oil. The farmers who need this enzyme are in a weak position to bargain over price.
- Industrial buyers can also decide to vertically integrate along the supply chain by purchasing the company that supplies its raw materials. Organisations such as Coca-Cola and Pepsi Cola own their own bottling plants in various countries.

Consumer buyers

There is a larger number and wider variety of consumer buyers than industrial buyers. Organisations grapple with different ways of understanding segments of consumers so that some sense can be made of behaviour patterns and the forces that consumers can create within industry sectors and on companies. The points below illustrate this:

- Consumers can exhibit collective buyer power when they group together to purchase items from manufacturers.
- Consumers carry considerable power as they can choose whether or not to buy a product. They can also decide to switch from one product or brand to another. Understanding this power, marketers are forever trying to understand consumer segments and their buying motives so that organisations can position themselves sensibly in the marketplace.

■ Consumers may or may not be price sensitive, depending on their make-up as a segment. Consumers are also increasingly sophisticated and are ready to search for information regarding the best prices and quality for a range of products and services, with the Internet increasingly used to facilitate the search.

Supplier power

Supplier power is similar to buyer power, as one company will be a buyer and the other a supplier. Suppliers are often smaller organisations supplying components or raw materials to larger corporations. The factors that are pertinent to suppliers are the same as those discussed in the previous section.

Threat of substitutes

As technology advances, it becomes increasingly difficult for organisations to predict the changes that could take place within their own industry sectors. For example, the new biotechnology companies, which offer more effective treatments against diseases such as cancer and Alzheimer's, are challenging pharmaceutical companies. Many individuals are searching for alternative methods for curing ailments, rather than relying on drugs. The Swiss watch industry was decimated in the 1970s as a result of the advent of digital technology. Within the travel sector, rail and air travel could substitute for one another.

Overview of analysing the industry

Industry analysis enables an organisation to understand how market forces are driving the sector within which it competes. At the same time it helps to highlight the significant ways in which the organisation can target and segment its consumer base once it understands the power these segments wield in the marketplace. The following section discusses a range of other analyses that can be performed by organisations. It is important to remember that there are links between these and industry analysis.

Portfolio tools

The product life cycle

A range of portfolio matrices is also available to marketers for segmenting markets. The most common of these is the product life cycle (PLC) concept. The PLC has been used for many decades and continues to be discussed in marketing theory. Depending on the stage a product is at in the life cycle, various strategic alternatives are available to organisations. These are summarised in Table 2.1. The strategies are taken from the classic paper by Day (1986). These competitive positioning stances can be linked to the Boston Consulting Group (BCG) matrix, and the possible strategies are also illustrated in Figure 2.2. It should be remembered

Table 2.1 Product life cycle and potential strategies

	Embryonic	*Growing*	*Mature*	*Ageing*
Dominant	All-out push for share	Hold position	Hold position	
	Hold position	Hold share	Grow with industry	Hold position
Strong	Attempt to improve position	Attempt to improve position	Hold position	Hold position or harvest
	All-out push for share	Push for share	Grow with industry	
Favourable	Selective or all-out push for share	Attempt to improve position	Custodial or maintenance	Harvest
	Selectively attempt to improve position	Selectively push for share	Find niche and attempt to protect	Phased withdrawal
Tenable	Selectively push for position	Find niche and protect it	Find niche and hang on or phased withdrawal	Phased withdrawal or abandon
Weak	Up or out	Turnaround or abandon	Turnaround or phased withdrawal	Abandon

Source: Based on Day (1986)

that many organisations will have a range of products and thus may be dealing with different market segments. It is therefore important to use the BCG analysis to understand the product portfolio and to ascertain whether an organisation has a balanced set of products or not.

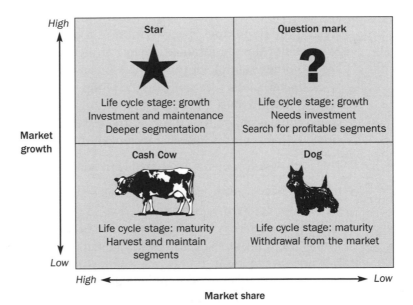

Figure 2.2 The BCG matrix and associated lifecycle analysis
Source: Adapted from Rowe *et al.* (1986)

The characteristics of each stage of industry maturity are as follows (Hax and Majluf 1984):

- *Embryonic industry*. This is characterised by rapid growth, changes in technology, vigorous pursuit of new customers, and fragmented and unstable market shares.
- *Growth industry*. This exhibits rapid growth, clear trends in customer purchase patterns, a growth in competitors' market shares, technological developments and increasing barriers to entry.
- *Mature industry*. This shows stable purchase patterns, a growth in technology and market shares (however, the industries themselves may be highly competitive).
- *Ageing industry*. This is characterised by falling demand, a declining number of competitors and a narrowing product line.

At each of these stages, the following competitive positions could be adopted:

- *Dominant*. In any industry, only one organisation can dominate, for example Boeing in the aircraft industry and Microsoft in computer software with its Windows products.
- *Strong*. This includes organisations that are leaders within their sector of industry, but do not exhibit absolute dominance. They have large market shares and are strong competitors. Examples of such organisations are Unilever in the toiletries market and Volkswagen in the car sector.
- *Favourable*. This describes a particular competitive position reached by an organisation in a fragmented industry by pursuing a differentiation strategy or by exploiting a particular market niche in which the company excels. An example of this is Dell Computers which has created a particular differentiated product in the PC market through its just-in-time, customised direct-marketing strategies.
- *Tenable*. This describes a position that can be maintained profitably through geographic or product specialisation in a narrow or protected market niche. Examples of this are localised organic farmers in Europe who supply local markets. Another example of this is the Morgan car for which there is a waiting list (see Chapter 5 for a case study on the Morgan Motor Company Limited).
- *Weak*. This describes a position that an organisation cannot sustain given the competitive economics of the industry. In such a situation, an organisation can strive to improve its position or it can exit the sector.

There are some problems associated with analysis using the BCG matrix:

- It is not always easy to determine market share. In industry sectors such as automobiles and pharmaceuticals, market share data is available and since the number of players is known, market shares can be determined. In many other sectors it is difficult to determine actual market shares.
- It is not easy to use in the service sector, where both services and clients can be varied (for example, in accountancy firms). The value of the clients rather than absolute market shares may make more sense in this sector.
- Life cycles may not always follow the classical shape of growth and decline. Some products may grow very rapidly whereas others may take time to grow. An

example of rapid growth is computer games such as 'Lara Croft', which then declines rapidly as new games are released.

- Organisations could make hasty decisions on products and fail to invest in potential stars.
- Products sometimes take time to diffuse into the marketplace and need initial investment.

Under these circumstances, Rogers' diffusion curve should also be considered. Rogers (1995) argues that products diffuse into the marketplace according to five factors. These are:

- *Relative advantage.* Organisations developing products or services need to consider the relative advantages offered by the new products. Economic factors, status aspects and incentives can all contribute to an innovation's perceived advantage. For example, the Dyson vacuum cleaner offers a relative advantage over conventional vacuum cleaners with its innovative technology.
- *Compatibility.* A new product or service needs to be compatible with consumers' values and beliefs, needs and previously adopted innovations. For example, a consumer familiar with a computer that uses the Windows operating system is most likely to upgrade to a computer that is compatible with their previous experience of PCs and allows them to transfer and use files created using their old computer.
- *Complexity.* The rate at which a new innovation is adopted is, in general, related to the complexity of the product. Complex products are less likely to be adopted by consumers – consider the case of the new mobile technology.
- *Trialability and observability.* Trialability and observability are usually positively related to adoption. Trialability is of particular importance to early adopters since they do not usually have peers to ask for advice. If individuals can try a product or can observe the way it works and benefits their lives, they are more likely to adopt it. Companies such as Microsoft often bring out beta versions of their new software so that consumers can observe and trial the software.

Figure 2.3 shows the typology of the consumers who are willing to adopt new products or services. The consumers tend to fall into the following categories:

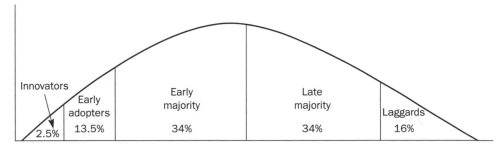

Figure 2.3 Typology of new product users

- *Innovators*. These are individuals who are venturesome and who may also have the financial means to try out new inventions and innovations. When new products are introduced, they are often priced at a premium rate to try to recoup development costs as organisations are aware that a new product may not always diffuse into a marketplace.
- *Early adopters*. These consumers are willing to observe and trial a new product. As new, similar products enter the market, they will start purchasing and will follow the innovators. Once a product or service reaches this stage, further progress can often be achieved.
- *Early majority*. This segment of the population is value-driven and tends to make a considered choice when purchasing a product. It is likely that economies of scale have made the product cheaper and more accessible through the distribution network by this stage. This set of consumers will wait for this to happen before making the decision to purchase.
- *Late majority*. By the time the product reaches this segment of the population, it will have matured. The late majority (or the sceptical consumers) are those who are not convinced by a product or service offered. They may or may not adopt it. If they do, it may be adopted grudgingly because everyone else has the product. Mobile phones were resisted by a section of the population, but many have been forced to adopt them, perhaps because friends and relatives already possessed them or perhaps because they are the only means of communication when travelling.
- *Laggards*. Laggards comprise a section of the population that never seems to move in line with popular opinion. They are usually the last to adopt an innovation, usually grudgingly.

As a product diffuses through the marketplace, from the innovators to the laggards, it moves through the life cycle of its existence. It is important to remember that not all products follow the smooth, bell-shaped curve shown in Figure 2.3. Some products may take a long time to reach maturity and some products may never reach the early majority stage, so caution should be exercised when using this model in conjunction with the PLC.

The GE/McKinsey business screen portfolio matrix

This analysis tool is a development of matrices originally devised by General Electric (GE) and the consultancy firm McKinsey.

The GE/McKinsey business screen portfolio matrix, shown in Figure 2.4, is composed of two main axes, depicting industry attractiveness and business competitive position. Depending on what strengths a company exhibits for either its products or its strategic business units (SBUs), particular strategies can be followed.

The various portfolios can be plotted on the grid in circles, indicating the market shares within particular sectors. The directions in which an organisation could decide to move are indicated. In using matrices such as these, it is important that the factors that are most important to an organisation within a particular sector are considered and analysed (see Table 2.2).

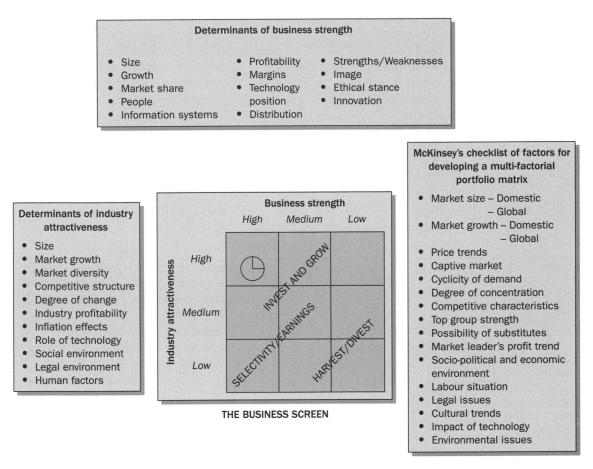

Determinants of business strength

- Size
- Growth
- Market share
- People
- Information systems

- Profitability
- Margins
- Technology position
- Distribution

- Strengths/Weaknesses
- Image
- Ethical stance
- Innovation

McKinsey's checklist of factors for developing a multi-factorial portfolio matrix

- Market size – Domestic
  – Global
- Market growth – Domestic
  – Global
- Price trends
- Captive market
- Cyclicity of demand
- Degree of concentration
- Competitive characteristics
- Top group strength
- Possibility of substitutes
- Market leader's profit trend
- Socio-political and economic environment
- Labour situation
- Legal issues
- Cultural trends
- Impact of technology
- Environmental issues

Determinants of industry attractiveness

- Size
- Market growth
- Market diversity
- Competitive structure
- Degree of change
- Industry profitability
- Inflation effects
- Role of technology
- Social environment
- Legal environment
- Human factors

Business strength

High   Medium   Low

Industry attractiveness

High

Medium

Low

INVEST AND GROW

SELECTIVITY/EARNINGS

HARVEST/DIVEST

THE BUSINESS SCREEN

Figure 2.4 The GE/McKinsey business screen portfolio matrix

Source: Adapted from Kerin *et al.* (1990)

The directional policy matrix

The directional policy matrix (DPM) is useful for analysing an organisation's prospects in particular markets. It was originally conceived and used by Shell Chemicals UK (Hughes 1981). The matrix, shown in Figure 2.5, is based on:

1 Business-sector prospects – the profitability and growth potential of the sector within which the organisation operates.
2 The competitive position of the business in that sector.

The DPM offers a flexible and sensible way of analysing an organisation's competitive strengths and prospects within markets. The key points made in the matrix show the directions in which an organisation could proceed depending on whether it is making money (*cash generation*) or losing it (*disinvest*). On the other hand, it may wish to invest in potentially lucrative markets (*double or quits*). Again, these possible directions are not meant to be prescriptive; they are suggestions based on various other factors that an organisation needs to consider (see Table 2.3).

Table 2.2 Factors contributing to market attractiveness and business position

	Attractiveness of your market	*Status of your business*
Market factors	Size ($, £, €, ¥, or units, or both)	Your share in equivalent terms
	Size of key segments	Your share of key segments

	Growth rate per year:
	     Total
	     Segments
		Your annual growth rate:
		     Total
		     Segments

	Diversity of market	Diversity of your participation
	Sensitivity to price, service features and external factors	Your influence on the market
	Cyclicality	
	Seasonality	Lags or leads in your sales
	Bargaining power of upstream suppliers	Bargaining power of your suppliers
	Bargaining power of downstream suppliers	Bargaining power of your customers
Competition	Types of competitors	Where you fit, how you compare in terms of products, marketing capability, service
		Production strength, financial strength, management
	Entries and exits	Segments you have entered or left
	Changes in share	Your relative share change
	Substitution by new technology	Your vulnerability to new technology
	Degrees and type of integration	Your own level of integration
Financial and economic factors	Contribution margins	Your margins
	Leveraging factors, such as economies of scale and experience	Your scale and experience
	Barriers to entry or exit (both financial and non-financial)	Barriers to your entry or exit (both financial and non-financial)
	General capacity utilisation	Your capacity utilisation
Technological factors	Maturity and volatility	Your ability to cope with change
	Complexity	Depth of your skills
	Differentiation	Types of your technological skills
	Patents and copyrights	Your patent protection
	Manufacturing process technology required	Your manufacturing technology
Sociopolitical factors in your environment	Social attitudes and trends	Your company's responsiveness and flexibility
	Laws and government agency regulations	Your company's ability to cope
	Influence with pressure groups and human factors such as unionisation and stakeholder acceptance	Your company's relationship and influence Your company's relationships

Source: Adapted from Abell (1979)

Business sector prospects

	Unattractive	Average	Attractive
Weak	Disinvest	Phased withdrawal Custodial	Double or quit
Average	Phased withdrawal	Custodial Growth	Try harder
Strong	Cash generation	Growth Leader	Leader

Company's competitive capabilities

Figure 2.5 The directional policy matrix

Source: Robinson et al. (1978)

Table 2.3 Factors underlying analysis of business-sector prospects and organisation's competitive capabilities

Factors relevant to analysis of business sector prospects	Factors relevant to analysis of company's competitive capabilities
1 Market growth 2 Market quality 3 Environmental aspects	1 Market position 2 Production capability 3 Product R&D
Guidelines for assessing market quality	**Guidelines for assessing market position**
A sector for which the answers to all or most of the following questions are yes would attract a four- or five-point star rating. *The following questions are more relevant for manufacturing companies and will need modification for other sectors:* a) Has the sector a record of high, stable profitability? b) Can margins be maintained when manufacturing capacity exceeds demand? c) Is the product resistant to commodity pricing behaviour? d) Is the technology of production freely available or is it proprietary and specialist? e) Is the market free from domination by a small group of powerful customers? f) Has the product high added value when converted by the customer? g) In the case of a new product, is the market likely to remain small enough, so that it is unattractive to other producers? h) Is the product such that the customer has to change his formulation or even his machinery if he changes suppliers? i) Is the product free from the risk of substitution by an alternative supplier?	*Primary factor*: percentage share of total market. *Secondary factor*: degree to which market share is secured. *Ratings associated with alternative competitive positions:* ★ Current position negligible. ★★ Minor market share. Less than adequate to support R&D and other brand development. ★★★ A company with a strong viable stake in the market, but below the top league. Usually when one producer is a leader, the next level of competition will comprise of producers meriting a 3-star rating. ★★★★ Major producer. In this situation, two to four organisations are equally strong. All merit a 4-star rating. ★★★★★ Leader. A company in a pre-eminent market position, likely to be followed by others, and also the acknowledged technological leader. The market share associated with this position is likely to vary from case to case. For example, in a field of 10, a company with a 25% share may be a leader, whereas a 50% share in a field of two competitors may not confer market leadership.

Source: Kerin et al. (1990)

Growth vector analysis

Growth vector analysis, shown in Figure 2.6, is a modified version of the more commonly used Ansoff matrix for segmenting products and services within organisations. An organisation has to determine how attractive or poor its products or services are in matching certain segments. It can then make a decision as to whether it would like to extend its product or service offerings. The direction of the arrows shows the level of risk the organisation may be committing itself to as it moves away from familiar segments and markets. The numbers indicate how the level of risk increases. Each case has to be taken on merit as a high-risk situation but may also produce high returns.

Key issues to consider when using portfolio matrices

Portfolio matrices have become significant tools in helping to understand the macro-environment when developing segments. They also enable an organisation to understand and develop its positioning strategies. However, the following caveats should be noted:

- A high-growth market may offer opportunities, but will also demand high investments.
- Many portfolio matrices are geared to understanding product markets and are based on manufacturing organisations.
- Portfolio matrices need to be modified for the non-profit and services sectors. For example, factors such as the experience curve may not have direct relevance. Also, market share may not be a critical issue; service levels may be more important.
- Portfolio matrices largely focus on the current capabilities of an organisation rather than stressing future possibilities.
- A blinkered approach to the use of portfolio matrices may result in narrowly defined strategies (such as invest, harvest, divest), based on a limited range of considerations. It also prevents innovation and creativity in developing segments and strategies.

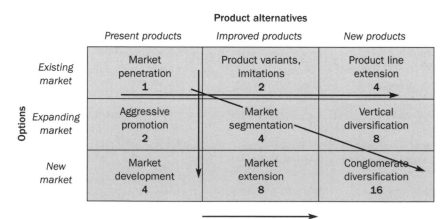

Figure 2.6 Growth vector analysis
Source: Rowe *et al.* (1986)

- New products and services could attract funding from venture capital markets and therefore it should not be assumed that strategies are constrained by resources (Wensley 1981).
- It is not always easy to define product/market segments.
- The judgements involved are largely subjective, but appear to be scientific when plotted in two dimensions.

This section has highlighted some of the key points that need to be considered when a macro-analysis of the environment is coordinated with a particular portfolio within an organisation. The next section considers segmentation in a more focused manner.

Segmentation

We have considered the main drivers of competition and the segmentation that an organisation could pursue as a result of portfolio analysis. It is useful to go beyond this and also consider the attractiveness of different segments. Understanding segments is a critical element of marketing. However, analysis of segments is rarely straightforward and demands a greater understanding of the segments that are being served. This section is going to consider some of the traditional methods of segmentation and also consider the ways in which segmentation is moving in the twenty-first century.

Figures 2.7 and 2.8 illustrate that segmentation requires consideration of:

- the macro-environment;
- the sectors in which an organisation operates;
- its portfolio of products/services;
- consumer characteristics;
- physical variables, such as geographic location and environment.

The next section will look at the bases that are generally adopted for analysing consumer groups in marketing.

Many authors argue that, when segmenting markets, it is important that the following factors be taken into account:

1 *Is the market segment **measurable?*** Has an organisation enough market research available to ascertain the size, buying power and profiles of the segments it is targeting? This is a difficult issue as appropriate measures and statistics may not always be readily available. It may also be costly to undertake specific market research. Under these circumstances, organisations often buy research from companies such as Mintel.

2 *Is the market segment **accessible?*** Most organisations will be anxious to know whether they can effectively reach and serve their designated market segments. In order to access certain markets, issues of distribution, advertising and branding need to be considered. Access to particular segments may be dependent on advertising followed by distribution strategies.

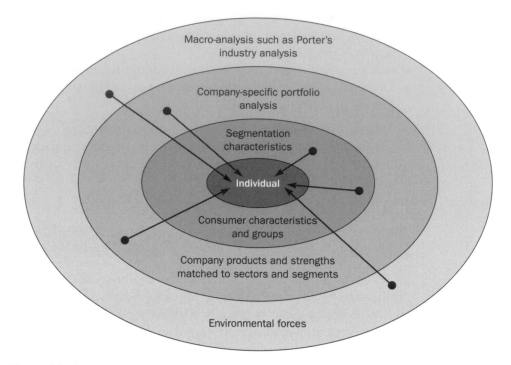

Figure 2.7 Segmenting markets

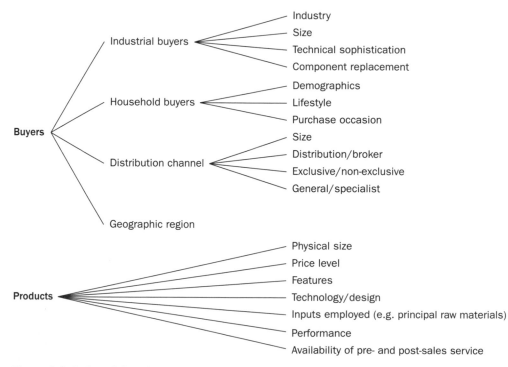

Figure 2.8 Industrial and consumer segmentation
Source: Grant (2002)

3 *Is the market segment **substantial**?* For most organisations, it is important to know whether a particular segment is large enough or profitable enough to service. For some organisations a large market segment may be important for market share development, yet for others the profitability of a niche segment may be more important. For example, a company like the Morgan Motor Company may be happy to serve a small but substantially profitable segment of car enthusiasts, whereas a company like Procter & Gamble may be interested in the size and distribution of the segment for anti-dandruff shampoos.

4 *Can marketing strategies be **actioned** to serve the market segments?* Every organisation has limited resources and it may not always be possible to serve all segments effectively. An organisation therefore has to be certain that it can implement marketing and targeting strategies for its chosen segments.

Understanding segmentation characteristics

There is no single way to segment a market. For both personal and business customers, however, there is a plethora of bases that may be considered when trying to segment the total market. The classification variables, or bases, are as diverse as the ways different researchers classify them into groups. A classification of segmentation bases presented by Frank *et al.* (1972) is shown in Table 2.4.

Frank (1972) and Wilkie and Cohen (1976) also indicate the distinction in terms of:

- **general customer characteristics** such as demographic, socioeconomic, personality, and lifestyle which represent relatively enduring characteristics, and
- more **market-dependent** or **situation-specific customer characteristics**, like tendencies towards brand loyalty or basic consumption patterns, as well as attitudes, perceptions and preferences.

In research, general lifestyle and general attitudes may be used, in combination with more product-specific variables.

A classification using behavioural measures as classifiers linked to other factors can also be used (Van Raaij 1982). The variables closely related to behaviour would be behavioural intention, attitudes and lifestyle, linked to sociodemographics, personality and neighbourhood characteristics.

Variables can be classified as being quantitative or qualitative:

Table 2.4 Segmentation bases

	Customer specific	*Product specific*
Observable	Cultural, geographic, demographic and socioeconomic variables	User status, usage frequency, brand loyalty, store loyalty and patronage, usage situation
Unobservable	Psychographics: personality and lifestyle	Psychographics: benefits, perceptions, attitudes, preferences and intentions

Source: Adapted from Frank (1972)

■ *Quantitative* – geodemographic, economic, size and type of customer;
■ *Qualitative* – psychographic, behavioural, benefit sought.

These may be used singly or in some form of combination.

Another classification scheme relies on factors being divided into two large groups (Cahill 1997): those based upon **physical attributes** (geographic, demographics, and the combination of the two, geodemographics) and those based upon **behavioural attributes** of the customers (lifestyle, life stage, psychographics and usage).

A marketer should try a range of different segmentation variables, alone and in combination, to find the best way to view the market structure. Some of the key characteristics of segmentation variables used for this purpose are explained below.

Geographic segmentation

Geographic segmentation schemes are probably the oldest segmentation method of all. Small manufacturers who wished to limit their investments, or whose distribution channels were not large enough to cover the entire country, segmented the market, in effect, by selling their products only in certain areas. As its root, geographic segmentation assumes that people have needs because of where they live that are different from those of people living elsewhere. Usinier (1999) has written a whole treatise on understanding how cultural attributes resulting from geographic locations may determine different individuals' propensity to purchase a range of goods. Geographic segmentation calls for dividing the market into different geographical units such as nations, states, regions, counties, cities or neighbourhoods. An organisation may decide to operate in one or a few geographic areas or to operate in all areas but pay attention to geographic differences in needs and wants (Kotler *et al.* 2001). Many organisations today are 'regionalising' their marketing programmes – localising their products, advertising, promotion and sales efforts to fit the needs of individual regions, cities and even neighbourhoods. Geographic segmentation has a lot to recommend it; it is simple to understand, simple to perform and implement, and simple to manage (Cahill 1997).

The type of neighbourhood facilitates or hinders the diffusion of an innovation. Lunn (1982) describes the ACORN (A Classification of Residential Neighbourhoods) approach in the UK, which is based on census data. Webber conceived ACORN when he was working at the Centre for Environmental Studies. He is now at CACI Inc. ACORN is based on the government's Census of Great Britain, conducted in 1981. Census neighbourhoods are updates derived from CACI's proprietary demographic model of Great Britain. ACORN represents a radical departure from previous types of geographic classification. These groupings, with their 38 neighbourhood type sub-groupings, have the advantage of being very easy to measure and relate to. In particular, it has been possible to give each postcode in the UK an ACORN classification, which is a descriptor of the predominant type of household to be found in that postcode. By relating financial services behaviour to type of household, for example, the propensity of each postcode to respond to a given financial services offer can be, in part, determined (Palmer and Lucas 1994). This type of segmentation can be helpful in siting retail outlets such as supermarkets, banks and other services. It can also help to identify groups of customers who may have similar lifestyle patterns as a result of the location in which they reside.

Demographic segmentation

Demographic segmentation offers an alternative method of segmentation. This methodology relies on age and lifestyle. Under this philosophy, targets were defined using variables such as young people, men or families with children. Unfortunately, a number of recent studies have shown that demographic variables such as age, sex, income, occupation and race are, in general, poor predictors of behaviour and, consequently, less than optimum bases for segmentation strategies. However, when market segments are first defined using other bases, such as personality or behaviour, their demographic characteristics must be known in order to assess the size of the target market and to reach it efficiently. Age is probably the demographic variable that most lends itself to credible, useful segmentation and targeting: consumer needs and wants change with age. Income is related to ability to buy; family size to quantity of purchases. Social class is a concept built up from age, the level of education and occupation. As the new century progresses, it may be easier to use social class and income as explanatory variables. Of course, demographic variables that can be used for segmentation and targeting purposes include more than just age: height and/or weight can work; race works for certain products, as does religion.

Sex segmentation has long been used in marketing for products such as clothing, hairdressing, cosmetics and magazines. For products and services such as automobiles, boats, clothing, cosmetics and travel, marketers have also used income segmentation. Many organisations target affluent consumers with luxury goods and convenience services, but many others profitably target low-income consumers with products and services such as discount shop chains. Handled properly, with a great deal of discretion and understanding, any demographic variable can be used.

A set of mostly demographic variables that has been around in social science research and the popular press for decades is 'social class'. The concept of a social class is constantly changing and the criteria that once defined a particular social category are now no longer appropriate. Also, previous assumptions about age and consumption have had to be drastically altered with the growth of the 'grey' market. Even this grey market is now so large and complex that only psychographics can be used to segment it into the smaller segments necessary to market to the different submarkets.

The demographic attributes used in segmentation may include dozens of elements, but the basic elements include age, income, home ownership, length of residence and occupation. Customer demographics are important because industry trends indicate that markets need to be carefully designated and are continually fragmenting.

The case study on PlayStation illuminates the issues raised so far.

The power behind PlayStation: going for old

Everyone's getting younger, older. Apparently. Thirty-plus-somethings continue on in the vein of teenage-somethings: coffee-table Hip Hop; Nike Shox; G Star Denim; the odd, wayward spliff; a desire to spend money rather than save – all manifestations of your average 35 year old. Youth 'lifestyle' has become every man's mantra. And included within this is video gaming's 'massification'. You're as likely to find a PlayStation 2 console in a 50-year-old architect's office as you are within a 13-year-old's bedroom. PlayStation has managed gaming – aggressively at times – into an age profile that extends way beyond the conventional tween, or early teen, territory.

Five years ago, gaming resided in male, teenage bedrooms. Gaming was nerdy. Masturbatory. An embarrassment. Something you wouldn't admit to. Today it enjoys mainstream acceptance; its aesthetic, or artistic appeal, is widely recognised and debated. Gaming has become a serious, mass market leisure pursuit. And PlayStation, in particular, has helped to accelerate this societal change.

How?

Back in 1995, Sony sought to command and conquer older individuals' leisure time, not just their gaming time, with its 32-bit console; 'micro' disruption of the category was sought through a four-fold strategy:

- 'older' communication targeting;
- 'older' technology (CDs not cartridges);
- launch of 'older', adult-themed games versus childish, platform titles;
- investment in 'serious' role-playing icons – like Lara Croft – rather than cartoon 'heroes' such as Mario or Sonic.

Consistently the brand was marketed, over and above the product's technical capacity. The reward in gaming, communication reasoned, rested within the benefit of experiential output, not the console's input, as previous hardware manufacturers had iterated. Powerful gaming experiences could change you, move you, reshape you.

Feeding off this desire to own leisure time ran a media strategy which *understood* the requirements for 'meeting points' between PlayStation and an older consumer. Building a skate park meant developing a touch point with skate fans in their late teens who were, simultaneously, gaming fans (the Tony Hawkes franchise continues to sell impressively). A roach card magazine insert delivered an acknowledgement of what older gamers did when they gamed, with their mates, in each other's homes. Further, an 'intelligent' brand voice told these audiences they could 'quote themselves'; they could 'be their own hero' or 'land on their own moon'.

The power of play through PlayStation was dramatically and compellingly told. Gaming was much more than gaming. It was a sport. An art form. An interaction that could terrify, fascinate and frustrate. More significantly, you – the gamer – decided on how your gaming 'escape' should manifest: you might choose to be David Beckham in one moment or fly a jet fighter plane in another. If not these, then you might prefer to role-play God, or at least a superhero; to become a deadly assassin or a triple-A snowboarder; why not a street fighter or a DJ? The choice – the possibilities – were infinite. An infinity made practical by the largest library of games. Games that were – and continue to be – uniquely positioned and marketed.

When we consider the consumer profile of PlayStation and PlayStation 2, today, we see a brand that enjoys an almost unnatural span of age profile. Where the junior console drops off – around the age of 14 – the senior, second-generation console picks up, and enjoys its largest number of gamers between the ages of 20 and 25. A healthy penetration continues, afterward, beyond the age of 40, however, and well into the grey market of 50, 60 and 70.

Breaking the targeting and brand rules of this category has – ultimately – changed the status of gaming. In six short years, PlayStation has evolved and grown the gaming category out of the kid's bedroom and into all of our lives. Let's give this some perspective. In terms of money, gaming now generates more cash than the American film industry. In fact, Datamonitor suggests that sales of games consoles and software in Europe and the USA will generate over $20 billion worth of business by 2003. Not bad for a category that was – according to 1995 business forecasts – rasping its way into extinction.

Source: Carl Radcliffe (TBWA)

Life-stage segmentation, also called the 'family life cycle', is the recognition that a family's needs and expenditures change over time as people leave their parents' home, marry and have children, who grow up to repeat the cycle. In a sense, life-stage segmentation represents family demographics, particularly ages and income levels. The focus on longitudinal changes in purchase behaviour is valuable for predicting macro demand for specific product categories, such as houses, education, household appliances, services, etc.

Examining the demographic make-up of your customers enables you first to understand who your customers are and whether you wish to pursue others like them (Coffey and Palm 1999). Andreasen (1984) explored the effects of life status change on attitudes, needs, wants and behaviour. He notes, 'for many people, the break with the past that is inherent in the occasion of a status change can represent an opportunity to rethink and organise their lives' and concludes that the transition from one stage of life to the next causes much stress in individuals. It is this stress that can make customers become more susceptible to seeking the suggestions of others (particularly marketers) and could make them prime targets for products and services which are viewed as necessary requirements for the next life stage. The greater the change in the life pattern, the greater will be the life cycle change.

Geodemographic segmentation

By combining geographic and demographic into 'geodemographics', marketers have built a new analytic base. Of what use are geodemographics? Geodemographics are based on an understanding that people with similar needs and lifestyles tend to live close together. As Weiss (1994) states, 'where we live affects our attitudes toward what we buy...'. Although this may be true, it reverses the direction of major causality; the statement should read 'what we think influences where we live' – at least at the micro level (Cahill 1997).

Developments in the area of geodemographic segmentation include systems such as FiNPiN coding (Pinpoint Analysis Ltd) and MOSAIC (CCN Marketing). In both cases, the approach was to cross-reference other research-based data on the uptake of financial services to the original geodemographic descriptor. For example, Pinpoint Analysis Ltd cross-tabulated its PiNCode against the usage pattern of financial services established by the Financial Research Survey (FRS is a national regular survey of respondents' usage of financial products). From this cross-tabulation, a more industry-specific classification of FiNPin types was produced (Palmer and Lucas 1994).

Psychographic segmentation

Psychographic segmentation became an important aspect of advertising and marketing research in the 1960s. Understanding psychographics is important as it is difficult to develop demographic categories for many products (e.g. clothes, cars). The difficulties associated with the use of demographic and socioeconomic charac-

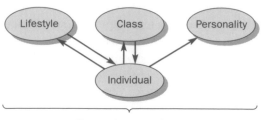

Figure 2.9 Psychographic segmentation

teristics as bases for segmentation have led to various attempts to segment markets based on psychographic characteristics. Often, demographic data is collected routinely and marketers are comfortable with this (Wells 1975). However, the reality is that even consumers categorised in the same demographic group can have very different psychographic characteristics. People tend to have differing behaviour patterns. See Figure 2.9.

According to Ziff (1971): 'some have used the term to refer to basic **personality** characteristics – aggression, anxiety, extroversion, masculinity – while some have applied it to **lifestyle** variables – community involvement, home entertainment, leisure activities, etc. Kotler (1988) says that social class, lifestyle and personality traits constitute psychographics. The most clear and complete definition is given by Gunter and Furnham (1992):

> *Psychographics seek to describe the human characteristics of consumers that may have bearing on their responses to products, packaging, advertising and public relations efforts. Such variables may span a spectrum from self-concept and lifestyle to attitudes, interests and opinions, as well as perceptions of product attributes.*

The case study on Lifestyle applications is an example of lifestyle segmentation for the mobile communications market.

CASE STUDY

Lifestyle applications

Lifestyle applications are typically services people use in the normal course of their day, i.e. buying train tickets, reading the paper, sending e-mail and looking up stock prices. These services, provided in real time, are a natural complement to mobile lifestyles. Some information services will fall within specific interest groups, i.e. 'The Socialites' or 'The High-fliers.' Packaging these services will therefore require intelligent market segmentation. A high-end market identified as the early adopter is the 'Mobile Professional' market.

Some examples of lifestyle packages are:

The Lost Traveller
This application provides the 'lost traveller' with locality information and directions. The user can follow street maps to get to the nearest bed and breakfast, check out what's on in town or simply find the nearest Japanese restaurant.

The Time Poor

We are experiencing a time where the working man and woman are so busy, they cannot find the time to go to the bank or even open their bills, let alone organise to pay for them. Applications that will make life easier for this segment are services such as checking account balances, transferring funds, paying bills, viewing transaction details, extending insurance policies and performing numerous other such tasks via a wireless terminal.

The Socialites

The teenage market is undergoing a social revolution. Never before has there been a greater desire to keep in touch and communicate with friends among the teenage market. In Europe there are reports of real-time communication, where youngsters call each other up to six times a day just to exchange details of their whereabouts and occupation at the time. A chat application (modelled on ICQ) allowing a number of users to communicate wirelessly at the same time is touted to be popular amongst this age group. Other applications such as selling movies, CDs and concert tickets online, interactive games, horoscopes and jokes would also be targeted at this segment. Nokia's Nigel Rundstrom states the demand (in Asian markets) has been for 'fun, disposable applications', such as downloading cartoons (IDG.net February 2000).

There are thousands of lifestyle applications around the globe, many of them in Japan. Japan's i-Mode has been studied to give an indication of what services are likely to emerge as WAP applications in other Asian markets, where the youth culture is often driven by Japanese trends.

Source: KPMG http://www.webcity.com.au/kpmg/page4.html

The Internet, postmodern marketing and globalisation

Marketers are always trying to understand how societal changes affect the markets that they are dealing in and how consumer trends are changing over time. In an attempt to understand cultural changes through economic prosperity and techno-logical changes, much discussion has centred around the concept of postmodern marketing. This in itself is a large and contentious area; however, no marketing text would be complete without some exploration of why the postmodern era needs to be understood and embraced by marketers (Ranchhod 1998).

Much of the discussion on postmodern marketing emphasises the growing importance of digital and communicative technologies, communication, con-sumption, images and symbols and hyper-reality (Venkatesh *et al.* 1993). According to Cova (1996), postmodernism champions individuality and the modern quest for liberation from social bonds. The fragmentation of society shows the consequence of postmodern individualism.

Cova argues that:

Paradoxically, the postmodern individual is both isolated and in virtual contact with the whole world electronically. Postmodern daily life is characterised by ego concentration, encouraged by the spread of computers.

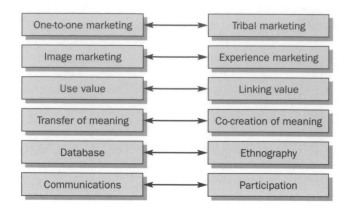

Figure 2.10 Postmodern marketing 'opposites'
Source: Adapted from Cova (1996)

Figure 2.10, adapted from Cova's (1996) article, shows the juxtaposition of opposites in the postmodern world. Cova goes on to say that, in postmodern marketing, one has to offer the following:

- *One-to-one marketing with the use of IT*. Unpredictable and individualistic customers could be retained this way.
- *Image*. Hyper-reality is the potential to offer experience similar to Euro-Disney's theme parks. Technology allows the postmodern consumer to be a participant in customising his or her own world.
- *Marketing images*. The era of postmodern marketing relies on image marketing (Venkatesh *et al.* 1993), emphasising cultural meanings and images. Cova (1996) feels that image marketing and brand management are closely related. Rather controversially, he argues that we are witnessing 'the obsolescence of advertising':

> *In postmodern markets, advertising simply misses the fundamental point: to be an interactive experience of co-creation of meaning for the customer.*

Market and technology shifts in the 1990s are pointing towards market **fragmentation** and mass communication (Müller-Heumann 1992). The fragmentation of markets is likely to herald a greater emphasis on smaller and unstable segments.

In many respects it could be argued that this type of postmodern world is not quite a reality for many people. Authors such as Clegg (1991) argue that we are seeing signs of modernity, with seamless societal changes taking place in different cultural contexts rather than complete paradigm changes. It would be facile to tackle this contentious issue in this book. Nonetheless, some of the arguments put forward have relevance in this new world of almost instant global communications.

Ironically, much of the postmodern emphasis on fragmentation and individualism seems to be borne out by the experience of organisations on the Internet. For example, companies such as Tripod and Geocities (Hof *et al.* 1997) have made a virtue out of helping to build 'community type' discussion areas which allow communication over large geographic areas. Tripod offers editorial content and discussions are grouped into fields such as politics, health and money. The target audience is the 'twenty-somethings' age group. Individuals are encouraged to design and build their own web pages. Larger companies such as Ford, Visa, Sony and Microsoft take banner advertising space in these locations. The demographics of the community play a large part in segmenting the advertising spend for these larger companies as the target group are mainly aged between 18 and 34, living in the USA and 75 per cent male.

Another interesting example of three community-based discussion areas is provided by Geocities, which has formed a 'virtual' city, allowing communities to develop and flourish, eventually exchanging or selling homes and settling into new neighbourhoods. Armstrong and Hagel (1996) discuss the merits of online communities and explain how the Garden Web area has evolved into a very successful community, where ideas are shared, plants are exchanged and links with related businesses and resources are forged. In this sense, this is a powerful area for an advertiser, rather than on a simple site that only allows transactions.

These discussions show the way in which technology is creating virtual communities and also determining the way in which consumers are reacting to marketing propositions. This makes segmentation increasingly difficult and it also means that new ways of segmenting markets need to evolve constantly. Chapter 4 on sustainability discusses how consumers are being segmented on their concern for the environment. In order to understand this in the new millennium, Firat and Schultz (1997) argue that, in the future, work life, domestic life, and life outside the home spent on recreation and leisure, far from being delineated from each other, will begin to merge. This will either create new configurations of life spheres or lives that cannot be differentiated into distinct spheres, but which are completely fragmented into dispersed moments. They also argue that there will be a merger of the consumer and the producer. Production and consumption are likely to be inseparable; the consumer will also be the producer (see Figure 2.11).

Marketers have to transform themselves from product to process. In other words, organisations must grasp the changing markets by embracing new technologies and creating both real and virtual images and move from product marketing to marketing a process and image. Processes can then be offered to customers which enable them to participate in designing the final product, customised to the images they seek. This will require a fundamental shift in thinking and demand a great deal of flexibility from organisations.

Summary

This chapter discusses the key approaches to segmenting markets. The discussion moves from a macro-analysis to a more focused understanding of marketing segments. It then concludes with the way in which segmentation is likely to evolve as technology allows individuals to become immersed in virtual worlds, demanding

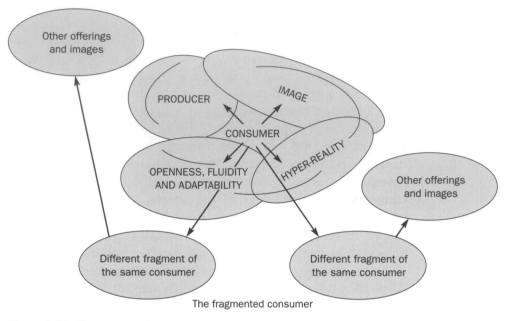

Figure 2.11 **The postmodern consumer**

increasing involvement with organisations producing goods and services. Segmentation strategies for business-to-business organisations will be different from those of organisations attempting to understand and deal with consumer markets. Segmentation is a difficult exercise for most organisations, but the checklist provided in the following segmentation exercise is an aid to developing better segmentation for most organisations.

Segmentation exercise

Macro-segmentation strategies

Assess the key market sectors that you are serving.

1. How good are the growth opportunities within these sectors?

2. How strong are your capabilities in the sectors?

Develop this after you have answered all the questions in Table 2.3.

Use the GE/McKinsey business screen portfolio matrix to plot the key positions for your organisation's portfolio.

Specific product market segments

Assess the key products/markets that you are serving using the growth vector matrix. How accessible, sustainable, actionable and measurable are each of the segments considered through the growth vector matrix.

Future segmentation strategies

- What is the degree of globalisation of the products/markets?

- What is the degree of competition in each of the product markets?

- How strong is your company vis-à-vis the competitors?

- What is your stance regarding virtual customers and developing images?

- How involved are consumers in your product processes?

3 Stakeholders and marketing

Introduction: Organisational stakeholders

Organisational stakeholders are many and varied in nature. Stakeholders are any groups of individuals that are in some way either affected by an organisation's actions or, in turn, can affect an organisation's actions. In many ways, understanding stakeholder interests and concerns and translating these into effective marketing strategies and organisational positioning within a marketplace is one of the great challenges facing organisations in the twenty-first century. It is no longer enough just to consider products, segments and markets. It is necessary to consider not only customer–company interactions, but also company–shareholder, company–community, company–environment and a host of the other interactions. Consumers are getting more intelligent and may want to consider not only the products on offer, but also an organisation's record on ethical issues and its image within the marketplace. The case study on Marks & Spencer helps to illustrate how stakeholder relationships contribute to either the success or the failure of marketing strategies. For example, at Marks & Spencer:

1 Customer choices and preferences were ignored.
2 Stakeholders such as suppliers were treated poorly.
3 The poor management of customers spilled over into poor staff management.
4 The original philosophy of product, people and property was not respected.

This resulted in poor assessments by shareholders and the stock market. Would Marks & Spencer have reached this state if it had managed its stakeholders better over a long period? Was the power base accorded to the managing director (a stakeholder) by the shareholders (another set of stakeholders) too great?

Slow decline of high-street champion

Some people bought everything at Marks & Spencer and some would buy nothing, but everyone has their theory about the retailer. When the rise and fall of Marconi or Invensys is written, few will care, but for M&S – Marks to its former fans – it is like reading the obituary of a once-great statesman. Judi Bevan is thus unpicking a rich seam in detailing the hubris and nemesis of the nation's favourite clothes shop. Michael Marks's arrival in Britain from Russia in 1882 and his progress from hawking penny goods to creating the national chain by which Middle England swore – then swore against – lends itself perfectly to a former City journalist and novelist. In 1997, *The Times* pointed out that the empire's new clothes were no longer smart. Suddenly everyone joined the critical bandwagon and sales slipped – but the seeds of the decline had been sown years earlier.

M&S was a paternalistic employer with a customer base as loyal as its staff. Richard Greenbury had joined at 17, became chief executive in 1988 and chairman three years later. His retailing skills were legend: he would walk the shop floors asking what was selling and telling staff what to do. But by the 1990s, this physically big man preferred lecturing to listening and not only did sales staff no longer dare answer back, neither did directors. His own deputy, Keith Oates, started plotting a coup to take Greenbury's seat. As Bevan writes, just talking to the press was as alien as wearing an Asda shirt. But Oates was allowed to stay and lead a policy of expanding out of trouble, increasing overseas exposure and paying GBP192m for 19 Littlewoods stores that eventually cost GBP450m.

But in dashing for profits to cover its problems – even considering mergers with GUS and Safeway – Marks forgot its basic formula and a public that could once find nothing wrong with the shops could now find nothing right. Belatedly introducing fitting rooms and credit cards did not help. Greenbury's answer was to cut costs and ranges. The non-executives' wives complained that

Marks no longer had the right garments in the right place – nor assistants to assist. Oates waited until his chairman was in India to make his bid for power, but Greenbury returned unexpectedly to confront him at the regular Monday meeting, forcing the non-execs to choose who ran M&S.

Bevan is at her best detailing the failed compromise of firing Oates and giving Greenbury's executive duties to another long-server, Peter Salsbury. But the overbearing Greenbury, retaining his office and a GBP450,000 chairman's salary, thought he still ran Marks and fired intolerant Rickograms at his many critics. Salsbury turned on his former mentor, refusing to talk to Greenbury or even have his portrait in the boardroom with the other chairman. Bevan paints Salsbury as a weak man who sacked staff and suppliers without compassion, paying consultants GBP40m to devise one restructuring after another.

Greenbury quit rather than be insulted and Salsbury was replaced by outsider Luc Vandevelde, but sales and profits have continued the fall that began in 1998. Simon Marks, who built the chain before and after the war, had a philosophy of product, people and property. Having let the product and the people go, the company is now selling the property – and undoing its overseas expansion.

Bevan compares Greenbury with Thatcher – leaders who hung on too long, pushed out by loyal lieutenants. Both possessed towering egos. Both failed to nurture a worthy successor. Their increasingly irrational behaviour was tolerated by their acolytes, she writes. Oates did for his chairman what Heseltine did for his prime minister. Both were great leaders whose tragedy was that they failed entirely to appreciate the impact of their personalities on those around them. It is a case study that should be read by any organisation – from Coke to the BBC – with a market share so big it can only fall.

Source: Northedge (2001)

Stakeholder theory

Stakeholder theory has many facets. Some theorists take a corporate governance view (Bailey and Clancey 1997), whilst others take a socioeconomic perspective (Hutton 1996). A more operational view argues that stakeholding issues should be considered at organisational level, where people work, rather than just at national level or welfare policy level (MacDougall 1995). A simple view of stakeholding would be to just consider the key players that affect an organisation's wellbeing. A more complex view would consider the interaction between an organisation and various players. This type of view considers stakeholding from the point of view of dynamic interrelationships. Resource availability, power and environmental turbulence can mediate these interrelationships.

Stakeholder interactions

To begin to understand the multiple relationships that interact in a complex manner, affecting both an organisation and its various stakeholders, it is perhaps important to go back to Freeman's (1984) seminal work on stakeholders and consider the definition of a stakeholder:

> ... *any group or individual who can affect or is affected by the achievement of the organisation's objectives.*

The OECD (Organization for Economic Co-operation and Development) starts from the perspective of corporate governance and mentions that a key element in improving economic efficiency is corporate governance, which involves a set of relationships between an organisation's management, its board, its shareholders and *other stakeholders*. The OECD (1997) statement goes on to say:

> *Corporate governance also provides the structure through which the objectives of the company are set, and the means of attaining those objectives and monitoring performance are determined. Good corporate governance should provide proper incentives for the board and management to pursue objectives that are in the interests of the company and shareholders and should facilitate effective monitoring, thereby encouraging firms to use resources more efficiently.*

Obviously these corporate governance issues cannot be separated from the wider macroeconomic issues within and outside national boundaries. These issues affect the nature of markets and the levels of competition within them, as do legislation and regulation (usually governmental). Business ethics and the social and economic interests of the communities directly affected by its actions have a considerable impact on the wellbeing of an organisation.

To make sense of the various interactions of stakeholders, it is useful to consider the various constituencies and their influences on the organisation. The relative inputs and outputs of the various stakeholders determine the level and power of the interactions taking place (Donaldson and Preston 1995). This in turn allows us to understand the relative impact of an organisation's strategies on other stakeholders. Figure 3.1 shows the key constituents at play.

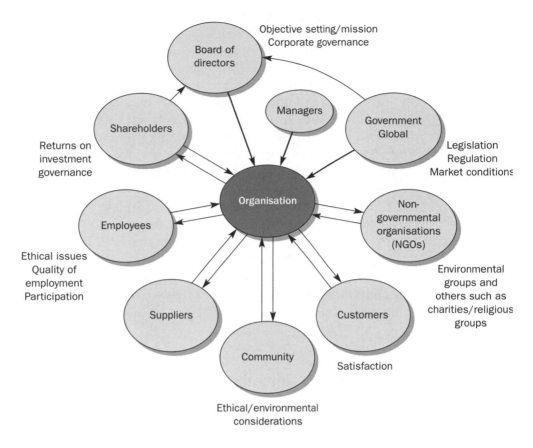

Figure 3.1 Stakeholder components

The board of directors

One could argue that this is the single most influential set of stakeholders of an organisation. The members of the board of directors are both internal and external stakeholders. They generally determine the strategic direction that an organisation will take and how it will impact on various other stakeholders. According to the OECD (1997) framework, board members need to act on a fully informed basis, with due care and diligence, in the best interests of the organisation and the shareholders. It also states that the board should ensure compliance with applicable law and take into account the interests of stakeholders. One of the key functions of the board should be to:

> ... *review and guide corporate strategy, major plans of action, risk policy, annual budgets and business plans; setting performance objectives; monitoring implementation and corporate performance; and overseeing major capital expenditures, acquisitions and divestitures.*
> (OECD 1997)

The board is also responsible for hiring key executives and setting their remuneration levels. Undoubtedly, this gives the board a great deal of vested power. However, board members themselves could wield disparate levels of power. There are also arguments that the chief executive officer (CEO) may have a disproportionate level of power compared with other board members (Pettigrew and McNulty 1995), though the level of power may be related to particular circumstances. In a recent survey (Stiles 2001), it was found that strategy is typically developed by managers at the business unit level (Bower 1970, Burgelman 1983, 1991). The board therefore is largely responsible for setting the strategic parameters within which the strategic activity can take place. The board is ultimately responsible for the vision, mission and focus of the organisation and acts as a gatekeeper and confidence builder. Interestingly, given the primacy of a board, Stiles' research, conducted in the UK, showed that a large proportion of the directors interviewed felt that their main roles were in developing strategies and responsibility for monitoring the health of the organisation. Only a few responses covered dialogue with shareholders/stakeholders, responsibility for an ethical framework or a review of social responsibilities. Within an organisation, the board is a powerful stakeholder. At the same time, this power is tempered by the interaction of managers and the CEO.

The role of board members

The earlier case study on Marks & Spencer helps to illustrate the interaction between the CEO and managers. What is not clear is how much of a role the board played in tempering the chief executive's management of the various stakeholders. To a large extent, the way an organisation is managed depends on corporate governance and the way this governance impacts on stakeholders.

Government and global pressures on corporate governance

Corporate governance has increasingly become a governmental and global issue. This is due to the increasing globalisation of capital flows and shareholding. The USA, UK and Australia are characterised by the Anglo-Saxon model of share ownership. Often large institutional investors such as pension funds or unit trust funds hold the majority of the shares in companies, with individuals holding fewer shares. These institutional investors are therefore the largest sets of stakeholders in many organisations. As a result, there is continued pressure for performance. Fundamental differences in the shareholding structure in European countries are the key to explaining the variations in the importance of their stock markets (Lannoo 1995). Table 3.1 shows that the largest shareowners of quoted companies in the UK are institutional investors (pension funds, insurance companies, banks

Table 3.1 The structure of shareholding in selected countries (% of total)

As at end of year:	Germany 1990	France 1992	Italy 1993	UK 1993	USA 1992	Japan 1992
Financial institutions – of which:	22.0	23.0	11.3	59.3	31.2	48.0
Banks	10.0	–	9.9	0.6	0.3	26.7
Pension funds/insurers	12.0	–	0.8	51.5	23.9	17.2
Others (unit trusts)	–	–	0.6	7.2	7.0	4.1
Households	17.0	34.0	33.9	19.3	48.1	22.1
Private companies	42.0	21.0	23.0	4.0	14.1	24.8
Public authorities	5.0	2.0	27.0	1.3	–	0.7
Foreign investors	14.0	20.0	4.8	16.3	6.6	3.9

Note: The comparability of data is affected by differences in definition used by the providers of the data and differences in regulatory structures when comparing data. For example, a bank is a universal bank in Germany and a high-street bank in the UK.
Source: Lannoo (1995)

and unit trusts). These possess an average equity of 59 per cent. Households are the second largest group in the UK with 19 per cent, and industry (including unit trusts) owns 4 per cent. In Germany, on the other hand, the situation is rather the reverse: industry is the largest owner of quoted companies with 42 per cent, institutional investors possess a much smaller shareholding with only 22 per cent (of which banks hold 10 per cent) and households possess 17 per cent. Households or families are the most important stockholders in France, Italy and the USA. In Italy, the government is a major stockholder with 27 per cent ownership.

Protection for stakeholders

Traditional structures in Europe are designed to protect the stakeholders against hostile takeovers. The firm as a coalition of both internal and external stakeholders needs control over its environment in order to protect stakeholders (Groenewegen 2000). This protection is often country specific. For example, in the Netherlands, the legal aspects of the structure of the corporation are organised in a manner that creates a control mechanism over shareholders. The structure tends to favour other stakeholders, especially the employees. In Germany, close ties between banks and industry provide stability and protection against takeovers. In France, control is in the hands of the president director general (PDG). He or she is often elected by the board (*conseil d'administration*), which in turn is appointed by the shareholders. The PDG is often the only person who represents the organisation externally and is often isolated from the other stakeholders of the organisation The PDG often has good connections at his or her level in the government and the sector. Shares are often sold to friendly banks and industrial firms, reflecting cross-stockholding. This creates the core shareholders (*noyau dur*). Sometimes shareholders in companies in France and the Netherlands enjoy multiple voting rights. As can be seen, the different structures in different countries are complex and therefore any organisation's analysis of stakeholders has to take corporate governance, board structures and shareholding structures into account. These are often country specific rather than universal. However, the growth of globalisation is changing the nature of stakeholders, largely as a result of increased shareholder activism. The key main developments are:

- the growing role of institutional investors as more companies are privatised in Europe and around the world;
- the integration of financial markets and the global movement of capital;
- increased shareholder activism.

The role of shareholders

Shareholder activism is encouraged in the UK and USA. As key stakeholders, shareholders are urged to exercise their voting rights. Shareholders join forces to strengthen their position against company management. As companies are privatised, more American shareholders with overseas shareholdings are demanding a greater say in the governance of companies in Europe. The advent of the euro and the single market is expected to hasten the move towards a more Anglo-Saxon model of open shareholding and transparency of disclosure. In reality, there are strong national interests at play, with a tussle between globalisation and national interests. In this sense, the government and key shareholders should be seen as major stakeholders wielding a great deal of power. Much of the European system favours a slower, stable form of organisation, compared with the rapidly changing, market-led entrepreneurial organisations that exist in the UK and USA. In any study of any organisation, this area of stakeholding should be considered carefully.

Read the following case study and consider the key stakeholders that are important in different countries. How can marketing be affected by poor stakeholder management?

CASE STUDY   FT

Image in the balance

The past year has seen a serious run on business reputations. Uncertainties after September 11, corporate scandals such as the collapse of Enron and the decline in economies across the world have all had an impact on the image of business and of CEOs. In spite of this, a survey in Europe and North America shows that chief executives still believe their own reputation is vitally important to their company's image. Hill and Knowlton's Corporate Reputation Watch 2002, conducted by Harris Interactive, examined the views of more than 800 CEOs and senior managers in nine countries. Eighty per cent of US business leaders see their reputation as a significant influence, compared with 56 per cent in the UK and 50 per cent in Europe as a whole. Of course, it is not just about the boss. Nine out of 10 CEOs said the customer's opinion was the most important factor in shaping reputation. Employees' attitudes were rated as the second most important determinant.

For business leaders, reputation is not an abstract concern. The survey showed there is a growing tendency for CEOs to be at least partly remunerated according to their ability to affect corporate reputation, ranging from 13 per cent of CEOs in Germany to 44 per cent of those in Italy; in the UK and the US, the figures were 26 per cent and 29 per cent respectively. Where CEOs do receive cash for corporate kudos, the proportion of compensation can be significant. In the UK and Germany it was more than 40 per cent and in the US just over a third.

Furthermore, reputation management increasingly has a place at the boardroom table. The UK and Belgium led the pack on this, with 62 per cent and 69 per cent respectively reporting that the board was involved in monitoring corporate reputation. In the US the figure was just over a third. But here is the challenge. Reputation, rather like beauty, is something that largely exists in the eye of the beholder. For corporations, that beholder is the myriad stakeholders whose perceptions combine across interests and geographies to create a corporate reputation. So while companies may be remunerating chief executives on the basis of their ability to affect reputation, how are they measuring something that exists in a million different minds?

Well, measuring it they are. According to the survey, more than 75 per cent of international companies have corporate reputation measurement systems in place. For those based in the UK and the US, the figure is at 80 per cent or above. These systems are a mix of formal and informal metrics, although a significant number of companies measure only on the basis of informal systems such as word of mouth. And here is a potential problem: word of mouth is one of the most powerful marketing and communications tools but to measure reputation purely by what the corporate ear picks up suggests that reputation management may not, after all, be receiving the attention it deserves.

There is no denying that word of mouth has an important place in the measurement of corporate reputation. But it alone cannot provide the balanced view that international companies in particular need. Sensibly, most companies go beyond word of mouth, opting for formal research such as financial performance, media coverage, industry rankings, analyst commentary and even price/earnings ratio (the higher the p/e, the more positive the market). But across different markets, different measurement techniques enjoy different priorities. Formal customised research is undertaken by 50 per cent of international companies and is, on average, the second most popular technique. In Italy and the Netherlands it tops the bill.

In Germany and the UK financial performance ranks as the second most important measurement. German companies are more likely than others to use media coverage and published rankings to measure corporate reputation. With the exception of those in Belgium, international CEOs are more likely than those in the US to use p/e ratios to measure corporate reputation. Despite the plethora of measurement techniques, the survey reveals some gaps. CEOs in all countries appear to pay more attention to influences on reputation with which they have most personal contact, such as customers, employees and print media. They are less concerned by those with which they have less personal contact, such as the internet and campaign groups. Nevertheless, there is grave danger for them in underestimating the power of such groups. The survey shows the continuing ways in which CEOs are attempting to manage their reputation. What the data cannot reveal is how long it will take for those techniques to reverse the damage done by corporate scandals.

Source: Andrew Pharoah (2002), managing director, public and corporate affairs, at Hill and Knowlton

Non-governmental organisations

For most profit-oriented organisations, non-governmental organisations (NGOs) are a real force to be reckoned with and are key stakeholders who often determine the success or failure of particular strategies adopted by an organisation. Examples of this are the pressures put on organisations by environmental protection groups such as Greenpeace and Friends of the Earth and by charities such as Oxfam and Christian Aid. Such organisations play a key role in putting the issue of social responsibility firmly on the agenda of organisations involved in profit-seeking activities in any corner of the world. For example, Monsanto's recent, very public foray into publicising genetically modified (GM) foods, and even setting up an expensive website for this purpose, ended in a public relations disaster. The demise was hastened by very public denunciations of its activities by groups such as Friends of the Earth, which also used a website to present graphic images. A grotesque, Frankenstein-like image of a ripe tomato with a blue, rotating eye and a leaf 'tail' that wiggles captures the notion of the introduction of a fish gene into the vegetable. A secondary powerful and emotive argument used by opponents of genetically modified organisms (GMOs) is that modified genes introduced into particular foods such as oil seed rape could 'migrate' to other species and to wild plants. They argue that, if a mistake occurs, the danger will be spread to all flora and fauna. Paul Moroney, Hampshire spokesman for Friends of the Earth, said: 'Genetic pollution is irretrievable and unlike an oil spill, cannot be cleaned up' (Simpson 1998).

The pressure applied by NGOs can turn company policies around. For example, see the case study on the environmental group Greenpeace.

CASE STUDY

Novartis buckles as Greenpeace reveals GE soya in its baby products

Dear Mr Heinzer,

With respect to today's demonstration at the St. Johann, Basel, headquarters of Novartis AG, we understand that representatives of Greenpeace allege that our affiliate Gerber is selling in the Philippines products intended for consumption by infants which contain genetically modified ingredients.

We will investigate these serious allegations without delay and once we have a full understanding of all the facts, we will take appropriate actions.

Very truly yours,
Felix Raebe
Head media relations Novartis International

Basel, Switzerland, 21 August 2001 –
Gerber/Novartis will investigate its products sold in the Philippines after Greenpeace revealed scientific evidence showing that the company's baby food products contained massive amounts of GE (genetically engineered) soya, despite its promise a year ago to stop using GE ingredients worldwide.

The company's decision follows a Greenpeace action earlier today in front of the Novartis headquarters in Switzerland where activists blocked the main entrance of the building with hundreds of baby-puppets. The puppets were holding protest signs saying: 'Novartis/Gerber, keep your promise!' and 'Novartis/Gerber, stop genetically modified baby food!'.

Earlier, Greenpeace sent three products to the internationally certified Hong Kong laboratory, DNA Chips, where very high levels of GE contamination were found. The following percentages of genetically engineered soya were found in these products: Green Monggo's (66.7 per cent), Cream of Brown Rice (52.2 per cent) and Mixed Fruit (34.3 per cent).

These levels of contamination demonstrate Novartis' deliberate intention to use GMOs (genetically modified organisms) in its Gerber baby food products, which are manufactured in Indonesia, in the Philippines.

'Are Novartis' promises only valid in rich countries and not in poor ones such as the Philippines?' asked Greenpeace Southeast Asia campaigner in the Philippines, Beau Baconguis, while presenting the test results at a press conference in Manila (Philippines) this morning. The Philippine Congress filed a bill on 15 August 2001 requiring the labelling of GMO derived food and food products, under which the penalty for failing to label would be 6 to 12 years in jail.

Food products in Europe are mostly GE free but unlabelled GE food is sold to consumers in other parts of the world. 'We demand an immediate stop to Novartis' double standards policy,' said Bruno Heinzer, of Greenpeace Switzerland, in front of the Novartis building.

On 11 June 1999, Novartis Consumer Health head Martin Stefani wrote in a letter to Greenpeace: 'Our consumers can be sure that our baby food does not contain any GMOs or parts derived thereof.'

This was reiterated by Novartis US spokesperson Al Piergallini, who was quoted in the *Wall Street Journal*, Europe, of 30 July 1999 as saying: 'I want our mothers to be comfortable'.

In a letter to Greenpeace dated 2 August 2000, Novartis declared it would not use any more GMOs in its food products worldwide.

Greenpeace is now urging Novartis to respect its own pledges, not only in rich nations but in all countries.

Scientific understanding of the impacts of genetic engineering on the environment and human health is extremely limited. Greenpeace believes that citizens and consumers worldwide have the right to know how their food is produced and to refuse to eat genetically engineered food.

Source: http://archive.greenpeace.org/~geneng/highlights/food/Aug21_2001.htm

In other instances, organisations such as the World Wildlife Fund (WWF) exert pressures on organisations to improve their products so that energy resources are not wasted. These examples illustrate that NGOs need to be considered as serious stakeholders when developing and executing company marketing strategies. Adverse publicity will not only harm the organisation's image, but will also deter future investors and consumers. The results of pursuing environmentally friendly activities impinge on the whole range of stakeholders, from suppliers, who have to manufacture the required components, to the surrounding community, who benefit from lower levels of pollution, and to consumers, who gain access to eco-friendly products and energy-efficient equipment.

The case study about WWF considers the impact of company strategies on a range of stakeholders. Identify the key stakeholders affected and the level and power of interactions.

CASE STUDY

Keep cool, keep clean: a deal to save the climate

Most of us try to do what we can to fight global climate change, but a deal between WWF and AEG, the German appliance manufacturer, aims to show how companies can use energy saving technology to work towards the goals of cleaner power and efficient energy use

Gland, Switzerland: Innovative and environmentally friendly products are now part of our daily lives. We use fuel-efficient cars, better housing insulation, energy saving light bulbs and domestic appliances. This is all helping to achieve the targets for cleaner power production and more efficient use of energy proposed by the conservation organization WWF.

Germany has ambitious goals in the fight against climate change. It aims to reduce carbon dioxide, the main global warming gas, by 25 per cent by 2005. At the same time, however, it wants to phase out carbon-free nuclear power production, which accounts for a third of domestic electricity. So if a dramatic increase in carbon dioxide emissions caused by new coal-fired power stations is to be avoided, an improvement in energy efficiency is needed. That is why WWF–Germany has been working with selected companies to commit themselves to less and greener power consumption.

'It was clear that if we wanted to have an effect on power consumption, it was not enough just to target the consumer,' says Dr Stephan Singer, Head of the Energy and Climate Department at WWF–Germany. 'It was vital to get the manufacturers on board.'

In 1997 WWF struck a deal known as Consensus 25 with AEG, the German maker of domestic appliances, which has an overall market share of 10 per cent and is already well-known for its green policies, its transparency and its openness. Publicly supportive of WWF's climate and energy policy objectives, AEG was also in favour of ecology tax. So it was no surprise that, unlike more conservative companies, AEG committed itself to reducing the energy consumption of five of its leading products between 1995 and 1999. Its commitment has been recognized by making Consensus 25 a Gift to the Earth in WWF's Living Planet Campaign.

'It was calculated that if these appliances sold as preceding models had, the energy equivalent of the annual electricity consumption of a small city in Germany of up to 10,000 inhabitants would be saved,' said Dr Singer.

Two years later most of AEG's new 'green line' appliances have proved to be both energy efficient and successful, saving between 20 per cent and 50 per cent of the usual consumption of electricity. The limits of energy efficiency for some products, however, were demonstrated by cookers which, while saving electricity, took ten hours to bake a cake. This suggests that the logical next step is to increase the availability of renewable energy sources, which is why improving the supply side of energy is the second target of the WWF campaign.

Meanwhile, AEG has committed itself to an even more ambitious target after negotiation with WWF. Within the next four years the company has undertaken to sell only fridges and freezers classified 'A' under the compulsory European Union labelling scheme. This means that products are classified from 'A' to 'G' based on their power consumption, with 'A' products consuming at least 45 per cent less electricity than average.

'The AEG agreement is a very good indication of what the domestic appliance industry can do if it has a mind to,' says Dr Singer. 'It also supports moves towards an EU-wide ban on inefficient appliances and will set strong energy efficiency standards.'

AEG is now marketing efficient, environmentally sound cooling appliances. Currently neither ozone depleting substances nor fluorinated super warming gases (HFCs) are used for cooling or insulation in the EU. About half of AEG products are already labelled 'A', and some of these consume between 70 per cent and 80 per cent less energy than average.

It is estimated that if all new technology is category 'A' from 2003 onwards, the annual saving

Case study *continued*

will be in the region of 16 million kilowatt-hours of electricity. Careful calculation of Germany's energy consumption reveals that if all German producers marketed only the 'A' models, one coal-fired power station of a capacity of at least 50 megawatts, the amount of energy consumed by at least 100,000 people, could be closed.

'If other appliances, such as dishwashers, washing machines, televisions, computers, videos and so on,

made similar technological improvements, the international debate on shutting down nuclear power plants and complying with climate targets would be much easier,' said Dr Singer. 'WWF is very excited by the possibilities that this kind of deal offers, and we hope it will show the way for other companies.'

Source: Kyla Evans (1999), a press officer with WWF International based in Gland, http://www.panda.org/news_facts

Customers

Customers are the lifeblood of any organisation. Organisations not only have to be receptive to their needs and wants, but also have to understand them (see Chapter 1). Customers as stakeholders are in a powerful position to either accept or reject an organisation's offering. It could be argued that organisations spend vast amounts of money to cajole and coerce this stakeholder group to purchase their goods. Generally this is undertaken through branding strategies. Customers are often attracted to organisations with a good brand image and to those that can offer good quality, long lasting products. Increasingly customers are also loosely connected to NGOs and in many ways can direct organisational strategy towards environmentally sound processes and developing environmentally friendly products.

Classical marketing theory regards customers as supreme entities whose needs should be profitably satisfied by an organisation. For many years organisations have tried to follow this philosophy. However, many organisations realise that customers could be their best ambassadors. Increasingly, therefore, organisations think of relationship marketing and of lifetime associations with customers. As a philosophy for the future, it could be argued that customers should not only be satisfied, but should be retained (Rust *et al.* 2000). Organisations should maximise customer equity by addressing its three key drivers (see Figure 3.2):

1 *Value equity*. This covers aspects of a customer's objective assessment of the utility of a brand, based on the perceptions of the value of the exchange process (money for goods or services).
2 *Brand equity*. This is the customer's subjective and intangible assessment of the brand above and beyond its objectively perceived value (see Chapter 5).
3 *Retention equity*. This is a measure of the customer's tendency to stick with the brand above and beyond their subjective assessment of the brand.

In the twenty-first century, the marketing focus is increasingly moving away from brand management and transactions between organisations and customers and moving towards actually understanding the relationship. An organisation's value lies in the lifetime value of its customers rather than just its brands. This reflects the importance of customers as stakeholders in an organisation. Of increasing impor-

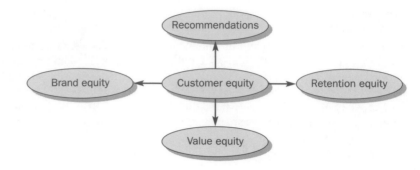

Figure 3.2 Drivers of customer equity

Source: Adapted from Rust *et al.* (2000)

tance to these stakeholders is the growth of the Internet, where information and product exchange processes can be undertaken in a virtual setting. Customers are also able to post their feelings about organisations and their products in discussion areas, thereby either enhancing or degrading an organisation's image.

Suppliers

Suppliers generally have a symbiotic relationship with an organisation. They are major stakeholders who help in the production processes by supplying components or systems. The way in which a supplier can affect an organisation's wellbeing is dependent on its power (Porter 1985). Suppliers can influence production costs. If there are only a few suppliers in the marketplace, then they can be powerful; if the suppliers' products are necessary for production, they can wield considerable power. For most organisations, suppliers are a complex group of stakeholders. Some may carry a great deal of power, whereas others may be less powerful. A quick overview of an organisation's suppliers shows the complexities. For example, a clothing manufacturing company is often dependent on:

- electricity companies;
- water companies;
- machine suppliers;
- textile manufacturers;
- packaging companies;
- designers;
- thread manufacturers;
- gas suppliers (for heating);
- vehicle dealers (for transportation);
- computer suppliers;
- robot designers and suppliers.

This is just an illustrative list and is by no means exhaustive. Nevertheless, it underlines the fact that, when we consider the word 'supplier' for an organisation,

Losses cut as Martin wins back M&S deals

Shares in Martin International received a boost yesterday when the clothes maker announced it had regained its Marks & Spencer knitwear contract. Martin also reported that half-year pre-tax losses to June had fallen from GBP1.85 million to GBP236,000. The shares rose 1p. The company cited heavy knitwear losses and restructuring costs as reasons for the previous year's poor performance. It spent GBP1.27 million downsizing the knitwear arm in the first half of 2000. First-half sales dropped by 10 per cent to GBP46.7 million, blamed on the lack of a spring knitwear order from M&S, its major customer.

But the retailer is reinstating its knitwear deal with Martin this autumn and will use the company as a menswear supplier from 2002. Martin currently supplies M&S with lingerie, nightwear and ladies leisurewear. Finance director David Sadler said: We're not pleased to be reporting a first-half loss but we are encouraged by the reinstated contract and are looking for a profit of about GBP250,000 at year end. Analysts said that, despite difficult market conditions, a small profit might be realistic now that Martin had regained the important knitwear contract. Martin is not supplying materials for the new M&S womenswear range Per Una launched yesterday.

The ailing retailer is hoping Per Una will be instrumental in turning its business round.

Source: Brown (2001)

we usually mean a range of suppliers with differing inputs into the organisation's products. An organisation is also dependent on advertising agencies that supply it with its branding and advertising strategies. Without this complex web of supplier interaction, most organisations would not be able to survive. In any strategy, therefore, the power of the key suppliers needs to be assessed and understood. Organisations today are often networks of alliances, and the suppliers are therefore part of these networks and value chains. As stakeholders and suppliers value these networks, they look for long-term, stable relationships.

The case study about Martin International shows the mutual relationship between suppliers and buyers. In this example, the interaction between the buyer and the supplier as stakeholders is the crucial factor. The power of the buyer (Marks & Spencer) nearly brought Martin to its knees and, paradoxically, may help to revive Martin's fortunes in the near future. The article illustrates the evolving nature of stakeholder management and the importance of power and time in understanding relationships.

Employees

Employees are important stakeholders in any organisation. This stakeholder group is made up of individuals who have made a commitment to work for a particular organisation and to devote their time and skills to it in return, for monetary reward and satisfaction. Employees are rarely homogeneous and every organisation requires a range of skills that add to its value (Doyle 2000). A good mix of key skills sets an organisation aside from its competitors. Employees are also board members in many companies in Europe. Their roles range from management to secretarial support to shop floor work, each operating in a complex web of interaction. A particular and unique web of interactions helps to create competitive advantage for an organisation.

Its particular web of interaction distinguishes each organisation and organisations are often defensive about public exposure of their systems of working. In many cases, employees are also shareholders in the organisation either by design (company share options as bonuses or rewards) or by choice (individual purchase of shares). In each case, as shareholders, employees will be looking for long-term growth in their shares. As shareholders, they also play an important role in determining this potential growth (or decline). As Hamel (2000) says: 'Entrepreneurs won't work for peanuts, but they will work for a share of the action.' Research by Strategic Compensation Research Associates found that the average Internet company had issued enough share options to employees to dilute normal shareholders by 24 per cent, if exercised (Krantz 1999). This shows that employees are an important but complex group of stakeholders.

Shareholders

Shareholders are often the key stakeholders within an organisation as they are the institutions and individuals who actually risk their funds to support it. The shareholding body's interests vary, as do their goals and investment horizons. In almost all OECD (Organization for Economic Co-operation and Development) countries, basic shareholder rights include the right to:

- secure methods of ownership registration;
- convey or transfer shares;
- obtain relevant information on the corporation on a timely and regular basis;
- participate and vote in general shareholder meetings;
- elect members of the board;
- share in the profits of the corporation.

Shareholders are entitled to vote in general meetings and have to be consulted when any fundamental corporate changes are undertaken. Shareholders may have different voting rights according to the class of shares they hold. By risking their funds, shareholders are looking for growth and can influence an organisation's chances of success by acquiring more shares or by disposing of them. As stakeholders, they are generally quiet when the returns on their holdings are reasonable. Doyle (2000) argues that the shareholder value principle is that a business should be run to maximise the return on the shareholder investments. The most powerful group of stakeholders in any organisation, shareholders are increasingly moving their capital around within a global environment. They can be fickle and can look for short-run equity growth within organisations. For this reason, shareholder communications is an important part of most organisations' marketing communications strategies.

Community

Communities are generally stakeholders who are affected by the economic impact of organisations within their locality. In many cases these organisations also affect the environment in their vicinity. The issue of community as stakeholders is discussed in more detail in Chapter 4 on sustainability and strategy.

Developing competitive marketing strategies

This section is concerned with understanding how the interactions between stakeholders can help an organisation to gain a degree of competitive advantage in the marketplace.

Management of the different stakeholders' interests is a potential source of competitive advantage (Donaldson and Preston 1995, Jones 1995), in part because of the reduction of relational costs (Dyer and Singh 1998, Preston and Donaldson 1999). There are also arguments that stakeholder management is a condition for long-term survival, given its moral dimension (Jones 1995). Proper management of the different stakeholders therefore:

- helps to reduce the costs of managing relationships;
- adds a social and ethical dimension;
- helps an organisation to take a long-term view;
- helps to develop a competitive advantage over an organisation's rivals;
- helps to enhance and develop marketing relationships.

Stakeholder management is also an important issue in today's organisation given the multidimensional nature of each stakeholder. This is expressed in Freeman's (1984) conceptualisation (see Table 3.2).

Table 3.2 The power of each stakeholder group

<table>
<tr><td></td><td></td><td colspan="3">Type of Power</td></tr>
<tr><td></td><td></td><td>*Legal*</td><td>*Economic*</td><td>*Political*</td></tr>
<tr><td rowspan="3">**Stake**</td><td>*Financial*</td><td>Shareholders
Directors – CEO</td><td></td><td>Dissident shareholders</td></tr>
<tr><td>*Economic*</td><td>Banks</td><td>Consumers and clients
Competitors
Suppliers
Unions
Banks</td><td>Consumers' association</td></tr>
<tr><td>*General*</td><td></td><td></td><td>Consumers
Lawyers
Government</td></tr>
</table>

Source: Adapted from Freeman (1984)

There are three steps involved in developing the management of stakeholders:

1 Identify an organisation's stakeholders as fully as possible.
2 Understand and examine the relationships between how stakeholders are managed and an organisation's goals and objectives.
3 Incorporate the interests of the various stakeholders into the development of a corporate and marketing strategy.

The key question here is the *level of involvement* that each stakeholder has in processes and decisions. Involvement also means that organisations must be prepared to spend money or time on lavishing attention on the stakeholders. Therefore the question of which groups will or should receive more attention is important. Organisations can take either a narrow or broad view of stakeholders.

Narrow view

Only select stakeholders that have a direct relevance to the organisation's core economic interests. These can be regarded as business stakeholders. They are task-related stakeholders. In general, organisations are more likely to shower attention on these task-related stakeholders since they are central to its economic activity (Mitchell *et al.* 1997, Steger 1998; see also the recent empirical work of Berman *et al.* 1999).

Broad view

Consider the full range of stakeholders and their likely impact on the company from either an economic or an image and ethical point of view on a long-term basis. Recent research (Greenley and Foxall 1997) suggests that orientation to the varied and diverse interests of stakeholder groups is central to strategic planning. In many cases, failure to address the multiple stakeholder groups may be detrimental to an organisation's performance. However, most organisations are not only constrained by resource availability, but are also subject to the external environment, including competitor hostility and general economic activity such as market growth. Their research showed that the external environment moderates the impact of multiple stakeholder orientation. Therefore the following factors should also be considered:

- competitive hostility;
- market turbulence;
- market growth;
- technological change;
- ease of market entry.

The argument, therefore, is that the Miller and Lewis (1991) model of achieving a balance when addressing stakeholder interests is more important than selectively prioritising attention and resources just on particular stakeholders. Interestingly, the research shows that simple orientation towards particular groups, such as consumers, and giving priority to their interests does not appear to be associated with enhanced company performance.

The managerial implication of this is that managers should try to map their task-related stakeholders and then try to go further with the integration of other institutional stakeholders. This is linked to the idea of prioritising according to how each group might interact with the others. Certain writers (Rowley 1997) advocate a network theory of stakeholder influence:

> ... *firms do not simply respond to each stakeholder individually; they respond, rather, to the interaction of multiple influences from the entire stakeholder set.*

Organisations therefore have to consider carefully the effect of the different level of attention paid to different stakeholders, as the stakeholders themselves are likely to interact with each other.

Understanding stakeholder evolution and management

As discussed in Chapter 1, the issue of time is important in any issue relating to stakeholder management for competitive positioning. Neither organisations nor stakeholders stand still. Add to this the fact that stakeholder patterns may change as a result of the evolution of an organisation. Understanding an organisation's approach to its multiple stakeholders through the stages of formation, growth and maturity, decline and revival or death may help to foster a better understanding of its strategies (Jawahar and McLaughlin 2001). An organisation's survival and continued success depends on the ability of its management to satisfy its range of stakeholders and give them wealth, value for money or the satisfaction of having their concerns incorporated into strategy development and implementation. This has to be achieved without recourse to favouring one group over another (Clarkson 1995, Jones and Wicks 1999). However, this may be a static view and the stakeholder strategies of any organisation are likely to evolve over time. The management of stakeholders is likely to be dependent on:

- *Resources*. Organisations are dependent on resources for their survival. As an organisation grows and prospers, its need for resources will change and so will the range of stakeholders providing particular resources to the organisation. In many cases, the power exercised by the key stakeholders such as equity providers will be considerable (Frooman 1999). Organisations are likely to focus their attention on stakeholders who control the resources necessary for survival and growth (Pfeffer and Salancck 1978, Kreiner and Bhambri 1991).
- *Opportunities and threats*. There are many opportunities and threats associated with managing stakeholders. The way these opportunities and threats are handled often creates situations of loss or gain for an organisation.

In managing stakeholders, organisations can adopt the following strategies:

■ *Proactive.* This means that they actively work with stakeholders and address their concerns. This would include anticipating and understanding the key issues involved.

■ *Accommodating.* This is a less active approach to dealing with stakeholder concerns. This strategy involves general interaction with stakeholders with little extra activity or anticipation of their needs. An example of this may be where an organisation willingly pays attention to the needs of the community, but does little to anticipate its needs.

■ *Defensive.* This strategy involves doing the minimum required to keep a stakeholder happy. Often an organisation will do the minimum required by legislation to address environmental concerns.

■ *Reactive.* This strategy involves fighting particular stakeholders, or ignoring them completely.

Again, organisations may need to consider pursuing different strategies for different stakeholders, depending on the stages of evolution – see Figure 3.3.

As you read the case study on page 67, consider the evolution of British Biotechnology and how it should have dealt with the various stakeholders.

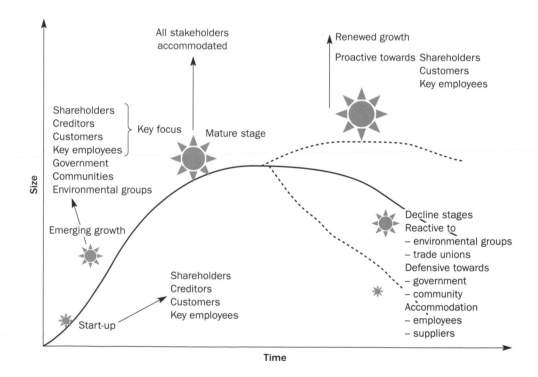

Figure 3.3 Organisational cycle and stakeholder strategies

CASE STUDY

British Biotechnology

British Biotechnology began life in Oxford, approximately 13 years ago. As Figure 3.4 shows, the company shot to prominence in the biotechnology sector as a company to watch and was even predicted to join some of the top companies in share value. The share price, from a high of 326p in 1996, is now languishing at around 20p. The company was the darling of the stock market in 1996, when it released a statement which was bullish about the prospects for Marismastat, the anti-cancer wonder drug. The potential market was enormous and this led to a wave of optimistic buying, sending the shares to dizzy heights. The euphoria settled down on 12 May 1997 when the press release in the *Financial Times* announced 'British Biotech set for first drug launch'. Senior managers, including Dr. Millar, were concerned that the *Financial Times* article would lead the EMEA (European Agency for the Evaluation of Medicinal Products Shareholders) to believe that the company would be seeking product approval imminently. This was not the case. The company at this stage sought and received assurance that media coverage would not affect the progress of the MAA. Products can only be marketed in Europe once the EMEA extends an MAA (Marketing Authorisation Approval). A similar set-up exists in America and marketing is controlled by the DDMAC, the Division of Drug Marketing Advertising and Communications within the FDA (Federal Drug Administration). By this time, the genie had been let out of the bag. In 1998, the head of clinical research Dr. Millar was sacked for opening the debate on how valuable Marsimastat could be. He expressed his concerns to Perpetual, the leading fund holder. This created a rift between him and Dr. McCullagh, the founder, who remained bullish about the prospects. With the rift becoming public, it was inevitable that investors would be nervous about the company's prospects. Dr. McCullagh was forced to leave by worried shareholders, as trials of the drug did not show significant advances over existing treatments. The company now has a new chief executive, Dr. Goldstein, who is to continue the Marismastat trials and trials for the new drug Zacutex. Dr. Millar felt that the original team was too enthusiastic about the prospects for the drugs.

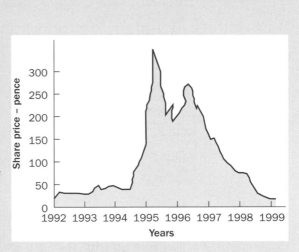

Figure 3.4 British Biotechnology

The New York and London Stock Exchanges are investigating share dealings.

From a PR point of view, it is not uncommon for companies to offer possible positive progress reports to the press. The problems with the stock market arise when the press reports do not match the promised results. For some biotechnology companies, there is only the *promise* of products and any adverse publicity can affect their standing in the market. Consumers generally do not understand the intricacies of drug delivery systems, only their efficacy. They only want news which clearly exposes the prospects or the time frame in which products could reasonably be expected to get to market. Many private investors are now sophisticated enough to wait for greater returns in the future. However, institutional investors may press for shorter-term growth. There are often pressures on management only to divulge good news, as they may be worried that any neutral or negative news would mean falling shares when money is desperately needed for research. Such news could also be wrongly interpreted as poor competency on the part of management. The key managers themselves may also own a considerable number of shares and their levels of motivation could also be affected.

Source: Ranchhod and Gurau (1999)

		Power			Strategy			
		High	Medium	Low	Proactive	Accommodating	Defensive	Reactive
Stakeholder	Consumers		*		*			
	Shareholders	*				*		
	Employees	*				*		
	Press	*					*	
	Marketing Authorisation Authority (MAA)	*			*			

Figure 3.5 Stakeholder power/strategy analysis for British Biotechnology

When considering a comprehensive strategy, it is important to try to understand both an organisation's stakeholder strategy and the power exercised by each stakeholder. To help with this, it is useful to use a power/strategy matrix, as shown in Figure 3.5.

The analysis in Figure 3.5 shows the various ways in which key stakeholders were communicated with and dealt with by British Biotechnology. Many of the stakeholders should have been dealt with in a proactive manner. The problems that have arisen as a result of poor stakeholder management have led to a lack of trust. The company actually underinvested in trust. There is always a range of interdependencies between organisations and specific stakeholder groups (Wicks *et al.* 1999). Therefore, in addition to considering the power/strategy matrix, the level of trust offered or generated should also be considered. Lack of trust is likely to hamper British Biotechnology's strategic positioning and marketing activities for many years to come.

Positioning products in markets

As can be seen, competitively positioning an organisation in the marketplace is dependent on many factors. These factors have to be considered over the short, medium and long term. Only by undertaking a detailed analysis of these issues can the proper positioning of an organisation be achieved. Success at this corporate level lays the foundations for strategic marketing. The key factors that have to be considered in conjunction with the power/strategy matrix are:

- competitor hostility;
- market turbulence;
- technological change;
- ease of market entry.

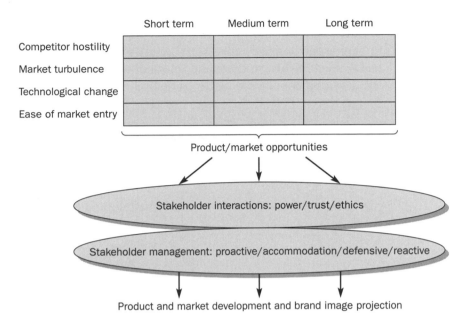

Figure 3.6 Competitive positioning: stakeholder management and environmental factors

Through a clear stakeholder analysis and assessment of the key factors shown in Figure 3.3, organisations can develop competitive positioning strategies that *evolve over time*. Figure 3.6 illustrates the way in which the various stakeholders and environmental factors interact and should be considered while developing products and markets. The ways in which power is handled and trust is developed with various stakeholders contribute to the overall brand image of an organisation. In considering competitive positioning and developing market advantage, it is useful to remember that stakeholder interests will change over time. Organisations that have analysed the main factors will have a clear understanding of the windows of opportunity available to them as a result of certain favourable factors and sensible management of stakeholders. These organisations are the ones most likely to succeed this century. Out of this positioning flow the product/market strategies.

Summary

This chapter takes a stakeholder approach to understanding how organisations can position themselves in the marketplace. Simple product/market strategies are not sufficient as we move further into the twenty-first century. When dealing in markets, organisations must work on a range of issues which have an impact on the products or services offered. Stakeholders have a major impact, as we have shown in this chapter, and they can be dealt with by being either proactive or reactive.

The turbulence in the environment offers both opportunities and threats to organisations. Being successful in the marketplace means that these opportunities have to be grasped and combined with a clear stakeholder management strategy as this has a direct impact on the brand image of the organisation. This in turn helps with the development of a product's positioning within particular market segments.

Chapter questions

1 How can stakeholder management affect customer relationships?

2 What are the limitations of a power/strategy matrix?

3 Discuss the ways in which stakeholder management can improve the brand equity of an organisation.

4 Sustainability and strategy

Introduction: Limits to growth

As the world's population grows and some 90 million more individuals are added to the planet each year, many marketers are questioning some of the basic tenets of marketing. Is it right to expect continued growth? Should we be marketing goods that are likely to harm the planet? Should marketing concentrate on products that are 'green'? These and many other questions are being asked not just by marketers but by general consumers themselves. In recent surveys, it has been shown that consumers are concerned about the products that they purchase; however, cost may also be a factor in purchasing products.

Nonetheless, in Germany, 88 per cent of consumers are ready to switch brands to greener products; the corresponding figures in Italy and Spain are 84 per cent and 82 per cent respectively (Wasik 1996). In the USA, the green market is estimated to include 52 million households (Ottman 1993). In 1996, MORI categorised 36 per cent of its British poll respondents as 'green consumers' on the basis of their claim to have 'selected one product over another because of its environmentally friendly packaging, formulation or advertising' (Worcester 1997). This compared with 19 per cent in 1988 (although it continued the steady decline from a peak of 50 per cent in 1990). This makes it important that marketers actually understand and respond to customer needs.

Furthermore, are the provisions of certain products and services sustainable? Sustainability is about understanding the interactions of the various stakeholders in an organisation. Maximising profits and looking for short-term gains in market share may, in the long run, be so harmful to certain groups of stakeholders that the organisation itself suffers bad publicity. These stakeholders are the employees, the local community and government agencies. The main stakeholder is probably the planet itself, and increasingly the public feels that business organisations should take responsibility for environmental damage inflicted on parts of the earth in the pursuit of profit. An example of this is the cost to the General Electric Company (GEC) in the USA for removing two million cubic metres of contaminated sludge from the Hudson

River (*New Scientist* 2001). For 35 years the company poured some 500,000 kilogrammes of polychlorinated biphenyls (PCBs) into the river, before they were banned in 1977. Residents living near the river bank claim to have suffered from a variety of PCB-related illnesses ranging from cancer to physical deformities. As a result of this, the US Environmental Protection Agency has decided to remove the sludge and has asked GEC to foot the $500 million bill.

In a situation like this, the factors are complex; however, the fact remains that the consumers of the period actually bought electrical equipment that was manufactured by GEC, and were generally unaware of the pollution problems. The onus, therefore, is on organisations to consider whether their products and services are environmentally friendly or not and whether their practices are environmentally sustainable or not. This information also needs to filter through to the consumer. In this chapter we will explore various notions of sustainability, ranging from 'green' products to sustainable production. The aim of this chapter is to understand the implications of being environmentally friendly and how, by taking such a stance, an organisation could create a sustainable competitive advantage in marketing.

Understanding environmental marketing

For many consumers, the term 'green' may evoke a range of different emotions and understanding. For some it may mean products that do not harm the environment; for others it may mean products that have been made without harming the environment. Many may consider ethical and moral considerations such as fair trade with developing nations. For some it could be charitable ventures such as Oxfam. From these examples, it can be seen that the term 'environmentally friendly' encompasses a myriad of meanings for individuals, depending on their range of experiences and perspectives. The main issue here is the merging of social concerns as well as ecological concerns. Many in marketing would argue that these are now inseparable (Peattie 1995), see Figure 4.1. Others argue that simply being green is not enough and that ethical issues also need to be taken into account. This is backed up by research into the notion of 'environmental justice' within the USA (Oyewole 2001). The main contention is that many companies site chemical plants and dump toxic waste near poor or deprived communities. This is also part of a global concern about some products being cheaply made by communities which are too poor to complain about environmental issues because they need jobs and money to sustain themselves.

Hand in hand with this, crisis-ridden governments such as Indonesia, the Philippines, South Korea and Thailand cut back on environmental spend (French 2000). For instance, in Russia, the budget for protected areas was cut by 40 per cent. The globalisation of commerce is intensifying the environmental agenda, with many countries increasingly concerned about the effect of global consumption trends on the environment. This is illustrated by the following quotes provided by the Worldwatch Institute, and Figures 4.2, 4.3 and 4.4.

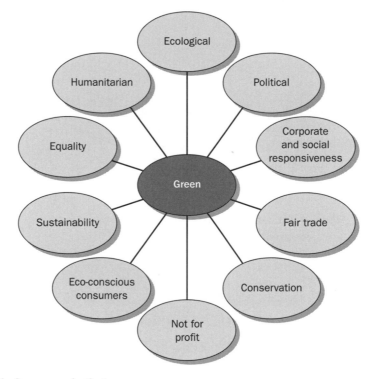

Figure 4.1 Green marketing
Source: Peattie (1995)

Energy and the climate

As our growing population increased its burning of coal and oil to produce power, the carbon locked in millions of years worth of ancient plant growth was released into the air, laying a heat-retaining blanket of carbon dioxide over the planet. Earth's temperature increased significantly. Climate scientists had predicted that this increase would disrupt weather. Indeed, annual damages from weather disasters have increased over 40-fold. (See Figure 4.2.)

Chemicals and the biological boomerang

Our consumption of chemicals has exploded, with about three new synthetic chemicals introduced each day. Almost nothing is known about the long-term health and environmental effects of new synthetics, so we have been ambushed again and again by belated discoveries. One of the most ominous signs of this is the evolution of pesticide-resistant pests as the use of pesticides increases. (See Figure 4.3.)

Commerce and the oceans

The global economy has more than doubled in the past 30 years, putting pressure on most countries to increase export income. Many have tried to increase revenues by selling more ocean fish – for which there is growing demand, since the increase in crop yields no longer keeps pace with population growth. Result: over fishing is decimating one stock after another, and the catch is getting thinner and thinner. (See Figure 4.4.)

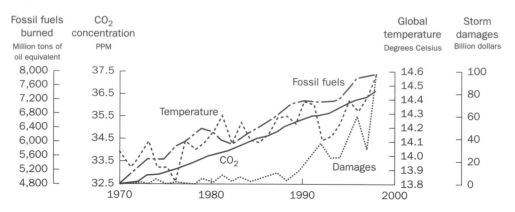

Figure 4.2 Energy and the climate

Source: Worldwatch Institute (2000)

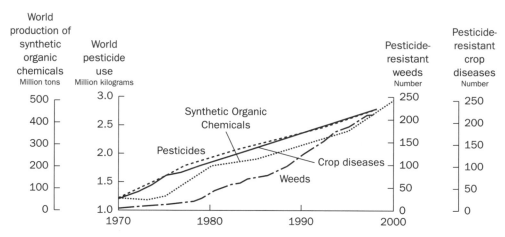

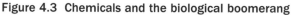

Figure 4.3 Chemicals and the biological boomerang

Source: Worldwatch Institute (2000)

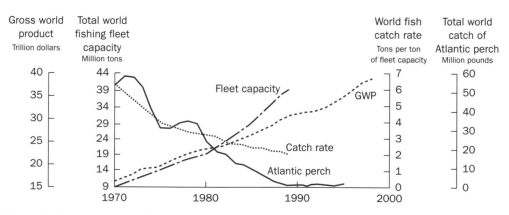

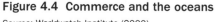

Figure 4.4 Commerce and the oceans

Source: Worldwatch Institute (2000)

As production, marketing and consumption become increasingly global, environmental issues affect every one of us. For marketers, who are often concerned with single products or brands, it is often difficult to disentangle the various interconnecting strands affecting the production of a single product. A complex piece of machinery, such as a car, may well have components which have not been produced using either ethical or environmentally friendly processes. Some marketers would even say that the production and use of a car itself is environmentally unfriendly, as each car in use adds to local and global pollution. Given this range of views, we need to understand the different ways in which green marketing is perceived.

In many ways, to be totally green means that the human population must eschew any luxuries, using only what is necessary for self-sufficiency. As the history of marketing shows, consumption has always played a large part in human existence. For this reason, many marketers feel that being totally green is unattainable, therefore the term 'greener' should be used (Charter and Polonsky 1999). Figure 4.5 also shows the way in which many products are now global and the way in which consumption at the local level also has global implications.

In order to understand how products can be considered as being green, many complicated systems have evolved over the years and many multinationals are now taking green issues more seriously. McDonald's, for example, has spent a great deal of money on improving its ability to recycle materials, but has been quiet on the impact the company has on the environment as a result of the mass production of beef. McDonald's has instituted the following programmes in order to combat energy wastage (Wasik 1996):

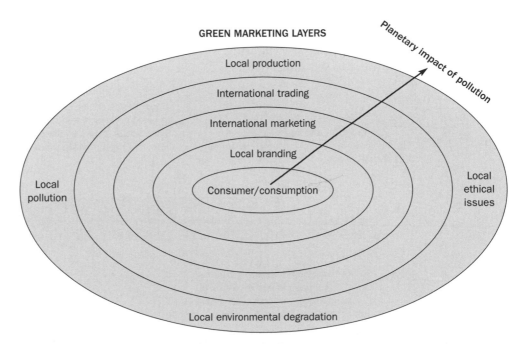

Figure 4.5 Global implications of green marketing

- **McRecycle USA Programme**. The company claims to purchase over $100 million of recycled packaging. Switching from white to brown bags has saved bleaching costs and prevented a greater degree of chemical pollution.
- **Recycled Materials in Construction**. The company sets aside 25 per cent of its construction budget for recycled materials in construction.
- **Energy Efficiency**. In partnership with the US Environmental Protection Agency, the company instituted a 'Green Lights' programme. Eco-efficient lighting was used in stores. The stores themselves were made more energy efficient. The energy saved has resulted in preventing over 30 tons of carbon dioxide being released into the air.
- **Waste Reduction Action Plan (WRAP)**. The focus of this programme was to cut the amount of waste materials going to landfill sites by using recycled materials and paper.

Interestingly, the biggest failure of the many programmes instituted was in the recycling within the shop environment. Consumers were generally oblivious to this! So the final question is, is McDonald's a green product? This is a difficult question to answer because the company has obviously tried hard to improve its products and services through the various ecological efficiency programmes. On the other hand, the morality of mass-producing beef remains unresolved. Some would argue that this brings necessary employment in poorer areas; others would argue that such farming is harmful to the environment. In the light of these fundamental questions, we can only argue for greener marketing.

Greener marketing may well colour different organisations in different shades of green (see Figure 4.6). Again, it is important to note that both social and ecological issues are inextricably intertwined and a truly green organisation should address both areas simultaneously in order to create sustainable businesses and environments. The Nike case study illustrates the particular problems faced by an organisation caught exploiting workers and then, as a result of public pressure, attempting to set things right.

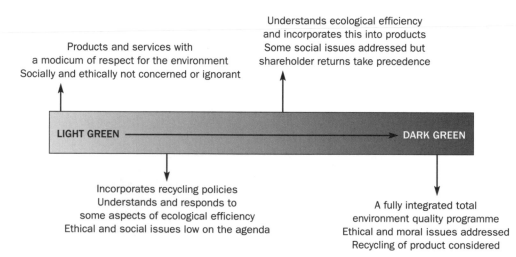

Figure 4.6 Measuring the green policy of organisations

CASE STUDY

Nike Corporation

Consider Nike, the $8 billion footwear and clothing company, which has become a lightning rod for activists, consumers, the media and others, who have taken aim at the company's workplace, environmental and human rights practices. According to its critics, Nike has engaged in a variety of practices that have exploited Third World workers and the communities in which they live. The images proffered by Nike's critics are vivid: women and young children toiling for long hours for low pay in squalid conditions, breathing fumes of toxic chemicals, unable to protest for fear of losing their jobs, manufacturing goods whose price tags exceed their monthly pay.

Nike acknowledges that in the past it was less than vigilant in monitoring the practices of its factories – although nearly all of these are contracted to independent manufacturers. It has now launched an aggressive and ambitious effort not only to correct such situations but also to set a shining example for its industry. The company has begun using sustainability as a design criterion to reduce the use of toxic materials and generation of waste in its manufacturing processes. Nike cut the use of solvents in its adhesives by 800,000 gallons in one year and set a goal of reducing its use of volatile organic compounds per unit of production by 90 per cent by 2001. The company also supports organic cotton farming by providing incentives for farmers to switch to organic production.

None of this seems to have stemmed the tide of criticism. In recent years, Nike has been named among the 10 'worst' international corporations by *Multinational Monitor* magazine. It had an Indonesian factory looted and burned by protesters and suffered criticisms by US women's groups, who pilloried the company for commercials that call for women to be empowered, while poorly paying its predominantly female overseas workers. Its hometown Portland, Oregon, adopted a resolution urging its troubled school district to 'respectfully decline' a $500,000 cash donation because of the company's alleged human rights abuses.

The experiences of Nike, and of other companies that have come under intense public scrutiny because of perceived wrongdoings, suggest that consumers' expectations of brands are changing. It is no longer enough that a company delivers high-quality products. In the search for differentiation, the battleground shifts from the tangible – pounds of chemicals and other wastes released into the environment – to the intangible – ethics, values and corporate culture.

Source: Rand Corporation (2000)

So, ethics are part of understanding sustainable marketing strategies. The other part of understanding sustainability lies in taking a different view on the commonly quoted product life cycle.

The life cycle analysis (LCA) concept

One way of considering the creation and utilisation of products and services which are environmentally friendly is the LCA concept. The LCA is recognised both as a concept and as an analytical environmental management tool (SPOLD 1995). This concept, sometimes termed life cycle thinking, helps everyone (consumers and producers alike) to understand the overall environmental implications of the services required by society. This promotes the consideration of the cradle-to-grave implications of any actions taken, forcing us to move beyond the narrow vestiges of supply chains and sector-based considerations of the environment and consider the wider implications of our activities.

The case study on APRIL illustrates the various factors involved in a company striving to be green.

APRIL takes a leaf out of the green book

Asia is not renowned for being the most advanced region as far as environmental awareness goes. Just think of the car-clogged, highly polluted streets of many of Asia's big cities, the lack of paper recycling systems throughout much of the region or even the poor quality of drinking water in some places further off the beaten track.

But a mixed track record is no excuse for Asian industries today and many of the region's major pulp and paper manufacturers are facing up to the 'green challenge'. One such company is Indonesia's Riau Andalan Pulp and Paper (RAPP), part of the Asia Pacific Resources International (APRIL) group. On the environmental front, RAPP was arguably helped along by its cooperation, albeit short lived, with Finland's UPM-Kymmene. 'The presence of a European company helped raise environmental awareness and performance,' according to Canesio P Munoz, the company's environmental manager. But since the the alliance broke down and RAPP was left standing on its own two feet, there has been no let-up in the company's momentum for greener and cleaner operations.

At present, RAPP is constructing a second pulp line at its Kerinci mill in the Riau province on the Indonesian island of Sumatra. As the company starts to expand toward a two million ton/yr pulp capacity target, the mill is becoming increasingly aware of the need to meet stringent environmental targets to satisfy both local and international demands. The company is targeting a first quarter 2001 startup date for the new line at the Riau mill.

As part of its environmental commitment, APRIL is working on its first annual environmental report. But it is not just a moral sense of concern for the mill's surroundings which is driving APRIL – pressure is coming from many quarters. Local people have lodged complaints about skin-related

diseases and fish depletion in the nearby Kampar river. As a result of these allegations, non-governmental organizations (NGOs) have leveled criticisms at the pulp and paper mill. There have also been some critical voices from overseas, for example in Europe.

In an attempt to put these fears and accusations to rest, APRIL has appointed independent bodies to carry out research and help prove that the Indonesian mill operates in line with international standards, and in some cases, beats these targets (Table 4.1).

Outside approval

One independent body that RAPP selected was the Finnish Environmental Research Group which carried out an environmental impact assessment at the mill. The report was published last September and concluded that RAPP's industrial complex contained low levels of pollutants and that the external treatment seemed to work efficiently, although improvements of nutrient dosage could be carried out. The Finnish group also came to the conclusion that the risk for humans coming into contact with the Kampar river water was 'negligible or non-existent'. As for the river's fish life, investigations suggested that the level of pulp mill effluent contaminants was low enough not to have any serious effect on the animals.

Soon after the Finnish report, RAPP launched a one-year program with local NGOs to carry out further studies into the effects of the pulp and paper operations on the quality of the local river. The gist of these investigations is to sample biodata from the Kampar river every three months and compare examples taken from upstream, downstream and at the point of effluent discharge from the pulp mill.

Table 4.1 RAPP effluent load as compared to international standards (kg/ton)

Parameter	Indonesian (early 2000)	Canada (BC)	Sweden	Cluster rules Existing mills	New mills	RAPP (October 1999)
BOD5	8.5	4.5	8.7	8.05	5.5	2.93
COD	29.75	No spec	31.00	No spec	No spec	11.22
TSS	8.5	7.0	4.0	16.4	9.5	4.41
pH	6–9	5–9	5–9	5–9	5–9	7.1–8.2
AOX	No spec	1.5	0.23	0.623	0.272	0.12

Note: No spec = No specification

Source: Jenkinson (2001)

The research is a three-pronged effort, with local NGO Riau Mandiri assessing the water quality, the Fisheries department of the University of Riau in charge of the river biology/ecology and the University of Singapore investigating health-related matters.

The preliminary results are good news for RAPP, with no strong condemnations being thrown in its direction. The water quality is described as 'generally good', although Riau Mandiri is looking further into the COD (chemical oxygen demand) and BOD (biological oxygen demand) readings which have recently started to rise. The University of Riau has not noticed any significant difference to the natural river life either. In fact, fish stocks actually increased due to higher nitrogen and phosphorus levels in the effluent treatment. The university team continues to assess the quality of the fish stocks as it seems that sulfur levels are slightly higher than normal, though.

On top of that, the reports from local people about skin irritations are not being blamed on RAPP and it is thought that plants may be the problem. The findings of one Riau University study suggest that it is 'unlikely' that river water is a cause of inflammatory skin problems among villagers. Monitoring will continue, though, until a more conclusive verdict is reached.

It is certainly in RAPP's interests to cooperate with the NGOs and prove the mill's case wherever possible, as the NGOs can act as a powerful lobbyist. As Riau Mandiri spokesperson, Anny Hardiyanti, says, 'After a year's monitoring, if we find negative results, we will urge the company to address the problem. And if the problem is not addressed, we will launch a campaign against the company responsible.' Added to that, the NGO is not afraid of carrying out threats of action. It has already launched several campaigns against other companies, which were found to be polluting another nearby river in the region.

Forest sustenance

A key tenet of APRIL's environmental policy is striving toward fully sustainable forest management. The Indonesian mill's long term goal is to achieve sustainable forest management certification. But as an interim step, the mill is focusing on an ISO 14001 certificate for its forestry operations, which it hopes to receive by the end of this year. If the company sticks to the timetable, certification would come just a few months after RAPP was awarded ISO 9002 for its pulp and paper operations.

ISO 14001 is an environmental management system, which provides criteria for assessing a company's use of air, water, soil and resources. The drive toward this certification comes from RAPP's customers around the globe, and particularly from European consumers.

Part of the company's efforts toward full sustainability is the development of its acacia plantations. Planting started back in 1993 and some of the plantations are already mature, but the company is waiting until next year before

▶

harvesting the area for strategic reasons. RAPP aims to make a full switch from mixed tropical hardwood to acacia plantations by 2008.

The company has also carried out extensive tests on the plantations and is extremely pleased with the yield and quality results. The plantations are expected to yield 210 m³/ha at harvest and achieve a wood to pulp conversion rate of 4.5 m³/ton/ib. As a result, RAPP hopes to gain the double advantage of higher yields and limiting any adverse effects on the environment.

By RAPP's calculations, the mill will need 127,500 ha of plantations to supply pulp line #1 which has an 850,000 ton/yr capacity (Table 4.2). Pulp line #2A is due to come on line by the first quarter of 2001, bringing total capacity up to 1.3 million tons/yr. RAPP calculates that it will need 195,000 ha/yr of acacia plantations to meet this pulp capacity, and it is no surprise perhaps that the company happens to have exactly this amount available. Originally the government allocated 280,000 ha of land to RAPP for conversion into plantations. The area chosen by the government was so-called 'non-productive land' – in other words the land had already been logged over and exploited. Some of this area must be maintained as a greenbelt area to protect wildlife and ensure biodiversity in the area, leaving the company with the magic number of 195,000 ha/yr for converting into plantations.

Indonesia's social scene

On paper, the land transfer sounds like a relatively simple procedure – the government allocates land and the company decides to convert the area into plantations. In practice, though, there are many more hurdles to be cleared. For example, some of the allocated land is next to local settlements and the communities claim that the ground is theirs in accordance with 'community rights'. Companies such as RAPP are only able to operate effectively by avoiding conflicts with these local communities. This involves talking with the people, suggesting alternative sources of income and convincing them that they will not lose out. As environmental manager, Munoz, says, 'We don't drive people out. Resolutions are always reached by consensus.'

Of the total area allocated to RAPP, some 60,000 ha of land were termed so-called 'problem areas'. So far, the company has resolved approximately half of the issues. RAPP is all too aware of the need to work with the local people to avoid potentially serious problems. For example, last December the Kerinci

Table 4.2 Plantation supplies at RAPP

		Line 1	Line 1+2A	Line 1+2A+2B
Pulp mill capacity		850,000	1,300,000	2,000,000
Acacia growth rate mean annual increment	m³/ha/a	30	30	30
Rotation	Yr	7	7	7
Yield at harvest	m³/ha	210	210	210
Wood to pulp conversion – acacia species	m³/ton/ib	4.5	4.5	4.5
Wood and HTI requirement				
Annual acacia input	m³/yr	3,825,000	5,850,000	9,000,000
Total net HTI area required	ha	127,500	195,000	300,000
Land resources for tree plantation development				
RAPP HTI concessions area	ha	195,000	195,000	195,000
Associated companies/joint ventures	ha	0	0	85,000
Tree farms	ha	0	0	20,000
Total area	ha	195,000	195,000	300,000

Note: HTI = hutan tanaman industri (local industry requirement)

Source: Jenkinson (2001)

mill was brought to a standstill as demonstrators took to the streets in protest over a labor dispute. And in the new era of 'reformation' which is flourishing in Indonesia, local communities are becoming increasingly aware of their rights and companies such as RAPP clearly want to avoid conflicts wherever possible.

To date, RAPP has employed a host of community development (CD) projects to try and keep the peace with the locals. The CD programs have existed since 1993, although the initiative was significantly expanded in 1998. Last year alone, the company implemented programs in six local villages. RAPP has carried out initiatives such as building a mosque, providing drinking water, building bridges to overcome transportation difficulties and training the villagers to cultivate unused land for productive and profitable uses.

RAPP's budget for CD programs in 2000 is $2 million and the company's management believes that

it is money well spent. Not only does it benefit the local people, but it also promotes good relations with neighboring communities and improves the skills of potential employees for the pulp and paper mill.

One village called Gunung Sahilan chose to develop oil palm plantations with the company's CD program funds. As a result, APRIL teamed up with an associated company, Asian Agri, which is active in the oil palm industry. The alliance has worked well and the villagers seem extremely pleased with the project's success. But when asked if he was satisfied, the village chief replied, 'We don't need more, but we want more.' A note of warning to RAPP, perhaps, that it cannot sit back and relax. The company must constantly remain attentive to the demands of the local people just as much as, if not more than, those of the international community.

Source: Jenkinson (2001)

According to SPOLD, life cycle thinking reflects the acceptance that key company stakeholders cannot strictly limit their responsibilities to those phases of the life cycle of a product, process or activity in which they are actively involved. It expands the scope of their responsibility to include environmental implications throughout the entire life cycle of the product, process or activity. The implication of this type of thinking is that all processors, manufacturers, distributors, retailers, users and waste managers in the life cycle share responsibility.

The individual share of responsibility for each of them will be greatest in the parts of the life cycle under their direct control, and least in other stages of the cycle. Life cycle thinking has been applied to much of the legislation emanating from the European Commission, especially in product and waste policy. The concept of producer responsibility is at the heart of waste strategy, and it follows life cycle thinking. The example given in Figure 4.7 is drawn from the case study on page 78 on pulp and paper manufacture, which illustrates the various factors involved for a company striving to be green. Note that the chain to the final consumer can be quite long.

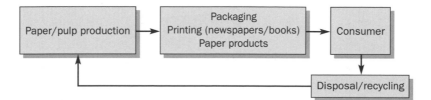

Figure 4.7 **Responsibility throughout the life cycle**

Currently there are a number of different concepts related to developing ecologically sound products. Some of these are as follows:

Design for the environment

There are many initiatives for reducing the various environmental impacts that a product may unleash. These could be at the production stage, the usage stage or the disposal stage (see Figure 4.8). In designing for the environment, technologists are concerned with reducing energy consumption (both in the production of an item and when it is in use) and generally conserving resources. The main trends are:

■ the incorporation of information from LCA into design;
■ the definition of environmental objectives;
■ a focus on the relationship between the product and the consumer and how the design can encourage environmentally responsible behaviour in the consumer.

According to the US Environmental Protection Agency (EPA) (1992), life cycle design is:

A systems-oriented approach for designing more ecologically and economically sustainable product systems which integrates environmental requirements into the earliest stages of design. In LCD, environmental performance, cost, cultural and legal requirements are balanced.

Clean technology

A definition of 'clean technology' is that it is the means of providing a human benefit which, overall, uses fewer resources and causes less environmental damage than alternative means with which it is economically competitive (Clift 1995).

Industrial ecology

This is generally concerned with the evolution of technology and economic systems in such a way that human activities mimic mature biological systems so that they are self-

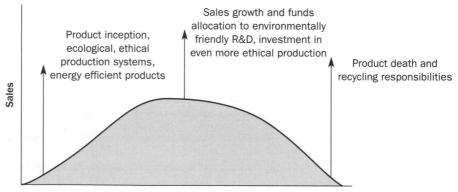

Figure 4.8 Green life cycle analysis

contained in their material and resource use (Allenby 1994). Governments and non-governmental organisations often use this idea when they assess industrial processes.

Total quality environment management (TQEM)

This concept synthesises environmental management and total quality management (TQM) (GEMI 1993). TQEM relies on the following precepts:

- *Identify customers.* The definition of quality is dependent on what customers want (a broader definition of customers is taken, and they include consumers, legislators, environmental groups and society at large).
- *Continuous improvement.* A systematic approach to continuously improve processes.
- *Do the job right the first time.* In terms of the environment, eliminate problems at the outset. Quality failures may be detrimental to the environment and also incur financial costs, without providing benefits to the consumer.
- *Take a systems approach.* Each part of environmental management is considered to be a 'system'. This includes people, equipment and processes. Weak links in the system are addressed.

In general, the plan–do–check–act (PDCA) cycle is followed, in common with typical TQM programmes.

All these concepts are interlinked. There is now a concerted approach to take a more holistic view and incorporate each of these concepts into a general framework for sustainable development (SETAC 1998).

Implications for organisations

It is becoming increasingly important for organisations to incorporate green thinking into their processes and products. They need to consider very carefully how much their activities impact on the planet. Any improvement creates a net benefit for both the consumer and the planet.

Organisations have been charged with embracing a green attitude at a superficial level and generally 'greenwashing' the public through clever advertising and public relations activities. Even companies like the Body Shop have been criticised for exaggerating their claims to promote sustainable development and to use pure ingredients (Stauber and Rampton 1995). In many cases, organisations that pursue even a modicum of green policies are not rewarded in the marketplace (Wong *et al*. 1996). Such criticisms could be levelled at almost every corporation. Nevertheless, it is important to realise that corporations can, by implementing some of the concepts discussed above, have a major impact on the environment. For example:

- Anheuser-Busch has developed an aluminium can that is 33 per cent lighter. This reduced use of aluminium combined with an overall recycling plan saves the company $200 million a year.

- Ford Motor Company used more than 60 million two-litre plastic soda bottles in the manufacture of grille reinforcements, window frames, engine covers and trunk carpets. In 1999, this effort accounted for 7.5 million pounds of plastic.
- Kellogg's plant in Bremen, Germany, employs a waste-water recycling operation that reduces water consumption and waste-water effluent. In India, a Kellogg vapour-absorption system is used to provide plant air conditioning, eliminating the use of ozone-depleting substances. Fluorescent bulbs at the Kellogg plant in New Jersey are sent for recycling, removing potentially hazardous materials from landfills (Rand Corporation 2000).

Despite the views of cynics, these efforts not only save the organisations concerned millions, but also save resources. These types of savings are not easily obtainable through individual customers, so it is important that organisations pursue such strategies. This is especially important when you consider that a study showed that, of the 100 largest economies in the world, 51 were global corporations – only 49 were countries (Anderson and Cavanagh 1996). Mitsubishi was larger than the fourth most populous nation on Earth, Indonesia. General Motors was bigger than Denmark, and Toyota bigger than Norway. Often large chunks of world trade are actually transactions between different parts of organisations. Organisations, therefore, have to be proactive in pursuing ecologically friendly processes and also in producing ecologically friendly products. In addition to this, they are also under pressure from consumers and non-governmental organisations (NGOs, such as Greenpeace). Bennet and James (1999) suggest that companies have become much more sensitive to such pressures because of:

- the growing economic value of a good corporate reputation and a strong, positively regarded brand. These can be put at risk by adverse criticism of environmental and social performance (Fomburn 1996).
- the growing number of customers who are becoming more 'green conscious' (this is discussed later), taking social and environmental criteria into account when purchasing goods or services.
- the tremendous flow of information, at unprecedented levels, through satellite TV stations such as CNN and the Internet. In the future it is likely that information will also be transferred 'on the move' through mobile communication devices such as WAP phones. This flow of information increases the visibility of any enterprise.
- highly educated and more environmentally 'literate' workforces, on which companies depend.

Interestingly, a recent survey of ethical funds showed that they have performed strongly over the past three years. Many funds have shown growth ranging from 73 per cent to 50 per cent (Bien 2001). These are early days, but the recent results bode well for ethical and green investments. What, then, should organisations strive to achieve? Some of the key questions that organisations should be addressing are given at the end of this chapter. In many ways, organisations have to strive to get into a virtuous circle and constantly look forward to the future with their research and development (R&D), see Figure 4.9.

If organisations operate in this virtual way, they could gain considerable competitive advantages. Various authors have tried different types of categorisations.

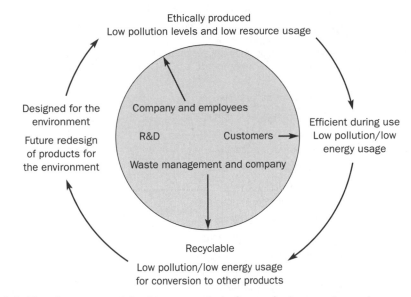

Figure 4.9 The virtuous, sustainable green circle for product management

For example, Hart (2000) has developed the sustainability portfolio where organisations can rate themselves on the following scale: 1 – nonexistent; 2 – emerging; 3 – established; or 4 – institutionalised. Based on this assessment, each organisation can look for gaps and attempt to understand their sustainability credentials and begin to plan both internal and external strategies for the future.

Another way of assessing the total commitment of an organisation to sustainability and ethical consideration is to utilise the matrix shown in Figure 4.10. The questions in Figure 4.11 help to determine into which section of the matrix an

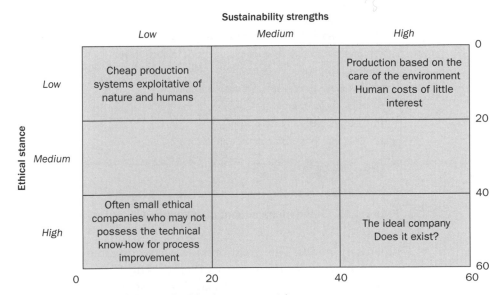

Figure 4.10 Sustainability and ethical stance matrix

Green management

Rate the organisation on a scale from 1 to 5 for each of the issues listed below.	Very poor 1	Poor 2	Adequate 3	Good 4	Very good 5
1 Design for the environment	☐	☐	☐	☐	☐
2 Energy efficiency in manufacturing	☐	☐	☐	☐	☐
3 Waste in manufacturing	☐	☐	☐	☐	☐
4 Pollution during manufacturing	☐	☐	☐	☐	☐
5 Recyclability of packaging	☐	☐	☐	☐	☐
6 Lifespan of product	☐	☐	☐	☐	☐
7 Energy efficiency during use	☐	☐	☐	☐	☐
8 Recyclability of product	☐	☐	☐	☐	☐
9 Total quality environmental management	☐	☐	☐	☐	☐
10 Search for new green product opportunities	☐	☐	☐	☐	☐
11 Use of pollution control equipment	☐	☐	☐	☐	☐
12 Compliance consulting	☐	☐	☐	☐	☐

Total points ☐

Ethical considerations

Rate the organisation on a scale from 1 to 5 for each of the issues listed below.	Very poor 1	Poor 2	Adequate 3	Good 4	Very good 5
1 Working conditions	☐	☐	☐	☐	☐
2 Staff welfare and health care	☐	☐	☐	☐	☐
3 Limitation of exposure to pollutants	☐	☐	☐	☐	☐
4 Sustainability of operations within local ecology	☐	☐	☐	☐	☐
5 Involvement of stakeholders in environmental issues	☐	☐	☐	☐	☐
6 Continuous pollution monitoring	☐	☐	☐	☐	☐
7 Management of the end of the life cycle without affecting others (prevention of dumping in poor areas)	☐	☐	☐	☐	☐
8 Respect for fauna and flora	☐	☐	☐	☐	☐
9 Adequate compensation to local suppliers	☐	☐	☐	☐	☐
10 Honesty in advertising	☐	☐	☐	☐	☐
11 Discussions with NGOs	☐	☐	☐	☐	☐
12 Environment restoration post production	☐	☐	☐	☐	☐

Total points ☐

Figure 4.11 Green management questionnaire

organisation falls. This questionnaire was formulated by understanding the various cases for greener organisations (Peattie and Charter 1997, Piasecki *et al*. 1999, Crosbie and Knight 1995). Organisations scoring 12 points in both sets of questions fall into the top left-hand box; organisations scoring 60 in both sets of questions fall into the bottom right-hand box. This analysis also points the way for future improvement and suggests opportunities that might be available.

Organisations scoring in the medium/medium range (middle of the matrix) may resort to strong advertising campaigns and PR in order to 'greenwash' the public. Consumers often have to rely on specialist journals or articles in newspapers for a true indication of an organisation's policy. There is a great danger that organisations will pay lip service to green strategies and not necessarily address the key issues. These issues are explored in detail in the hard-hitting book *Toxic Sludge is Good for You* by Stauber and Rampton (1995). As discussed before, an organisation that truly follows sustainable principles has to be both ethically and environmentally sound. Customers are also realising that we do not live in a world with infinite resources. In fact, the new-world paradigm reflects the fact that we are *a part* of nature and not *apart* from it (Wasik 1996). The postmodern consumer is more concerned about nature and is likely to look at issues holistically; Table 4.3 illustrates this. For a further discussion of the postmodern consumer, see Chapter 2.

Green consumer behaviour

According to a survey carried out by the Wirthlin Group (Wirthlin Worldwide 2000), two-thirds of American consumers agreed that 'environmental standards cannot be too high and continuing improvements must be made regardless of the costs'. In 1999, a Gallup poll survey found that 68 per cent of Americans worried a great deal about the pollution of drinking water and 53 per cent about the contamination of soil and water by toxic waste.

Understanding the complexity of the human/ecological interface requires a degree of scientific understanding. Yet surveys conducted by the National Science Foundation suggest that, even using lenient standards, only about 11 per cent of citizens understand enough of the vocabulary and concepts of science in general to be considered scientifically literate (National Science Foundation 1998). This is a

Table 4.3 Old versus new paradigms

Old world view	New world view
Continuous, unbridled growth	Sustainable, green economics
Conquer nature, reap resources	Biophilia (affinity for nature)
Environmental compliance	Eco-auditing
Marketing to fill needs	Marketing to sustain life
Materialism	Personalism
Industrial production	Industrial ecology
Design for obsolescence, disposal	Design for environment
Cost accounting (profit/loss statements)	Full cost accounting
Departmentalism, reductionism	Holism

particularly important issue when organisations are advertising the green benefits of their products. How many consumers will actually understand their claims? Are they likely to understand the scientific reasoning behind particular policies or will they be emotionally manipulated by the press? Quite often, people are very likely to understand simple cause-and-effect relationships. According to Coyle, the NEETF (National Environmental Education and Training Foundation) president:

> *[People] understand that cars pollute, or that species become extinct when habitat is destroyed. But when there are two or more steps involved ... such as energy production from fossil-fuelled power stations contributing to climate change, thereby warming ocean waters sufficiently to inhibit the production of plankton for fish, thus impairing the survival of marine life ... public understanding drops precipitously.* (NEETF/Roper Starch Worldwide 2000)

Each year, NEETF issues a 10-question survey on environmental awareness. In a typical year, Americans averaged fewer than 25 per cent correct answers to basic environmental literacy questions. Furthermore, myths and misconceptions persist. Surveys indicate that many Americans still believe that trash bags can be made to biodegrade in landfills (virtually nothing degrades in landfills). Many people still believe aerosol cans contain ozone-destroying ingredients (chlorofluorocarbons were banned from aerosols in 1978) and that landfills are brimming with plastic (plastic accounts for just 9 per cent of municipal solid waste; paper and cardboard account for four times as much).

This can be illustrated by the 'Energy and Environmental Profile Analysis of Children's Single-use and Reusable Cloth Diapers' carried out by Franklin Associates in 1992 and explained in Fuller (1999). For many consumers, the intuitive understanding is that plastic/paper diapers are extremely energy consuming and polluting. The comparative scientific analysis, however, shows that the environmental answers are not clear cut. The results show the following:

- Home cloth diapers consume 33 per cent more energy than single-use diapers and 12 per cent more energy than commercial cloth diapers.
- Single-use diapers produce about twice the total solid waste by volume of home or commercial cloth diapers.
- Home cloth diapers produce nearly twice the total atmospheric emissions of single-use diapers or commercial cloth diapers.
- Home or commercial diapers produce about seven times the total water-borne waste of single-use diapers.
- Home or commercial cloth diapers consume more than twice the water volume of single-use diapers.

Many criticisms can be levelled at such an analysis and some authors argue that single-use diapers also contribute to air pollution via incineration. They may also be the cause of allergic skin reactions. Nevertheless, the case illustrates the complexity of the issues involved when undertaking some sort of life cycle analysis for products. Consumers also need to be able to follow complex arguments in order to make valid judgements.

Roper Starch Worldwide (Rand Corporation 2000), who produce the *Green Gauge Report* on the environment and environmentally conscious purchase decisions, showed a breakdown of consumer attitudes in the 2000 survey:

- *11% True-blue Greens*: The recyclers, composters, letter writers and volunteers of the world, the ones most likely to go out of their way to buy organic foods, recycled paper products, rechargeable batteries, less toxic paints and other goods with environmentally preferable attributes.
- *5% Greenback Greens*: Those who will contribute to environmental organisations or spend more for green products, but not consider changes in lifestyles or housekeeping due to environmental concerns.
- *33% Sprouts*: Those who care about the environment, but who will only spend slightly more for environmentally sensitive products.
- *18% Grousers*: These are people who care about the environment but view it as someone else's problem; Grousers don't seek environmentally sensitive goods or consider green-minded lifestyle changes.
- *33% Basic Browns*: People who are essentially unconcerned about the environment.

There is another way of breaking down consumers, and that is the traditional method of classifying consumers as:

- *Traditionalists*: Those who believe in the nostalgic image of small towns and conservative churches.
- *Moderns*. These are individuals who are more materialistic and consumer oriented. They are generally individuals who see life through the same filters as *Time* magazine.
- *The cultural creatives*. This is a new category, discussed by Dr Paul Ray (Rand Corporation 2000) as a result of market research studies in consumer behaviour. The cultural creatives (CCs) have often been involved in, or care about, three to six social movements. These are:
  - very strong environmentalism;
  - the condition of the whole planet;
  - civil rights;
  - peace;
  - social justice;
  - new spiritualities;
  - organic food;
  - holistic health.

Many follow personal paths and spiritual goals. These individuals account for a high proportion of people using alternative healthcare and every other Lifestyle of Health and Sustainability (LOHAS) product and service. They are good at putting their own big picture together from diverse sources of information. They compare and contrast, are adept at understanding the real issues and are the least likely to be 'greenwashed'. To fully appreciate the sustainable lifestyle, Natural Business Communications and the Natural Marketing Institute believe that the greater paradigm of such existence is LOHAS, or Lifestyles of Health and Sustainability. The LOHAS market comprises five core market segments – Sustainable Economy, Healthy Lifestyles, Personal Development, Alternative Healthcare and Ecological Lifestyles. When combined, the five segments represented a $226.8 billion US market and an estimated $546 billion global market in 2000. Within each of these five segments are

Table 4.4 Key LOHAS segments and industry values

LOHAS market segment	Total in $ millions
Sustainable Economy	76,470
Healthy Lifestyles	27,811
Alternative Healthcare	30,698
Personal Development (mind, body, spirit)	10,628
Ecological Lifestyles	81,178
Total US LOHAS market	**$226.8 billion**

Source: Rand Corporation (2000)

many specific categories of products and services across a vast array of businesses and industries. Table 4.4 shows the total size for the five key LOHAS segments and the associated industry values:

If the US breakdown is emulated around the world, the Ecological Lifestyles and Sustainable Economy segments represent nearly 75 per cent of the global market. So, what exactly is a green consumer? Several interrelated factors have to be taken into account, as shown in Figure 4.12, since this is indeed a complex question. A new breed of consumer is emerging. This new consumer is influenced by many factors that are generally concerned with a need to protect the environment and to lead ethically correct lifestyles. Market trends show that these consumers are growing in numbers. Organisations wishing to understand this growing band of potential customers need to address their marketing offer in a sensible and honest manner. They also have to consider the way in which markets may move in the future.

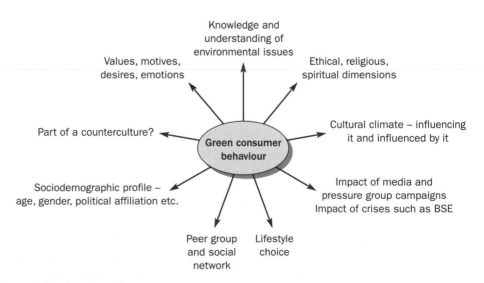

Figure 4.12 Factors affecting green consumer behaviour
Source: Adapted from Wagner (2001)

Green marketing strategies

Organisations often take reactive stances to green issues that damage the credibility of the organisation and the products it sells. It is therefore important for organisations that are seriously concerned about green issues to be more proactive and to pursue a market orientation that is green in its design. In order to gain competitive advantage, organisations have to exhibit the following characteristics:

- Offering products that address the ethical, moral and sustainability issues described above.
- Producing goods which are not only commercially viable, but which also meet consumer needs.
- Using some of the profits for environmental and social improvement at the source of production.
- Segmenting the markets effectively, so that the complexity of the niche markets and the 'new' consumer are understood and targeted accordingly
- Communicating honest and credible messages to the customers. These messages should be transparent and should be understood by internal stakeholders, external stakeholders and consumers.
- Developing transportation and logistics systems that mirror the organisation's aims and objectives of lessening pollution, being environmentally friendly, etc.
- Developing a marketing perspective that takes a cradle-to-grave approach for products.
- Offering certain levels of educational marketing literature in cases where products are complex.
- Advertising in a clear and concise manner.
- Understanding the *future* needs of customers and stakeholders.

Anticipating the *future needs* of consumers is of vital importance as the twenty-first century dawns. Future technological and biotechnological advances could spell either triumph or disaster for the environment. Already there is considerable disquiet over the introduction of genetically modified (GM) foods. Food production, distribution, commercialisation and perception has been radically changed in the last 20 years by the advent of new technologies such as genetic engineering.

The creation of genetically modified foods and organisms (GMOs) has increased general public awareness about the make-up and quality of foods. The main concern over GM foods centres on the fact that they have not conclusively been tested in people's diets using rigorous standards (Cottrill 1998). The negative perceptions surrounding GM foods lie deep within the myths and fears of modern civilisation; the expression 'Frankenstein Foods' is a good example (MacMillan 2000). Given these negative and, in many cases, serious concerns about the possible consequences of the environmental spread of 'rogue' genes via cross-pollination, the public is concerned about clarity of messages and clear labelling. As a reaction against GM foods and continuing health scares, organic food sales have grown rapidly. The growing and consumption of organic foods is seen by many as ecologically friendly and sustainable.

According to Datamonitor (1999), organic sales in the USA reached $5.4 billion in 1998 and were estimated at $6.4 billion in 1999. Datamonitor predicted that sales would continue to grow at approximately 20 per cent per year, reaching $7.76 billion in the year 2000, $9.35 billion in 2001, slightly more than $11 billion in 2002 and slightly more than $13 billion in 2003. Sales during the 1990s grew by between 20 per cent and 24 per cent per year. Organic produce still remains the leading category, although categories such as organic frozen foods, organic dairy products, organic bakery items and cereals, organic baby food and organic ready meals are growing at a faster rate. Another aspect of future consumer trends may be the need for convenience, access to product use and a desire to be free from material possessions.

It is quite possible that in the future organisations will have to design products that can be shared among different individuals. For example, cars could be pooled within cities and individuals could subscribe to a lease and use service, picking a car up when required and then leaving it at their destination. Many other items, including recreation products such as surfboards, could be leased in a similar manner. This type of consumption points the way towards a shared existence, away from the individualistic pursuit of gathering material goods.

Summary

This chapter outlines the major environmental threats to the planet through the consumption patterns of organisations and consumers. It also shows the way in which organisations can look at what being green means and how they can translate this into effective action and competitive advantage. It is clear that consumption patterns and consumer actions are going to change as we move further into the twenty-first century. Also, marketing has a key role to play in the greening of organisations and in the environment, and in developing consumer tastes that benefit the planet. At the same time, green and ethical policies offer a chance to improve the social status of poorer and less well-endowed sections of the developing world. Sustainability issues and ethics go hand in hand, and the opportunities that exist are immense for organisations that can think and act holistically in meeting the growing demand for greener products.

Chapter questions

1 What prevents organisations from developing 'green' strategies?

2 Explain how life cycle analysis can help an organisation in developing and designing new products.

3 Why should ethical and environmental stances be considered together when developing marketing strategies for an organisation?

4 What are the key roles that marketing can play in developing 'green' consumer tastes?

5 Building brand relationships

Introduction: Branding and communications – the 'last stand'?

The apparent necessity to differentiate various aspects of marketing diminishes the visible interrelationships between elements of the marketing approach. Experts in public sector marketing, communication specialists and marketing strategists abound. Yet the differences between, for example, public sector marketing and business-to-business marketing are almost as evident as the overlapping of the fundamental issues. As analysing the target market (however fragmented), selecting the target audience and positioning the product or service is the foundation for any organisation with a market orientation, the significance of the interrelationships between branding and communications in these sectors is of equal interest. Journal articles typically focus on the peculiarities of interrelationships – how branding affects loyalty or the way in which customer service affects equity. In reality, the wider context of marketing needs to be addressed (including the internal barriers to marketing, the external environment, cultural differences and social trends) with the adaptation of the marketing approach by various organisations measured not by short-term gain but viewed with long-term insight.

This chapter considers branding and communication as one of the key variables in marketing, challenging traditional thought and posing questions to facilitate lateral thinking. However, many organisations resort to branding and communication as a 'last stand' when every other marketing strategy fails to deliver the required results. Case studies are used to demonstrate the rhetoric and reality of marketing intent and practice.

Brand management

If branding, and the associated communication approaches, are the 'last stand' of marketing, arguably the following organisations would support the continuing strategic use of these marketing constructs. Coca-Cola, Walkers, Nescafé, Stella Artois and Persil began the millennium as the top five brands of the new century (ACNielsen, 2001). The image and quality of these brands matched the expectations and perceptions of the consumer and evolved within a changing environment. There is a strong argument that strong brands can also be created within services through integration of message and consistency of delivery (Berry 2000). Figure 5.1 shows four ways in which service organisations can build strong brands. Organisations with the strongest brands – Starbucks, McDonald's and Disneyworld are a few examples – typically use all four approaches.

Sensible organisations dare to be different by having radical advertising strategies and determining their own fame by providing specialised services. Emotional connections can be made by cause-related marketing (helping communities or causes) and internalising the brand means that every individual within the organisation provides an excellent service to the customer. In order to do this, employees need to fully understand the brand values and internalise them. This model could be equally applicable to a range of products. As brands come under growing threats from a range of different factors, they cannot remain immobile. Whilst 1999 saw the exponential rise of Procter & Gamble's fruit drink Sunny Delight, 2000 viewed the upsurge of organically made products, including food and dairy products. This demonstrates that a brand cannot remain immobile (Dru 1997) and needs to develop to remain contemporary. If branding and communications are so

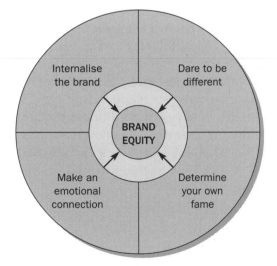

Figure 5.1 Cultivating brand equity
Source: Berry (2000)

fundamental to the strategic success of an organisation, how can a brand identity maintain brand equity in a climate of change?

A long-term view

If brands are to be successful, a long-term view of marketing decisions must be taken in order to ensure consistency and clarity. Whilst innovation in brand management is part of the brand dynamism, consistency of the marketing support (Bridges *et al.* 2000) is essential to provide uniformity and focus. Coca-Cola, for example, truly created a global brand 30 years ago by gathering 200 multiethnic youngsters on a hilltop in Italy and getting them to sing: 'I'd like to buy the world a Coke'. However, Coca-Cola has downgraded its ambitions as it continues to face challenges from local brands such as Thumbs Up in India. It is becoming increasingly difficult for organisations such as Coca-Cola to keep up with fragmenting markets (Tomkins 2000). Coca-Cola is trying to react to changes by launching a range of other soft drinks and bottled water (often not bearing the Coca-Cola brand). The consistency of Coca-Cola pays, but it also has a downside.

A frequently used example of how not to manage brand and brand innovation is epitomised by the case of Intel. A rare flaw in a Pentium chip was known occasionally to cause miscalculation problems with data. Instead of replacing the chip, Intel maintained the fault was extremely unusual and refused to publicise the problem or provide a replacement chip for a considerable number of weeks. When Intel finally did offer replacements to customers, it is estimated that only between 1 per cent and 3 per cent of customers actually requested an alternative. The brand image of 'power' and 'safety', however, had been dented. Consumers tend to retrieve brand-related information from memory and thus compute a brand-related rating on the basis of external information available at the time of judgement. Alternatively, they undertake a type of mixed retrieval–deduction process, in which some information is retrieved and some is deducted. The process is likely to depend on brand-related experiences (Alba and Hutchinson 1987). Therefore the lack of a PR campaign by Intel may have led to external information significantly contributing to consumer judgement.

Brand values

The apparent matching of brand promise with brand reality has been demonstrated by the 'top' brands. The consistency in approach towards managing a brand is critical, with brand association being key to enduring customer loyalty and awareness over a long period of time. Freshness, quality, longevity, simplicity and social acceptability are among the values associated with a given brand and the management of these values, once they are established, provides a platform for developing, growing and strengthening brand equity. Brand 'meddling' described by Mazur (2000) highlights the ineffective managing of brand and brand values, citing Levi Strauss, among others, as a significant offender. Branding, Mazur asserts, is more than a catchy phrase and quirky advertising.

Levi Strauss, which clearly differentiated itself in the marketplace for a number of years, lost its kudos when the brand previously associated with the 18–25-year-old market, Levi's, was displayed by Tony Blair (PM) and Jeremy Clarkson. Fine, upstanding men of the last decade they may be, but representatives of the brand values they were not. More importantly, Levi Strauss had failed to take notice of changes in the marketplace, including the rise of denim alternatives, as delineated by Gap, and the higher priced and positioned brand extensions by Calvin Klein and Armani, to name but a few.

Understanding brand positioning and perceptual maps is an integral part of brand research. An example of this understanding is provided by Dillon *et al.* (2001), who undertook research on fast moving consumer goods (fmcg) in the USA. This work looked at BSAs (brand salient attributes), which refer to general features, attributes or benefits that consumers link to a brand, thereby differentiating it from its competition. The GBIs (general brand impressions) refer to general impressions about a brand based on a holistic view. As brand perceptions depend on product attributes and impressions derived from memory, this is a useful way to measure positioning.

In the case of toothpaste, see Figure 5.2, Colgate's brand-building activities feature *hedonic benefits* such as good taste and breath freshening. Crest, however, concentrates on *preventative benefits* such as the prevention of cavities, plaque build-up and gum disease. The interesting issue here is that there is a variation between those consumers who have high brand knowledge and are more driven by brand attributes (BSAs) for positioning, and those with low brand knowledge and tend to be more driven by brand impressions (GBIs). Thus there are positioning differences between graph A and graph B in Figure 5.2. It is important, therefore, for organisations to develop consistent branding strategies for their target markets, whether aiming for hedonistically driven or attribute-driven consumers.

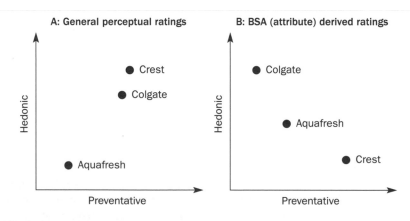

Figure 5.2 Toothpaste perceptual maps

Source: Adapted from Dillon *et al.* (2001)

To manage a brand effectively, it is necessary, therefore, to support the brand with marketing and monitor the difference between identity and image. Consistently observe the changing external and internal climate, be aware of the brand association and values analogous with the brand, and develop the brand, but make changes only when appropriate. These brand values are key to the internal functioning of an organisation as well as to the external perception of it.

Brand equity

Widespread public knowledge is not the only measure of true brand equity (Knapp 1999). Indeed, awareness, loyalty, perceived quality and identity all form part of brand equity. Ineffective brand management can have an adverse effect on a brand; for example, weakening a brand's impact through brand extension or stretching can decrease the equity of the brand. Risk managers must identify the drivers of brand value, define consumer perceptions of the organisation and its products, and scrutinise corporate decisions for their impact on brand power.

Brands are both risks and assets. However, as brands are rarely sold, value for insurance is not the same as value for sale. A number of methods are used to evaluate brand equity but the principal ones involve discounting future cash flows. These will be explored to a greater extent in Chapter 9. Interestingly, Ambler (1998) observes that there is allocation of brand equity responsibilities and that each segment (consumer, employee, etc.) has a duty to contribute to brand perception, loyalty and awareness. This can be done, for example, through the use of marketing and human resources for the aforementioned segments. Thus the brand is driven, developed and motivated by the stakeholders.

Brands have unique emotional and functional benefits for the consumer. Take, for example, the sweeping changes made to the names of confectionery products in the early 1990s. To the dismay of a number of consumers, Mars' Marathon bars became Snickers and Opal Fruits became Starbursts. The fate of a popular cereal may have followed a similar course, but with competent brand management Kellogg's CoCo Pops did not permanently become Choco Krispies. Loyal consumers who phoned to vote for the CoCo Pops name to remain were rewarded when thousands decided that the name CoCo Pops reflected the true nature of the product. Perhaps a cynical exercise, but awareness without differentiation is marginally profitable, and brands with little loyalty are more prone to decline.

The case study on the Morgan Motor Company demonstrates the significance of branding within a niche market in a saturated industry sector.

Considering branding as a key strategic function has attributed to the success of this niche organisation. Using Morgan as an example, branding can be seen to be effective as part of an ongoing, long-term strategy rather than being the 'last stand'.

Morgan Motor Company Limited

Retaining traditional brand values in an era of global lean manufacturing

Morgan Motor Company Limited, based in the town of Malvern in Worcestershire, England, is a private family-owned company. It has defied the forces of car manufacturing logic to survive as probably the only company in the world still making traditional, hand-built motor cars with an order book that will take four or five years to fulfil. On the one hand, the company has found a niche market to survive among the giants as a non-threatening manufacturer, riding out many decades of the global hi-tech, just-in-time, lean car mass manufacturing which produces the sophisticated vehicles of today. On the other hand, the company has kept going with a full order book when many other small-scale manufacturers of specialist cars have either disappeared from view of been the subject of numerous takeovers by enthusiastic multimillionaire entrepreneurs.

The company's core products are based on two-seater, open sports cars styled in the fashion of the 1920s and 1930s, built on conventional chassis compared with the monoque integral body/chassis design of modern cars. A range of engines, varying in size from a 1.6 litre Ford unit to the famous 3.5–4.2 litre Rover V8, are bought in, as are transmissions and axles. Recently, the Aero 8 model featuring a V12 BMW engine has been added to the range to provide an upmarket addition. For the first time in many years, the styling of this car reflects modern tastes rather than traditional values.

Most other components are made at the factory. Until recently, chassis members were made from ash wood, but recently the decision was made to buy them in, constructed of galvanised steel. A wooden framework is made for each car by craftsmen, and hand-formed aluminium body parts attached. Until recently, no power tools were used in the construction of the body parts. Craftsmen serve a traditional apprenticeship before becoming qualified to work unsupervised.

Despite the traditional methods of working, inefficiencies were highlighted during a visit by Sir John Harvey-Jones at the end of the 1980s. This was for the first series of the BBC TV programme 'Troubleshooter'. Sir John considered that the old-fashioned working practices were not always necessary for the car to retain its hand-built appeal with customers. He suggested that methods of stock and parts control lacked any coherent management system, that the five to six-year order lead time was far too long and that the company needed to raise prices in order to ensure adequate return on investment.

Sir John reiterated the importance of these changes during a second visit for the 'Troubleshooter' series at the end of the 1990s, and the company has not implemented all of Sir John's recommendations where it was felt that these might compromise the traditional values of the product. Nevertheless, changes have been made to production techniques and the factory layout which have increased work flow, efficiency and output. The Japanese *kanban* system of matching components to be delivered at the right moment to the production 'line' has been implemented.

Morgan cars have one of the highest proportions of vehicles manufactured still in use in roadworthy condition of any manufacturer. Typical buyers of Morgan cars are people who have a liking for traditional cars with a sporty feel and performance which require 'real driving' and lack the sophisticated handling and performance of modern cars, which tend to insulate the driver from the road. Morgan buyers are not necessarily terribly wealthy and the cars represent exceptional value for money, with the base 1.6 model costing just over £20,000 in the UK. The new BMW-engined Aero is expected to be premium priced, however, at somewhere between £55,000 and £60,000. The cars are rarely used for daily transport, being reserved for weekends and holidays.

The Morgan Owners' Club, which represents owners in many countries of the world, provides a sense of identity and community for many of the buyers. It has strong links and influences with the factory and is often consulted for advice on product and brand development. The owners' club is a powerful, though informal, symbol and promoter of the Morgan core brand proposition.

The core brand values of the product are tradition, quality, nostalgia, exclusivity, craftsmanship, fun and a sense of participating in something which is special and unchanging amidst a world of turmoil and constant change. These core values are augmented by opportunities for a personal relationship with the factory. Purchasers and prospects are able to tour the factory, and sometimes take delivery of their new car directly from the factory rather than from the premises of their local Morgan dealer.

Such values are often found amongst owners of vintage and veteran cars which are no longer in production, but a key differentiator for Morgan is continuity. Many features of the cars made today can be traced back directly to cars of the 1920s and 1930s, and it takes an expert eye to determine whether a particular model was made last week or twenty years ago. Morgan owners also tend to be loyal and are unlikely to indulge in brand switching, exhibiting extremely long-term commitment to the product.

The brand strength, identity and continuity is such that little advertising or promotion is required. The Morgan Owners' Club, and individual Morgan owners, do most of the product promotion through events and word of mouth. News about the Morgan factory or changes to the product line will result in a high level of friendly media interest. Whilst public relations does not have to be proactively managed in the way it does for volume production cars, the Morgan family place great importance on the maintenance of good public relations and other aspects of marketing communications. They are highly skilled at managing the whole promotional mix in an understated and subtle manner which results in high-profile but non-aggressive promotion of the key brand values, identity, image and attributes. It is probably not an exaggeration to say that no other car manufacturer has achieved such consistent branding over such a long period of time for so little communications expenditure.

Source: Mike Wilman, Senior Lecturer, Southampton Business School

Brand extension

Brand consistency is essential when maintaining the value and positive associations of the brand. Therefore, when diluting a brand, maintaining brand values is critical. Brand stretching is the introduction of a new product or service in the same (or a similar) market, whereas brand extension is the launch of an unrelated product or service with an existing brand name. It is almost impossible not to mention Virgin when alluding to brand extension. Virgin is a brand associated with music, airlines, cosmetics, finance, brides and trains – to name but a few of its operations. Each new venture has had its own measure of success or failure and, given the difficulties of Virgin Rail, it is a testament to the Virgin brand that it appears to have remained intact (Drummond and Ensor 2000).

The case study on Calpol overleaf highlights the issues of brand management, brand equity and brand stretching.

The significance of the referent groups in developing and enhancing brand identity is evident from this case study. Continuing loyalty and appropriate research appear critical to the success of developing or extending a brand. The risks of dilution are evident – as is the considerable strength of the brand. Where branding and the associated communication approaches are supported as a key strategic function, as with the example of Calpol, the 'last stand' of marketing demonstrates true strength. Issues of continuing brand equity, levels of awareness and strategic positioning are all factors raised in this case study.

Calpol™ – growing the brand

Background

The Warner Lambert Company is a global corporation with annual revenues of $12 billion. Since its merger with another pharmaceutical giant, Pfizer, in 2000, the company now has revenue in excess of $29.6 billion per annum.

The new Pfizer, which includes Warner Lambert, is primarily focused on its ethical prescription business. The second largest business for the company is the consumer healthcare business. North America is the largest region within the global consumer healthcare business, followed by Europe, of which the UK accounts for 38 per cent of sales and 54 per cent of the profit.

Warner Lambert Consumer Healthcare UK has an annual turnover of £110 million. The brand portfolio is made up of a number of market-leading brands. The upper respiratory category is the largest group and includes Benylin (28 per cent value share), Sudafed (42 per cent) and Benadryl (19 per cent) each of which is a market leader in the cough, decongestants and allergy category respectively. Warner Lambert has two other brand leaders within its portfolio: Calpol (65 per cent value share) in children's analgesics, and Listerine (34 per cent) in the daily-use mouthwash category.

Calpol*

Calpol is in many ways a unique brand. Not only does it hold a 64 per cent value share of the market, it has held this position for a number of years. It is the most recommended paediatric analgesic brand (OTC Bulletin 2001) by pharmacists, GPs and practice nurses, and has a place in the hearts of its consumers which the majority of brands can only dream of. Two pieces of research confirm this position.

Firstly a piece of qualitative research carried out by the Frontline Research Consultancy in 1999 revealed that to Calpol's consumers Calpol was thought of as 'the magic potion'. The brand was held in especially high regard. It was also described

* Calpol is a registered trademark of Warner Lambert Consumer Health Products Company

as 'miraculous' and clearly had a perceived efficacy far beyond that of mere paracetamol (the active ingredient). Calpol was the one medicine that consumers regarded as core to their drug repertoire and all of the respondents had a bottle in their medicine cabinet. In fact, to run out of Calpol was seen as tragedy. Emotionally, Calpol seemed to take on the guise of a talisman: to run out would almost certainly guarantee that your child would become ill.

Calpol was the one brand that all health professionals recommended – they use the brand somewhat generically. Most of the respondents knew that paracetamol suspension would be cheaper than Calpol or that there were other lesser brands that would cost them less. Yet they still put their faith, and their money, in Calpol.

The second piece of research was conducted by an agency called Brandz in 1999. This concluded that, within its own market, Calpol was at the top of the scale and compared favourably with other leading brands in the UK such as Heinz and McDonald's. Calpol was what they termed an 'Olympic' brand, similar to the BBC in that it was well known and well loved, with a large core following. It is talked about in everyday life and is part of the cultural fabric of the country.

With such a strong 'brand essence', ensuring Calpol's stability and growth is key to future success. Calpol is used primarily for children from 3 months to 6 years through its infant formulation and from 6 years to 10 years through the 6+ formulation. At this point children tend to move on to adult tablets and formulations. Two options therefore exist for Calpol to extend its franchise: to appeal to older children (via their parents) to extend the usage; to move into other related medicine categories.

Melt in the mouth tablets

Another concept was introduced which kept the brand within the traditional market segments of pain and fever; these were melt in the mouth tablets. This concept was generally strongly endorsed, particularly by Calpol users. It was felt that these filled a gap in the market and helped to bridge the gap between children's medicine and adult tablets. This concept was felt to be a natural extension to the existing Calpol 6+ range. The competitive benefits of the Calpol melt in the mouth tablet were perceived to be: better tasting than an adult medicine; easier to eat than an adult tablet; more grown up than medicine; for mums, less messy and much more portable.

The melt in the mouth tablets produced much debate about the optimum age range; many felt that this product was much more suitable for children aged 8 years or over. Having said that, most perceived that the tablets would be an alternative form of the existing 6+ products and endorsed the 6+ age positioning. The standard Calpol packaging approach for this product was felt to be perfectly acceptable since the tablets were considered an extension of the pain relief brand – 'melt in the mouth' should be the primary communication point.

Calpol vapour rub

Several new product concepts were tested on both existing brand users and non-users. The first product was a vapour rub designed to help young children breathe more easily when they are suffering from congestion brought on by a cold. This concept was generally well received across the sample. The non-sticky and non-staining aspects of the product were thought to be additional benefits but, more importantly, the natural and aromatic properties were considered contemporary and positive, and addressed the concerns of non-users that Calpol was sweet and sticky.

The key issue for the vapour rub concept was that of positioning and primary target age range. The research indicated that there is probably most potential for a product positioned for infants because that is where Calpol was most established.

Cough and congestion

Moving away from the traditional pain and fever relief that is Calpol heartland, new cough and congestion concepts were introduced. The reaction to these concepts was equally positive. The respondents saw these products as a natural development for Calpol and as an alternative and

specific form of relief for the child (and for mum) when the child is suffering from a nasty cold or flu. Competition in the children's cough and congestion sector is stronger than in the traditional pain and fever sector.

Calpol cooling patches

The final concept that was introduced took Calpol further away from its heritage as a medicine for treating pain and fever in children. A Calpol cooling strip was introduced, which, when placed on the forehead, reduced the temperature on the skin surrounding the patch. The initial reaction to the concept was that this was a new method of taking Calpol liquid. Respondents were well aware of nicotine replacement patches that deliver a stream of nicotine into the bloodstream through the skin and perceived that these patches would do the same.

The research indicated that whilst the general perception of a cooling patch was favourable, it was not thought to be suitable either for children or for Calpol. Calpol is seen as a brand that should produce products to cure childhood ailments. The patches were not perceived as having a clear and definite role and, as such, did not sit well with the current positioning of the Calpol range.

Concept research conclusions

Research confirmed that all three of the brand extension concepts had considerable appeal to both users and non-users.

The vapour rub was particularly appealing because it shows Calpol as the expert in decongestion and pain and fever relief. The focus on the natural and aromatic features were motivating for users and non-users as it challenged their negative perceptions of the brand. The vapour rub should be positioned similarly to the existing Calpol medicine range as it is likely to be used for younger children and probably for older children as well. Mothers stated that they didn't want a range of vapour rubs in the cabinet because they tend to last for some time.

The research indicated that a more overt infant positioning would be unnecessarily restrictive, particularly as Calpol has so much credibility for babies of 3 months and over.

▶

Whilst clearly the colour purple should be incorporated into the pack graphics in some way, it was felt to be important that vapour rub cues were used as well. Green was often suggested, particularly as this gives the impression of natural and aromatic properties.

The 6+ melt in the mouth tablets were considered to be a definite move forward, primarily because they offer a modern and novel delivery format but also because they are in a market segment that is part of Calpol's heritage. Unlike the medicine, the tablets were thought to offer the appeal of a grown-up format. Given that this concept was clearly thought of as an extension of Calpol's core pain relief sector, purple emerged as perfectly acceptable as the colour for the packaging.

The cough and congestion concept was well received, but the respondents felt that the brand would have to work harder because of the existing competition in the sector. However, they did confirm that if any brand was right to enter this market, it was Calpol due to its strength within paediatric medicines. Additionally, a significant proportion of consumers ask the pharmacist which he or she would recommend and it would therefore be critical to gain pharmacists' approval in this case.

More broadly, the research indicates that Calpol may have to work harder to project its points of difference in the cough and congestion sector. However, the strengths were widely percieved: Calpol would be more effective due to having children's pain relief and doctor recommendation heritage; it could be used in conjunction with Calpol medicine and would look and taste better than the existing competition. Additionally, it was thought necessary to develop Calpol imagery that appeals to children beyond the taste of the product.

Whilst these concepts were thought of as a natural extension to the existing Calpol range, the Calpol cooling strips were less well regarded. Traditionally, Calpol contains an ingredient which works to relieve the symptoms of childhood pain and fever. The Calpol melt in the mouth concepts and the Calpol vapour rub and cough and congestion concepts naturally extended this traditional viewpoint. The cooling patches, however, did not as they contained only menthol, which is neither systemic nor topical but rather cools through evaporation.

Source: Nick Burgoyne, Senior Product Manager

Advertising

Although it is acknowledged that advertising is more than quirky branding, building brands, positioning brands and brand values are generally supported by effective advertising campaigns. Indeed, without advertising, would brands be less recognisable and less profitable? Take Apple, for example. The choice of computer equipment centres on speed, availability of appropriate software, compatibility and future migration to new applications. Given the power and scope of Microsoft, a conventional approach to building the Apple brand would have been to find ways of reassuring all the target segments that the company was able to survive and be competitive in this industry environment.

However, the company adopted a different approach. The Apple brand was built by positioning Apple as a 'creative and innovative' company rather than a computer company. This has proved to be hugely successful. A clear example of this is the success of the iMac, which has become the best-selling computer ever, selling over 1.3 million units worldwide. In addition to this, the iBook has become Apple's best-selling laptop, selling 235,000 units worldwide in a six-month period. By considering and choosing alternative positioning strategies, Apple has demonstrated that through advertising it is able to build brand identity, awareness, loyalty and equity – often in saturated markets.

Additionally, it is becoming increasingly difficult to segment the market for television advertising. With low unemployment, low inflation and consumer spending forging ahead, there appear to be few reasons why advertisers should not be spending. Clearly, as media continue to fragment, organisations will consider alternative avenues. Procter & Gamble, which until four years ago principally used TV, now spends significantly on outdoor advertising. With zipping and zapping and the introduction of the TiVo (a new, interactive TV system that allows viewers to customise their viewing), the traditional methods of communication and segmentation require different approaches. Perhaps as Garry Lace, CEO at the advertising agency TBWA\, suggests, by recruiting people in the advertising industry who think creatively about the whole process of branding and advertising, branding strategies will continue to be innovative and original.

Ambient advertising

With outdoor billboards having been found in the ruins of Pompeii, it is reasonable to assume that advertising in not a new concept. Advertising has had a long and varied past, with adverts running during the Second World War encouraging consumers *not* to buy products. The advertising message then was one of guilt and sacrifice. Recession in the early 1990s shaped more reflective consumers, with the next decade producing a generation of 18–25 year olds who are more ad-literate and less likely to be attracted to a product because it bears a particular logo. ITV has reported its first ever slump in TV advertising revenue, and consumers are becoming desensitised towards shock advertising. Where, then, does advertising go from here? Down the toilet? Almost.

Ambient advertising has increased in the last few years. The term covers a multitude of approaches to communicating a message. Ambient advertising is using unusual or innovative locations for advertising messages, such as toilet doors, urinal walls, take-away carton lids, car-park barriers, shopping trolleys and the side of scaffolding. With the plethora of advertising messages that the consumer is expected to receive and understand on a daily basis, it is not surprising that ambient advertising focuses on short-term high impact and long-term strategic gain. Advertising revenue on ITV may decline, but with a more clearly defined consumer on digital and cable networks, the opportunities to access the target audience using alternative channels may be greater. With the addition of new media to the marketing armoury, advertising is not dead; it has simply been reincarnated.

Internet branding

The Internet is a myriad of facts, prices, data, product reviews, advice and how-to guides. Users now have virtually unlimited information about their prospective choices, but this sheer volume can be overwhelming. Rather than brands becoming less important and price more so, familiar brands, with their associated values and benefits, are likely to be recognisable, particularly for novices shopping online.

The rise and fall of dot.com companies highlights the necessity to effectively employ the principles of marketing. Whilst millions were being spent on brand building, sites were either under construction or unable to convey associated brand values. Mazur (2000) has indicated that there is little loyalty to sites among users and that, to entice consumers to return frequently to a particular site, products have to have more than physical characteristics. As an example, Mazur considers myhome.co.uk. Although the site reflects Unilever products, it also offers a cleaning service, encouraging brand loyalty and convenience for the consumer.

Internet branding, also considered under 'The impact of information technology' in Chapter 6, is a relatively new concept. As the audience grows, understanding the attitude of the target is increasingly significant. As organisations such as BT try to secure loyalty at an early age (Simms 2000), clearly practitioners are aware of the importance of this new media tool. Although the consequences of branding and advertising effectiveness on the Internet have yet to be fully explored, it is generally agreed that the Internet is not a replacement but a complement to existing marketing approaches.

Perhaps key to the success of Internet branding is integration of the brand message. Organisations took the opportunity to reposition themselves, probably to a younger target audience, when the Internet provided them with new access to a relatively elusive audience. In particular, financial services used different brand names to entice new customers online. The Co-operative Bank, for example, renowned for its policy on ethical investment (see Chapter 1), used Smile as its Internet brand for financial services. Whilst this may have allowed them access to a new target audience, existing users found the brand name change confusing. As a result of mergers and acquisitions, many financial services found themselves part of a major restructuring programme. Retail branches, for most banks, were a major casualty of the reconfiguration, with branch closures and a focus on telephone and Internet banking.

Although this suited the financial services providers, consumers were disconcerted and unhappy with the changes. Barclays Bank launched an advertising campaign to highlight how large the scale of its operations is, with an almost immediate announcement that over 150 retail branches were to close. The message to the consumer was, at best, confused. NatWest, however, used the opportunity to convey that it is a bank that listens to its audience. NatWest abolished its closure programme, maintained the same brand for Internet banking and provided a selection of overdraft facilities to match consumer needs. The integration of the communication could leave the audience in little doubt as to the message of the bank and the associated brand values. Perhaps integration within advertising agencies (NatWest Village) can assist in the consistency of message and approach to branding.

Loyalty

Does branding, and the associated communication approaches, encourage loyalty? Does true loyalty exist? Although supermarkets and other retail outlets have issued 'loyalty' cards in an effort to establish a platform for relationship marketing, is a loyalty card representative of customer loyalty? Or does a loyalty card merely confirm that a consumer uses the supermarket regularly because it is either more convenient, the nearest supermarket to the house of the consumer, or a familiar environment? What is loyalty in this scenario? Spurious loyalty? Is a loyalty card a cynical tool for sales promotion? How is loyalty measured in the retail environment? Fiona Debling considers these questions.

> There is a lot of confusion between loyalty and commitment in the literature and for practitioners. Loyalty has been defined in more behavioural terms (repeat purchases/patronage), whereas commitment has been focused on attitudes, emotional attachment or 'brand preference'. In recent years, though, Dick and Basu (1994) sought to integrate the two constructs so that 'true loyalty' (as opposed to habit/routine purchase) is seen as repeat patronage plus a high relative attitude towards the preferred brand.

> Knox and Walker (2001) also include both commitment and 'support' (repeat purchase) in their model of loyalty for fast moving consumer goods. Their model differs slightly from Dick and Basu's (1994) in that they allow for repertoire-buying (i.e. the notion that we are not necessarily 'loyal to a single brand' but that we buy from a portfolio of preferred brands. The latter also identify variety-seeking behaviour within their loyalty model (common in fmcg and the reason for brand extension/variations in pack size, colours, etc.).

Evidently, the extent of loyalty and commitment in the retail environment is evaluated to ensure appropriate tactics to direct consumer behaviour can be utilised. Critical to the success of brand building is not only identity and awareness, but also usage.

Business-to-business marketing

Business-to-business (B2B) marketing is infrequently referred to in academic texts, although a considerable amount of marketing spend is allocated to businesses attracting not consumer interest but the collective buying power of another business. B2B markets are often complex since the extent to which an organisation is centralised or decentralised affects business buyer behaviour. A software company, therefore, that wants to supply government departments not only has to comply with the tender principles but may not necessarily supply all departments (even if they are in the same building). It is patent, then, that communicating the benefits of software and software applications is complex.

IBM (quickly followed by Compaq) has produced a B2B advertisement for e-business solutions. This piece of communication, screened at the weekend and in the evening on terrestrial and cable TV, captures the intricacies of B2B buying.

With the number of people involved in the software, its design and its application, the advert shows an emergency board meeting to discuss the implications of fragmented software. The message of the advertisement is clear – expect software to operate without support at your peril. Possibly more interesting is the timing of the screening of the advertisement. In 2000 and beyond, is there an expectation that work will be taken home? Is B2B advertising on TV to continue and, if so, is this indicative of our cultural environment? This may not only widen the scope for communicating in a B2B environment, but may also highlight the approach to work in the twenty-first century.

Predicting future developments

Branding and advertising are functions that are fundamental to the continual evolution and success of consumer and business-to-business markets. Branding, advertising and associated communication approaches are not the 'last stand' of marketing but perhaps are now recognised as key in strategic development, rather than a tactical function to improve short-term gains.

How then will branding evolve in a continually changing environment? Superbrands have already started to emerge with Tesco providing food, clothing, music, entertainment, financial services and, as of September 2002, solicitors who will be able to practise within supermarkets. Tesco is becoming a 'life' brand – although loyalty will have to be significant for consumers to purchase all products and services from the same organisation. The associated brand values will be key to ensuring loyalty as the brand grows and develops in new market sectors.

Fragmentation

It is also likely that fragmentation of distribution will continue to increase. Thornton's chocolate bars are now distributed in supermarkets and Marks & Spencer sandwiches are on sale in selected W H Smith outlets, indicating a growing trend towards increased availability. Marketing associated products together in print, television or outdoor advertisements may suggest a particular lifestyle to consumers, afforded by combining brands. The joint promotion of, say, a particular coffee brand and a particular watch may become a more attractive proposition as brands become more self-selecting and brand 'recycling' becomes more evident.

Rebranding

Brands trying to reposition themselves in the marketplace could find advertising with an established branded product or service an added competitive advantage. In summer 2002, Black Tower, the 1970s classic dinner-party wine, 'reinvented' itself with a £1 million marketing campaign. As the eighteenth biggest seller in the UK, the necessity to rebrand is not immediately obvious. However, to require a new target audience that is not familiar with the image of the wine, a communications approach to develop the product was set in motion. In June 2002, the new Black Tower, in a redesigned bottle, appeared in the shops using two new grape varieties – the Pinot Noir and Riesling grapes. The wine's image has been updated by the introduction of the two new varieties in an effort to win over a new generation of drinkers (BBC Business 2002). Interestingly, the wine received a major boost during this period from exposure on Channel 4's *Big Brother* during the summer of 2002 (purchased by housemates). Sales of the wine over the fortnight rose by 40% (What the Papers Say 2002). On current form, it appears that the £1m rebranding and repositioning strategy has worked.

Branding and advertising could also assist in shaping an environment that is more equal in its approach to gender. Gender advertising – showing males to be either spineless or macho towards women and women depicted as ineffectual or manipulative – reinforces stereotypes that ought to have evolved. Providing branding and associated advertising that enhances independence and equality (epitomised in the most recent Levi's campaign) may not only support a change in consumer attitudes or beliefs, but also reinforce organisational philosophies concerning brand attributes. This would indeed be an effective form of both internal and external communication.

Summary

Branding, advertising and associated communication approaches, therefore, are key in determining long-term strategic gain. This chapter has looked at some of the main issues that affect branding and branding relationships. Many companies are beginning to understand that there is often little to differentiate between products in the 21st century. Branding remains the last bastion for differentiation. Therefore, the future development of organisations, their relationships with their customers, end-users, competitors and employees will be significantly affected by the concept, understanding and communication of the brand and brand values.

Chapter questions

1 To what extent is branding seen as a key strategic function of your organisation?

2 Does your organisation have scope for extending its brand? Would this be effective?

3 What type of communication approach does your organisation use? Is it fragmented? Why?

4 Are the employees within your organisation representative of the brand values?

6 Implementing marketing strategies

Introduction

Marketing strategy, and the formulation of this strategy, are important aspects of an organisation's long-term plans. Often, however, marketing strategy objectives fail to materialise. Is this because the strategy was unsound in the first place, or is it because the implementation was ineffective, or both? (Sashittal and Tankersley 1997). Organisations tend to spend a great deal of time planning strategies and sometimes fail to take into account the full implications of implementing these strategies. Several authors highlight the fact that much emphasis is placed on strategy formulation and little thought is given to implementation issues, even by marketers. Strategy may, or may not, drive actual marketing practice (Crittenden and Bonoma 1988).

With the explosion of new forms of communications that have a global reach, it is incumbent on marketers to consider implementation as an important issue in marketing, and at the same time consider the relevant speed at which implementation should take place. Technology drivers have become increasingly important over the last 10 years as the pace of information exchange increases. This has, in many ways, denied organisations the luxury of developing strategies over a long period of time. Shorter periods are available for strategy formulation and development; even shorter periods are available for the implementation of these strategies. This chapter will consider the neglected area of marketing implementation, taking into account organisational impediments, the utilisation of new technology and issues surrounding the relative power of the marketing function in organisations. This chapter needs to be read in conjunction with Chapters 7 and 8 which consider market orientation and the development of a learning organisation.

The environment

Many authors have argued that marketing strategies only result in superior returns for an organisation when they are implemented successfully (Bonoma 1984). Marketing implementation relies on people, first and foremost, and the way in which they adapt to the environment. Much of the literature tends to take a linear approach to strategy formulation and implementation, often regarding each area as a distinct step. Noble and Mokwa (1999), however, define marketing strategy implementation as:

> ...*the communication, interpretation, adoption and enactment of a marketing strategy or strategic market initiative.*

Many (for example, Cespedes 1991, Piercy 1989) argue that strategy formulation does not necessarily precede implementation. The relationship between the two is reflexive and iterative. As the environment is constantly shifting and changing, it is hard to consider formulation and implementation separately. If these processes are interrelated, then marketers have to be able to deal with the intricacies of the interrelationship in order to create strategic success. Research carried out by Sashittal and Tankersley (1997) highlighted the following key factors:

- Market planning and implementation are closely related, with managers making improvisations in nearly all elements of their marketing plans (including objectives, targeted customers and the marketing mix) and in their implementation actions. Plans are continually improvised to fit day-to-day marketing changes, and implementation actions are adapted to fit with changing marketing plans.
- Market responses to changing plans often trigger further changes in plans and implementation processes.
- The implementation process is fraught with uncertainty and few outcomes are achieved as originally intended.
- The constant need to improvise means that issues are often emergent and adaptations occur in real time, without being predetermined (Mintzberg and Waters 1985).
- Marketing plans and implementation procedures often lack a rational approach and are determined by 'gut' feel. This point was also made by Simkin and Dibb (1998) who found that many marketing managers followed short-term priorities.
- Interactive communication within organisations is important in volatile and changing environments.
- Competitor activities can trigger changes in strategy formulation and implementation.

The emergent strategic perspective (Mintzberg and Waters 1985) indicates a situation where a pattern of actions emerges without any prior plan. However, the actions may show a coherent pattern with an emerging strategic purpose (Figure 6.1). In many cases in marketing, it appears that implementation occurs as a result of incremental changes and emergent issues.

Table 6.1 shows differences between literature and actual research findings on the planning and implementation interface.

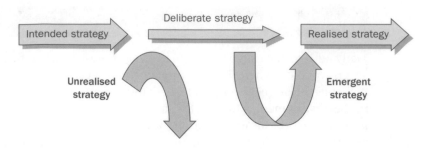

Figure 6.1 Deliberate and emergent strategy

According to research carried out by Simkin and Dibb (1998), many companies surveyed in the UK are quite happy to look for short-term returns and very few companies actually look for long-term marketing plans. They divided companies into the categories shown in Table 6.2. Their findings show that marketers, in general, focus on short-term financial measures of market attractiveness at the expense of longer-term issues and criteria relating to the external trading and marketing environment. Subjective measures take a greater importance.

Table 6.1 The planning and implementation interface: literature versus findings

The literature frequently depicts market planning and implementation as if:	*In the context of smaller industrial firms, the study finds that:*
■ Market planning and implementation are independent, sequential processes. Market plans lead to market implementation	■ Market planning and implementation are highly related. Their relationship is characterised by responsiveness
■ Market planning is a rational process, based on full market information and deliberate evaluation of alternatives	■ Market plans are often not much more than a set of sales goals, and a rough notion about action steps. Strategies are emergent and the nature of the market planning–implementation interface, and how it is managed, significantly impacts market outcomes
■ Formal strategies hold clear, well-defined actionable implications for implementation-directed actions	■ Formal market planning is not universally conducted. Clear and direct implications for implementation actions are largely absent
■ Future strategic gains in marketing are likely from improvements in implementation instead of improved strategy content (e.g. Bonoma 1985)	■ The relationship between market planning and implementation processes is complex, and isolating their impact on marketing outcomes is speculative at best
■ Effective plans lead to effective market implementation	■ Marketing implementation effectiveness is a result of (a) the interaction between planners and implementers (b) the responsiveness in planning and implementation (c) direct managerial actions
■ Market effectiveness is indicated by sales revenues, market share, customer satisfaction, and other market indicators	■ Marketing effectiveness is indicated by both market factors and psychosocial outcomes such as employee satisfaction, job security and creation of a good working environment

Source: Sashittal and Tankersley (1997)

Table 6.2 Diversity of criteria and approaches

Life is simple		Forward thinking	
How many customers		*Customer fit*	
– Where located		– Future potential sales volumes	
– Profit levels		– Customers' needs	
– Sales levels		– Likely differential advantage	
Short but effective		**Analytical**	
Brand loyalty contributions (£)		*Weight*	*Variable*
– Market growth rates		3	Market size
– Competitive intensity		3	Margin
		3	Market share
		3	Differential advantage/business strengths
		2	Competitive intensity
		2	Market size trends
		2	Propensity for long-term relationships
		1	Quality of customers

Source: Simkin and Dibb (1998)

The analyses seem to indicate a gap between theory and practice when marketers implement strategy. It could be that well-defined plans and segmentation analyses may actually be lacking in some instances, creating ad hoc responses to market changes and demands. Increasingly, environmental changes demand rapid and flexible responses, with organisations needing to be more flexible and collaborative, leading to a fusion of planning and implementation activities. The case study on Ovaltine illustrates the problems associated with a changing environment, reflecting changing consumer tastes that need to be accounted for in implementing new marketing strategies.

CASE STUDY

The life and death of a brand

Ovaltine has lost its market. Time to take a lesson from Lucozade

They were the Ovaltineys-der-der-der-der-der. The Ovaltine factory in Hertfordshire closed down yesterday and we must hope that the workers were allowed to drink away their disappointment with something stronger and more glamorous than the beverage they used to make.

First manufactured by a Swiss food organisation in 1904, the malt drink with added vitamins is now 98 and suffering commercially from the perception that most of its drinkers are of much the same vintage. Production will continue at a European factory but the Ovaltine brand was put up for sale earlier this year by a parent company that is now more keen on energy and health drinks and, if any buyers are sipping, none has yet swallowed. As the UK factory goes into the sleep, which its product induced in so many people, Ovaltine offers a fascinating study of brand decline.

The problem of this traditional bedtime cuppa is that it has become associated with two unpopular commodities: nostalgia and somnolence. The latter is unfair because, in its Swiss original, the refreshment was a forerunner of the isotonic drinks which athletes now fashionably swill down. Promoted for its energy-increasing properties, Ovaltine was the official sip at both the 1948 Olympics and on Hillary's Everest expedition, with absolutely no suggestion that a sprinter might snooze on the bend or a climber nap in a crevasse.

Indeed, all early Ovaltine folklore focused on the product as a drink which would help to keep you up and in more than one sense. The malt drink mixed with egg was reportedly favoured among males in the 1930s and 1940s as a cocktail which had the effect Viagra now has. Thought to make sex easier, it was also widely believed to relieve the possible consequences of intercourse: pregnant and nursing mothers took it to top up their supplies first of minerals and then of milk. Regrettably the times were too decorous for an advertising campaign promoting it in this way as the perfect his and hers drink: It gets him going and then keeps you going!

Mysteriously, though, this upper became reclassified in the popular imagination in the later 20th century as a downer: what wrinklies mixed with milk to make them nod. This connection of the beverage with the elderly probably happened because the product's marketing campaign insistently identified it with the past.

The singing kiddies of the radio show, winsome in their winceyette pyjamas, were accurate reflections of contemporary childhood at the time they started but, as they continued to be the official faces of the brand, kept sending the subliminal image that it was something your granny used to drink. In common with cocoa and Horlicks, Ovaltine took on the image of the sedative nightcap of veterans. Any potential buyer for the drink might reflect that the backwards-looking website Sterling Time – dedicated to 'British nostalgia ... Englishness and patriotism' – contains a large section memorialising the Ovaltineys.

Future anthropologists may also be interested in the fact that so many people were once drawn to draughts reputed to put you out for the night. Part of the reason for the decline of Ovaltine is surely that more recent generations exist in a habitual state of exhaustion, caused by longer working hours, the collapse of public transport and the cult of intensive, hands-on parenting among young mums and dads. They are also far more likely than their grandparents to drink wine nightly and have the option of late-night or all-night television: all reliable knock-outs. Graham Norton, Jacob's Creek and long-distance commuting now achieve much of what Ovaltine used to.

Because of this institutionalised tiredness in society, the soft drinks market has recently been taken over by energy-giving or health drinks. Though this was galling for Ovaltine, which had been the forerunner of these refreshments, it was unable to compete and suffered the double bind that, even among indulgence drinks, it came to be perceived as dull. Hot chocolate products have multiplied and now dominate the comfort-cuppa market. In the Far East, for example, Ovaltine was toppled as top tipple by the Australian chocolate drink, Milo.

Admittedly, faced with these changes, the brand didn't just roll over and go to sleep like a good Ovaltiney. Trend-chasing spin offs were launched, including Chocolate Ovaltine, Ovaltine Light and Ovaltine Power. A recent slogan – in ads using contemporary children rather than the smiling icons of the past – was: 'Tastes great – great for you!' Such repositioning can be achieved. For example, Lucozade, viewed by generations of children as the drink you got when you were sick in bed, has impressively reinvented itself as an accessory for the running track and the gym.

But, in that case, the extension was logical: a recuperative health drink being promoted as a preventative one. Ovaltine needs to make the greater leap from being associated with the past and the old to being linked with the young and the future. One market analyst has suggested that the drink which made the Ovaltineys whistle could be repromoted as a health bar – but can you really imagine snacking on one at the gym? Aged 98, Ovaltine won't have much to celebrate at 100 unless a new manufacturer can find a way of giving it some commercial Lucozade.

Source: Lawson (2002)

What marketing strategies should be implemented to change Ovaltine's fortunes? It is clear that the implementation of new strategies is vital to the company's long-term survival.

The impact of information technology

The implementation of many marketing strategies depends on the effective utilisation of sophisticated Internet technology (Hoffman and Novak 1996, Berthon *et al.* 1996, Kitchen 1999, O'Connor and Galvin 1997 and 1998). The rapid growth of the Internet and Internet marketing suggests that information technology has an important role to play in the process of implementing online marketing communications (Kassaye 1999). Internet-based technology can also facilitate information dissemination, file transformation, information gathering, and searching and browsing activities, etc. (Keeler 1995, O'Connor and Galvin 1997). Thus, a better utilisation of the state-of-the-art information technology for business and marketing becomes a fundamental task which is too important to leave to IT professionals (O'Connor and Galvin 1998).

Technological deployment corresponds to the way in which organisations plan and manage information technology to benefit from its potential and effectiveness in marketing implementation (Croteau and Bergeron 1991, 1998 and 2001). There are six components of information technology deployment (see Figure 6.2):

- *The strategic use of information technology* refers to the IT applications used to help the organisation gain a competitive advantage, reduce competitive disadvantage or meet other strategic enterprise objectives (Bergeron *et al.* 1991, Bergeron and Raymond 1995).
- *The management of information technology* examines IT-related activities such as the usage of current and new technologies, the development of specific IT applications and the degree of IT usage practised by employees (Bergeron and Raymond 1995, Das *et al.* 1991).
- *The role of Information Systems/Information Technology (IS/IT)* concerns the organisational importance of IT planning, the quality of the IT alignment with organisational structure, the effectiveness of software development and the management of communication networks (Bergeron and Raymond 1995).
- *The technological infrastructure* addresses the IT architecture and the formalised procedures used to guide and control the organisation's IT resources (Das *et al.* 1991).
- *The organisational infrastructure* refers to the internal functioning of the IS/IT development such as structure, processes, reporting relationships, support groups, and skills (Das *et al.* 1991, Henderson and Venkatraman 1999).
- *The administrative infrastructure* deals with the managerial policies and actions that influence and guide the work of employees involved with IS/IT development (Das *et al.* 1991).

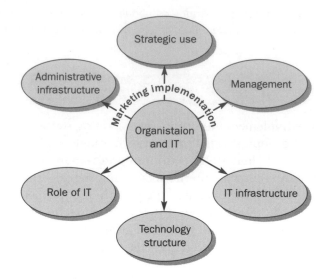

Figure 6.2 Components of information technology deployment

Marketing is, and will continue to be, heavily influenced by IT and marketers who do not adapt to the new technological era will not survive (Bruce *et al.* 1996, Komenar 1997). It can benefit organisations in many ways but it has to be successfully managed. The sensible use of IT allows creative and innovative strategies to cope with the new varied and dynamic marketplace (Schlegelmilch and Sinkovic 1998). IT helps with automation, information and transformation in marketing (Zuboff 1988, Remenyi *et al.* 1991):

- *Automation.* This argument is used to explain the fact that IT has been primarily used for automating manual systems of recording. It is useful for routine and tactical activities to improve efficiency (Peattie and Peters 1998).
- *Information.* This is the next stage of development, and translates data into useful information that can be utilised for developing marketing strategies. Information is also the stage when the data obtained through automation is scrutinised and converted into information.
- *Transformation.* This stage is reached when organisations embrace IT and start to 'think out of the box' (Schegelmilch and Sinkovic 1998). This is when organisations start to focus on new ideas and concentrate on adaptation and using knowledge to transform themselves into effective market-oriented organisations (Brady *et al.* 1999).

Information technology is now the key driver in most businesses and many organisations are conducting business through cyberspace. At the same time, with the growth of the Internet, organisations also need to be able to work and undertake transactions on a global basis. Many organisations that implement good systems to deal with value chains on a global basis show good returns on investment.

Information and knowledge creation

In addition to this, specific areas of application are also growing. One area is based on systems providing market intelligence on a global basis. As organisations become confident of their IT infrastructures on a global basis, they will increasingly be looking for access to systems that can provide them with business intelligence. Business intelligence gathering is becoming a complex issue for most organisations as technology develops. Increasingly, access to information is possible through hard-wired systems as well as wireless protocols.

Mobile technology will have to be integrated with these intelligence-gathering systems. Another important area of growth is knowledge management (KM). It is predicted that, by 2005, services for KM will be around $12.6 billion (Karhammar 2002). Knowledge management services include consulting, implementation, operation (outsourcing), maintenance and training. Corporations are beginning to realise that implementing a KM system is not merely a technical undertaking; it requires management endorsement and employee acceptance and buy-in. Increasingly, systems are about people, processes and technology. Implementation of a system needs to be tailored to the specific needs of an organisation. In the twenty-first century, organisations increasingly need to:

- build knowledge capital and invest in efforts that create long-term competitive advantage rather than short-term return on investment (ROI);
- link knowledge areas by developing conceptual and transactional areas of knowledge contained internally, by connecting planning, research, marketing, e-business and customer relationship;
- make sound business decisions based on knowledge.

An IT knowledge repository has many benefits, as shown in Figure 6.3. This type of model is suitable for most businesses, especially those in the telecommunications and financial services markets. In general, linking organisation data to market information can lead to greater insights and better planning. Better planning can lead to better relationships with vendors and customers, and help to minimise surprises.

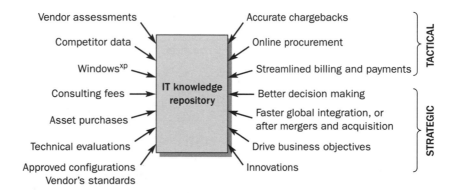

Figure 6.3 IT knowledge repository
Source: Flohr (2000)

Digital loyalty networks – e-differentiated supply chain and customer management

In a survey undertaken by Deloitte Hoskins, 850 manufacturing executives in 35 countries were interviewed across Asia-Pacific, Europe, North America, Latin America and South Africa. They found that manufacturers that successfully link their supply chain management (SCM) and customer relationship management (CRM) to create loyalty networks can generate significant competitive advantages. Organisations that perform far better than most other organisations analysed (see Figure 6.4):

■ collaborate extensively with their supply chain partners, both external (suppliers, distributors or retailers, and customers) and internal;
■ measure and exceed their goals for customer loyalty and therefore excel at CRM.

On the vertical axis in Figure 6.4, companies are classified according to their supply chain collaboration index. The index is based on answers from executives on how well their companies have integrated with suppliers, distributors or retailers, customers, and on how well their internal supply chain is integrated – all measured on a five-point scale. Because it contains four elements, the index can take on values from 0 to 20, with 0 being the lowest score and 20 the highest.

■ *Loyalty Networkers* (the upper right quadrant) are those companies that score 4 or 5 on customer loyalty/retention, and 14 or higher on the collaboration index. Only 13 per cent of all manufacturers in the survey are classified as Loyalty Networkers.
■ *Collaborators* (upper left quadrant) score 14 or higher on the collaboration index. However, despite these efforts, they are less successful in terms of building customer loyalty (scoring 3 or less) or do not measure customer loyalty/retention. Twenty-six per cent of companies are classified as Collaborators.

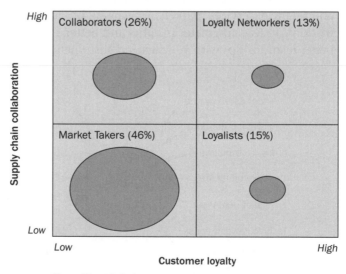

Note: Size of circles represents share of companies interviewed

Figure 6.4 Loyalty network quadrants
Source: Deloitte Research (2003)

- *Loyalists* (lower right quadrant) excel in generating loyal customers, scoring 4 or 5 on customer loyalty/retention. However, their supply chains are not well integrated (scoring 13 or below on the integration index). About 14 per cent of companies surveyed are Loyalists.
- *Market Takers* (lower left quadrant) constitute the remaining 46 per cent of all respondents. These companies are neither succeeding in integrating with supply chain partners (scoring 13 or below on the collaboration index) nor achieving much success in generating customer loyalty (scoring 3 or less) or do not measure customer loyalty/retention (from Deloitte Hoskins).

These results again demonstrate the importance of digital and information networks that straddle the globe and lead to effective customer management and marketing implementation. Companies surveyed in this research tended to be large multinational manufacturing enterprises. As IT investments grow and the technologies themselves become increasingly sophisticated, companies need to understand IT's potential in implementing marketing strategies. They also need to understand the possible flexibility that good information systems could offer to marketers by helping the fusion of the planning–implementation interface. Technology offers competitive advantage and is involved in achieving linkages among activities, affecting cost and potential differentiation of products and services. The Internet, apart from creating new industries such as online auctions and digital marketplaces, has had a great impact on reconfiguring existing industries and affecting their structure and therefore has had an impact on implementing marketing strategies (Porter 2001). In implementing marketing strategies, attention therefore needs to be paid to the impact of technology on a company 's value chain.

This section has illustrated the great impact that technology has on marketing implementation. In addition, it is necessary to consider its impact on customer relationship management.

Customer relationships

Kalakota and Robinson (1999) explain the value of integrating processes when building relationships, leading to three phases in customer relationship management (CRM). Their argument is that, as intimacy grows over time, a customer relationship can blossom. However, organisations need to implement marketing strategies speedily as the competition can 'lock in' potential customers. Customers, too, have a variety of partners with whom they can deal.

There are three phases of CRM (see Figure 6.5), each of which demands a different relationship over time:

1 *Acquiring new customers*. Customers can be acquired by promoting product or service leadership that pushes performance boundaries with respect to innovation and convenience. The value proposition to the customer is the offer of a superior product backed by excellent service.
2 *Enhancing the profitability of existing customers*. This relationship can be encouraged by excellence in cross-selling and selling upmarket products and services.

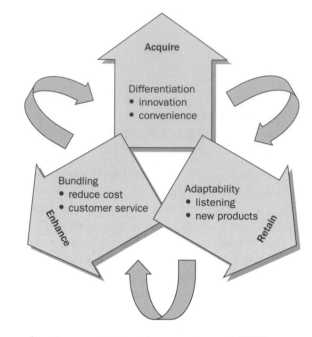

Figure 6.5 Phases of customer relationship management (CRM)
Source: Adapted from Kalakota and Robinson (1999)

3 *Retaining profitable customers for life*. Retention focuses on service adaptability and ascertaining customer needs. The value proposition to the customer consists of a proactive relationship that works in his or her best interest. Retaining customers costs less than acquiring new ones.

As all the phases of CRM are interrelated, systems integration and, more importantly, people and process integration is crucial for success. It is always difficult for organisations to align all three phases and implement them correctly. An organisation could try, therefore, to excel in implementing one particular area but must still keep sight of the other two. Organisations need to have the right technology and software to excel in one area and to support this with strength in the other two. The best organisations will be able to manage all the facets of CRM. This whole area is now under change yet again as a result of the rise of mobile communications. As more people shift towards mobile communications, organisations need to consider both radical and subtle changes to their marketing strategies.

Customer retention is an increasingly important aspect of CRM. The cost of retaining a current customer through the use of relationship marketing strategies saves an organisation five times the cost of recruiting a new customer (Rosenberg and Czepiel 1984). Organisations can boost their profits by 100 per cent if they retain 5 per cent of their customers (Reichheld and Sasser 1990).

One of the intangible aspects of having a good relationship marketing strategy is the ability to test market new products prior to implementing marketing strategies, with reduced risk (Shani and Chalasani 1992).

The technology drivers also create the following possibilities:

- Salesmen on the road can be updated on customer requirements. This information can be used to enhance CRM and logistics.
- As mobile devices become more sophisticated, customers will be able to access their suppliers' inventories. They can place orders and specify delivery times via links to an intranet or the Internet.
- Individuals, as well as talking to each other, will also be able to communicate with machines. This is already a reality, with consumers able to buy soft drinks, chocolates and car washes using mobile devices.
- Consumers will be able to pay for restaurant meals via secure transactions through a mobile device.
- Using 'Bluetooth' devices, retailers can market special offers to customers via their mobile devices if they are within a twenty-metre radius. This will also allow customers to undertake transactions with shops and restaurants.
- Radio will become an integral part of the mobile device, allowing an individual access to a myriad of radio stations. This has implications for advertising and branding.
- The incorporation of GPS (ground positioning systems, via satellite) into mobile devices means that individuals will easily be able to locate their positions and also the nearest outlets or services that they need.

Current IT systems (see Figure 6.6) are not fluid and dynamic enough to cope with customers who are constantly on the move and can contact organisations through mail, mobiles and the Internet. As customers become fluid in the way they contact and interact with organisations, organisations also need to be fluid in their approach. Often the links between IT and marketing are not good as the marketing function does not understand how IT affects service provision and prices. There is frequently a cultural gap between marketing and IT, therefore there is a need to integrate data and for computer experts to work side by side with marketers.

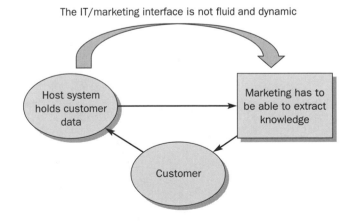

Figure 6.6 Current systems architecture

To achieve good customer relationship management, IT and marketing must work together so that IT understands the needs of this internal customer. A change of philosophy is required, where IT shifts from 'building solutions' to defining requirements from the front end with business and customers to build the best solutions. The one-to-one relationship means that a customer is known to, and interacts with, the enterprise, and the enterprise flexes and changes to meet the customer's needs. The enterprise will then have a unified view of a single customer across the entire enterprise.

As the relationship develops across boundaries, the organisation will become a learning organisation with which the customer develops a continuing relationship. At every given opportunity, the organisation can 'tailor' and refit its behaviour to suit the customer. If a relationship is successfully maintained, grown and nurtured, the customer is less likely to invest time in building a new relationship with a competitor. This means that relationship building needs to be regarded as a business process rather than a technology suite and technology needs to be able to support and enable this process (see Figure 6.7).

Many organisations have relied on CRM software. However, they are now realising the importance of people and processes. McKean (2002) comments:

Most firms cited personnel challenges as being the single biggest obstacle to success. In most cases, there was no specific plan to address the personnel issue. The people issue, which made up roughly 20 percent of the total transformation challenge, virtually went unaddressed.

Table 6.3 shows how companies have generally invested in IT versus what should really be done. It is important that investment in people and processes is generally increased by companies so that IT implementation can succeed.

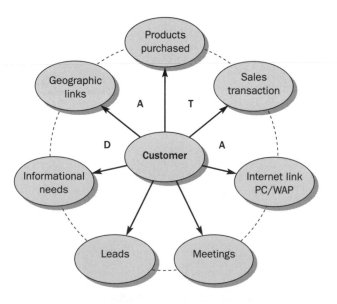

Figure 6.7 Creating a relationship web

Table 6.3 Investments and determinants

	Historical customer information investments (%)	Customer information competency determinants (%)
People	2	20
Process	2	15
Organisation	2	10
Culture	1	20
Leadership	1	10
Information	10	15
Technology	82	10

Source: McKean (2002)

How can marketing implementation be integrated with people and processes?

The discussion so far shows the importance of managing cultural issues when implementing marketing strategies. It also shows that, although technology is important, it has to be tempered by a sensible people approach. In understanding people, the cultural context within which they operate needs to be interpreted.

According to Deshpande and Webster (1989), organisational culture is defined as

the pattern of shared values and beliefs that help individuals understand organisational functioning and provide them with the norms for behaviour in that organisation.

Culture is often defined as a set of beliefs or standards shared by a group of people, which help the individual decide what is, what can be, how to feel, what to do and how to go about doing it. This definition probably suggests that most individuals *can* choose the culture in which to interact. However, the overriding culture that prevails in an organisation may be a more important aspect when an individual is interacting with it on a daily basis. If organisations are considered to be fully integrated with IT systems, then systems could be considered as knowledge systems (Weick 1995). As IS/IT is critical in marketing, this approach enables us to gain useful insights into understanding the culture of an organisation.

As markets become increasingly turbulent, the ability to learn more quickly than the competitors becomes even more important (Dickson 1992). In order to be effectively market oriented, higher order learning must take place. This higher order learning is discussed as double-loop learning in Chapter 8. Part of being a learning organisation is the ability to process information well. Mitroff (1983) discusses the 'frames of reference' managers use in assessing information. This organisational perspective focuses on the mind of the manager and views organisations as knowledge systems.

Cameron and Freeman (1991) state

Because cultures are defined by the values, assumptions, and interpretations of organisation members, and because a common set of dimensions organises these factors on both psychological and organisational levels, a model of culture types can be derived.

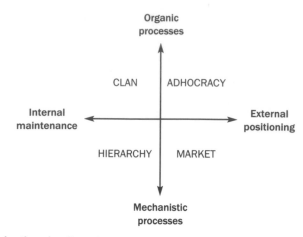

Figure 6.8 Organisational culture types
Source: Adapted from Deshpande *et al.* (1993)

Deshpande *et al.* (1993), building on earlier work by Quinn (1988) and Cameron and Freeman (1991), develop a model of organisational culture types, shown in Figure 6.8.

The four classifications of culture described in Figure 6.8 imply varying degrees of business performance in a competitive marketplace. The figure shows the Y-axis as a continuum from organic to mechanistic processes. This indicates whether organisational emphasis is more on flexibility, spontaneity and individuality or on control, stability and action. The X-axis focuses on the relative organisational emphasis on internal maintenance (smoothing activities, integration) or on external positioning (competition, environmental differentiation). The culture types that result are **clan**, **hierarchy**, **adhocracy** and **market**, labels that are broadly similar to those discussed and explained by Mintzberg (1979) and Ouchi (1980). The leadership styles adopted by each cultural type also match the leadership typologies and culture within organisational life cycles (Cameron and Quinn 1983). Figure 6.8 shows the relative positioning for an organisation, based on its dominant attributes. The key types are:

1 **Adhocracy**, exhibiting entrepreneurship, creativity and adaptability, supported by a risk-taking leadership style which in turn creates the climate for bonding. This type emphasises strategies that spur a company into growth, innovation and searching for new resources.

2 **Clan**, exhibiting cohesiveness, participation, teamwork and a sense of family, supported by a mentoring type of leadership, creating loyalty, tradition and interpersonal cohesion. The strategies that are emphasised are mainly internal, focused on developing human resources, commitment and morale.

3 **Hierarchy**, exhibiting order, rules and regulations and uniformity, supported by a coordinating, administrative type of leadership, creating bonds through rules and policies. The strategic emphasis is towards stability, predictability and smooth operations.

4 **Market**, exhibiting competitiveness and goal achievement with a decisive, achievement-oriented leadership, creating bonds through goal orientation, production and competition. The strategies adopted are towards competitive advantage and market superiority.

IT context	Strongly agree	Agree	Neutral	Disagree	Strongly disagree
	1	2	3	4	5
1 We utilise web-enabled customer management systems	☐	☐	☐	☐	☐
2 We incorporate mobile protocols into our systems	☐	☐	☐	☐	☐
3 We have the systems to disseminate information internally	☐	☐	☐	☐	☐
4 We can easily relay information to our suppliers	☐	☐	☐	☐	☐
5 We have a clear idea of our customer requirements	☐	☐	☐	☐	☐
6 Customers can easily contact us	☐	☐	☐	☐	☐
7 We can easily keep track of all customer contact	☐	☐	☐	☐	☐
8 Our field service managers can easily keep in touch with our systems	☐	☐	☐	☐	☐
9 Our systems are global, integrated supply chains	☐	☐	☐	☐	☐
10 Our data warehouse allows customer segmentation	☐	☐	☐	☐	☐
11 We have effective competitor intelligence data	☐	☐	☐	☐	☐
12 The marketing/IT interface is good	☐	☐	☐	☐	☐

Total points ☐

Organisational context	Strongly agree	Agree	Neutral	Disagree	Strongly disagree
	1	2	3	4	5
1 There are few blockages in information flow between functional areas	☐	☐	☐	☐	☐
2 The organisation is flexible and can reconfigure itself in a short time	☐	☐	☐	☐	☐
3 The people find it easy to implement information systems	☐	☐	☐	☐	☐
4 Change is readily embraced by staff	☐	☐	☐	☐	☐
5 There are good links between marketing strategy formulation and execution	☐	☐	☐	☐	☐
6 Customer requirements take priority	☐	☐	☐	☐	☐
7 It is easy to disseminate information formally and informally	☐	☐	☐	☐	☐
8 Creativity is accepted and rewarded	☐	☐	☐	☐	☐
9 The organisation is innovative	☐	☐	☐	☐	☐
10 There is an accepted vision for the development of marketing strategies	☐	☐	☐	☐	☐
11 Marketing and IT work together	☐	☐	☐	☐	☐
12 Competitor actions are monitored and acted upon	☐	☐	☐	☐	☐

Total points ☐

Figure 6.9 Questions to determine organisational and IT factors

Even though many SBUs or organisations may have a multiplicity of cultures, there is often one dominant culture which predominates over the others. These cultural types are regarded as modal or dominant, rather than mutually exclusive. Over time, it is expected that one type of culture will emerge as the dominant one.

The implementation matrix

To implement marketing strategies successfully, therefore, organisations need to understand not only their cultural attributes, but also their technological prowess, including the integration of IT into the processes delivering value to the customer. In order to integrate these two aspects of marketing implementation, a questionnaire has been designed to test an organisation's ability to be flexible and adaptive to customer needs (see Figure 6.9). It will also help to ascertain whether the organisation possesses the technology that will allow it to be adaptable enough when implementing marketing strategies. Once the scores to all the questions have been totalled for both the IT context and the organisational context, they can be plotted on the horizontal and the vertical axes of the implementation matrix, shown in Figure 6.10, to determine the organisation's position within the matrix. The implications of positions within each quadrant are:

- *Integrated marketing implementation.* Organisations in this quadrant will have well-balanced marketing implementation, based on good information technology systems and a dynamic, flexible organisation. The people, processes and technology work in unison. The organisation is likely to have a global information system.
- *Fragmented marketing implementation.* Organisations in this quadrant will have excellent organisational capabilities but their technology resources will be poor and not well integrated. Organisations in this quadrant will require extra investment in IT infrastructure.
- *Technology driven marketing implementation.* In this quadrant, organisations tend to rely more on technology. The people and processes tend to be poor and often mechanistic solutions are provided, leaving individuals within organisations alienated and poorly informed.
- *Poor marketing implementation.* Organisations in this quadrant tend to have outdated organisational practices and possess poor technology systems. These organisations need organisational change and investment in technology.

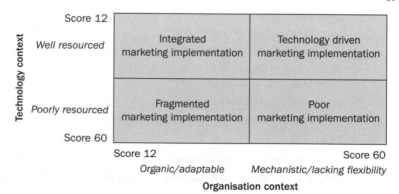

Figure 6.10 Implementation matrix

The implementation matrix provides a useful measure of an organisation's ability to implement marketing strategies within an environment which is increasingly driven by technology.

The global context

As the role of technology grows and evolves, many organisations are not confined to operating within national boundaries. Indeed, many organisations are now 'born global'. This type of organisation challenges the established notions of international marketing implementation. Based on a study conducted in Australia, the 'born global' organisations are classified by the following specific characteristics (McKinsey and Co. 1993, Knight and Cavusgil 1996):

1 Management views the world as its marketplace from the outset; unlike traditional companies, they do not see foreign markets as simple adjuncts to the domestic market.
2 'Born globals' begin exporting one (or several) products within two years of being established and tend to export at least a quarter of total production.
3 They tend to be small manufacturers, with average annual sales of less than $100 million.
4 The majority of 'born globals' are formed by active entrepreneurs and tend to emerge as a result of a significant breakthrough in some process or technology.
5 They may apply cutting-edge technology to developing a unique product idea or to a new way of doing business.
6 The products that 'born globals' sell typically involve substantial value adding; the majority of such products may be intended for industrial uses.

The authors argue that this phenomenon was determined by a series of recent trends that have facilitated the capacity of many organisations to initiate early export activities (Knight and Cavusgil 1996):

- *The increasing role of niche markets*, especially in the countries of the developed world (Holstein 1992, Robinson 1986), determined by increased demand for specialised or customised products.
- *The recent advances in process technology* which have created the possibility of flexible, low-scale and low-cost production. Holstein (1992) notes that technology is allowing small American exporters to increase their competitiveness in the global marketplace, while Robinson (1986) emphasises the new technological capacity to produce a diverse range of products on an ever smaller scale.
- *The recent advances in communication technologies* have reduced the costs of information transmission between distant markets. Through the use of computer-supported technology such as electronic data interchange and electronic mail, even small organisations can efficiently manage operations across borders (Holstein 1992).
- *The inherent advantages of small organisations*, such as quicker response time, flexibility, adaptability and direct customer relations, facilitate the international operations of 'born global' organisations and offer them an important competitive edge compared with larger multinationals (McKinsey and Co. 1993).

- *The means of internationalisation*, such as knowledge, technology, tools and facilitating institutions, have become more accessible to all organisations, regardless of their size or activity sector (Czinkota and Ronkainen 1995, Nordstrom 1991). The integration of the world financial markets, the globalisation of technology and the increased mobility of economic assets have become the driving forces of the global economy.
- *The recent emergence of complex transnational networks of strategic alliances* (Coviello and Munro 1997, Hakansson 1982, Thorelli 1990). Today, the implementation of a successful international commercial strategy is facilitated through partnerships with foreign businesses – distributors, trading companies, subcontractors – as well as more traditional buyers and sellers.

The 'born global' model is supported by numerous studies which show that these types of organisations are emerging in many national economies including France (Roux 1979), Canada (Denis and Depelteau 1985, Garnier 1982), Taiwan (Chang and Grub 1992), the UK (Buckley and Casson 1979) and the USA (*Economist* 1993, Holstein 1992, Norton 1994).

The definition of the 'born global' organisation emphasises its capacity to start and quickly develop international operations – mainly exporting activities. However, a global activity is more complex than this, and involves the implementation of an extensive network of transnational activities, as well as a restructuring of the organisation's internal environment (Bartlett and Goshal 1992, St. John and Young 1995).

Globalisation is a 'fuzzy', imprecise concept. It cannot be measured directly, because as a concept it reflects a composite of several dimensions. There are degrees of globalisation, and any given organisation, market or country can and has to be expressed on a scale to indicate its degree of globalisation. For organisations generally, the Organization for Economic Co-operation and Development finds that the concept of globalisation seems to reflect:

- the ability to move flexibly, and to identify and take advantage of opportunities anywhere in the world;
- the ability to source inputs, distribute products or services and move capital across borders;
- a lack of a home or national base (in the sense of not being committed to maintaining headquarters or a presence in a specific 'home' country);
- being present (usually as establishments, alliances or parts of networks) in a number of different countries;
- having management that thinks and acts 'globally'; and
- the ability to market products or services successfully in different nations (although the products or services may be adapted to specific markets).

The OECD study (1997) has defined five different degrees of globalisation for small and medium-sized enterprises (SMEs), shown in Table 6.4, based on the following three dimensions:

- the proportion of SMEs' outputs and inputs (including capital) that are traded across national boundaries, either directly or indirectly;

Table 6.4 The dimensions of SME globalisation

Description	Traded inputs and outputs	Establishments and affiliations	Market opportunities and competition
No globalisation *Domestic*	All inputs sourced from local area, all outputs sold in local area	Single establishment, no establishments or affiliations outside local area	No market outside local area, no potential competition from outside local area
Limited globalisation *Mainly domestic*	< 10% of inputs sourced across borders, and < 10% revenue from across borders, usually within a limited span of nations	At least one establishment or affiliate outside local area or outside national area	Barriers to entry to outside markets and to local market (for competitors) are significant and amount to > 50% of costs
Major globalisation *Internationalised*	> 10% but < 40% of inputs sourced internationally, and > 10% but < 40% of revenue from across borders, usually across two major international regions	Establishments or close affiliates in at least four different nations and in two major international regions	Barriers to entry are noticeable, make up to 10% of cost disadvantage, but can be overcome fairly easily
Extensive globalisation *Globalised*	> 40% of inputs sourced internationally, > 40% of revenue from outputs traded across borders, across all major international regions	Establishments or close affiliates in at least one country in all three major international regions	Barriers to entry to international markets are not significant impediment for firm or competitors, make up < 5% cost disadvantage
Complete globalisation *Fully globalised*	Majority of inputs of any establishment sourced across borders, large majority of outputs traded across borders	Multiple establishments or affiliates in many countries and in all major international regions	Markets in all major international regions, competition likely to be present or come from any international region

Source: OECD (1997)

- the number of establishments or affiliations in different regions or countries; and
- the number and range of regions which management perceives as market opportunities and/or competitive threats.

On the other hand, Bartlett and Goshal (1992) suggest that a global organisation is also defined by the implementation of an extremely complex and flexible management strategy. This allows an efficient allocation of the organisation's resources on a transnational basis, as well as a free flow of information and experience among the different units of the organisation.

These arguments should be sufficient to highlight the danger of a limited understanding of the global concept. In the real world there are different degrees of globalisation and many small and medium-sized organisations can be considered internationalised rather than globalised. In fact, the application of a stricter definition of globalisation to many 'born global' organisations would eliminate

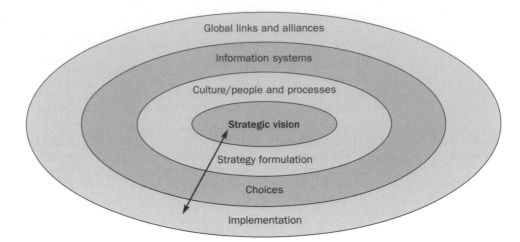

Figure 6.11 Implementation layers and dynamic interaction

them from the global category (OECD 1997), or reclassify them in different classes of globalisation.

Secondly, the consideration of exporting activities as the main criterion to define the degree of globalisation of an organisation artificially narrows the number of options available to a high-technology organisation in real life. Drawing a parallel with the similar limitation of the classical theories of internationalisation (Carstairs and Welch 1982, Hakansson 1982, Nordstrom 1991, Reid 1984, Root 1987), there are many alternative ways in which small and medium-sized companies can become global. Some of the alternatives are important and specific for the high-technology sectors, such as exchange of information, research partnerships, licensing, fund sourcing and foreign investment (Madsen and Servais 1997).

Considering the definition of global companies presented by the OECD (1997) study (see Table 6.4), it must be emphasised that one of the main criteria of globalisation is the proportion of inputs and outputs traded across borders. These outputs usually represent more than a simple export of finalised products or services. In implementing marketing strategies, organisations need to consider the impact of globalisation and strategic alliances, together with culture and information systems development (see Figure 6.11).

Consider the difficulties in implementing Islamic banking marketing strategies highlighted in the following case study. How far would technology be able to help in the implementation process?

CASE STUDY

Implementation of Islamic banking in Pakistan – a marketing challenge

Before I share my views, let me first give a brief background of myself as that may help explain my approach to the subject. I was the Marketing Director for Citibank, when Citibank started consumer banking in Pakistan. After six years with Citibank, I joined Johnson & Johnson as the Managing Director of its business in Pakistan. Presently I am working for Al-Meezan Islamic investment bank, the only premier Islamic investment bank in Pakistan supported by a group of strong sponsor shareholders of Middle Eastern origin. The point is that I have worked within an interest-based banking system, I have been a commercial user of a banking system and now I am working within an interest-free banking system. This gives me hands-on experience of all the aspects around the implementation of Islamic banking in Pakistan. Therefore, I believe, my views are not a representation of a single stakeholder like a banker, an academician, a commercial user of banking services or an Islamic banker. They are, in fact, a representation of a well-rounded and well-informed point of view. Combine this with over 20 years of experience in the marketing arena, across various industrial sectors, with leading multinationals that include Exxon, Lever Brothers, Reckitt & Coleman, Citibank, Johnson & Johnson, and you have a market-driven, realistic and practical point of view.

Implementation of Islamic banking in Pakistan is unique in the sense that it envisages a complete transformation of the economy led by a complete transformation of the banking system. The scope of this change is therefore very wide and the consequences far reaching. Despite the fact that it is viewed as a religious or a legal and financial issue, I believe it is neither. If one can identify the problem correctly, the chances of finding the right solution increase tremendously.

So what is the problem? The problem is that implementation of Islamic banking in Pakistan is actually a change management issue but it is being handled as a religious and legal issue. There is a tremendous need for this type of banking both at

the micro and the macro level. If we do not handle it appropriately, we will lose a major opportunity in terms of fulfilling a covenant of God and an important need of the people.

Is Islamic banking really a need of the people? Meezan bank conducted research last year to ascertain just that. This research was carried out by the Marketing Research Link, an outstanding research organisation. Market research consisted of a product concept test carried out in April 1999 based on eight focus groups in Lahore and Karachi. This was followed by a segmentation study in November 1999 based on 175 interviews, of which 100 respondents were able to invest a minimum of Rs 100,000 and 75 respondents did not have an interest-bearing financial relationship.

The main findings of the research were that there is a strong need for a riba-free (interest-free) banking system. Where the product concept was not acceptable, it was primarily due to confusion between riba free and profit free. People perceive a number of emotional benefits from a product that is based on the tenets of Islam. The objective is to alleviate the feeling of guilt by following the tenets of Islam. There is also a belief that Islamic banking will help fight the ills of the economy of the country.

From a marketing point of view, we need to have a winning brand positioning strategy in place. Based on our experience at Meezan bank and the research we undertook, the winning brand positioning strategy is to position Islamic banking as offering functional benefits while being in line with the tenets of Islam. By branding the financial system as Islamic banking, the functional benefits offered by the proposed banking system cannot be communicated well because of the overwhelming religious connotations.

Does the proposed banking system offer any functional benefits? Interest-based banking is all about money management and money is the subject matter of the business of banking. In the proposed banking system, money management is not the subject matter of the bank's business; it is

▶

the economy that is the subject matter of the bank's business. To give an analogy, the difference between the present banking system and the proposed banking system is like the difference between junk food and a balanced diet. Junk food is convenient, at times cheaper, tastes good and satisfies one's hunger. It has no apparent problems in the short term and therefore all its features make it very popular. However, you cannot support a healthy body on junk food because the ingredients required by the body are not available in the right proportions. A balanced diet may not be convenient, cheap or very appealing to the taste buds. It may not even offer any visible advantages over junk food in the short term and therefore may not be very popular. However, only a balanced diet can support a healthy body because all the ingredients required by the body are present in the right proportions.

As such, interest-based banking is somewhat like the junk food of banking. It may have all the attractive features of banking, but it has the major drawback of not being able to support a healthy economy because it does not allow efficient allocation of resources. It accumulates wealth with certain stakeholders in the economy and deprives certain other stakeholders of their fair share. Therefore, interest-based banking cannot support a healthy economy as it does not permit equitable distribution of wealth. Only the proposed banking system has the capability of supporting a healthy economy because it ensures an equitable distribution of the resources in the economy. It thus becomes imperative that we move to the proposed system of banking if we want to have a stable and healthy economy.

If the proposed system is a balanced banking system, then why is it branded as Islamic banking? There are two reasons for this. First, for us the prime motive for using this type of banking is based on conviction, hence the name Islamic banking. The second reason is that the proposed banking system does not allow any interest-based contracts. It is perceived that only Islam prohibits interest, therefore any banking that does not allow interest-based contracts is Islamic banking. But the belief that only Islam prohibits interest is incorrect. In fact, Judaism and Christianity also prohibit interest

(for reference, please see Exodus 22:25, Leviticus 25:35–36, Deuteronomy 23:20, Psalms 15:5, Proverbs 28:8, Nehemiah 5:7 and Ezekiel 18:8, 13, 17 and 22:12).

What is the issue in branding the proposed banking system as Islamic banking? Let us see this in the context of the customer decision-making process. When you have a single brand in the market, the customer does not evaluate the brand in any detail. Not having a choice, customers therefore accept the brand, whatever it is. However, when a second brand is introduced in the same market, then the customer starts to evaluate the whole proposition because now there is a choice. The second brand has the daunting tasks of first explaining the assumptions of the first brand and then justifying its own existence.

The new brand carries a huge amount of baggage in terms of having to explain the problems of the first brand. The same applies to the proposed banking system. Up until now, we only had interest-based banking. There was no choice, therefore people accepted interest-based banking without evaluating the proposition. However, with the introduction of the new banking system, people will have a choice and therefore will evaluate the whole banking proposition, not just the new system. In fact, interest-based banking will be evaluated in comparison with the new system. Therefore the proposed banking system will first have to answer for the shortcomings of interest-based banking before it can justify its existence. By calling it Islamic banking, it not only has to explain the shortcomings of interest-based banking, but it also has to explain the assumptions of Islam as a religion. Any brand proposition based on religion has a very limited appeal at best, and becomes very controversial at worst. Therefore the baggage that the proposed system has to carry, purely because of inappropriate positioning, is formidable.

What should we do? We must redefine the brand positioning strategy for the proposed banking system. One way to look at the new system is in terms of the basic advantage that it offers compared with the existing system. As explained earlier, the key difference is that the interest-based system has money as the subject matter of business whereas the proposed system

Case study *continued*

has economy as the subject matter of business. Could we therefore brand it as 'business banking' rather than Islamic banking?

Business banking is short, easily pronounceable, easy to remember and, most importantly, explains the nature of the product well in terms of its unique selling proposition. This branding strategy will also enable us to position it as functionally viable banking because any banking system that supports business is considered functional. With such positioning, the proposed system is removed from the religious platform and is positioned on the business platform. This will then allow us to focus on the functionality of the system while simultaneously receiving all the benefits of religious connotations by emphasising its non-interest-based nature. This strategy will also provide a sound basis for building up a change management programme, which is the answer to implementing Islamic banking in Pakistan.

Source: Pervez Said, http://www.islamiqmoney.com/money _matters/mon_mat01_17052000.htm#top

Summary

This chapter considers a wide range of issues related to the effective implementation of marketing. Successfully implementing marketing strategies lies at the heart of successful organisational management. However, the process is fraught with challenges as the marketplace is generally turbulent and ever changing. This places an emphasis on developing flexible and responsive organisations. Research also indicates that many organisations do not follow strategies through according to the traditional model and may implement them in an ad hoc manner. Improved technology helps to speed up processes. It also helps organisations to become global within a short space of time and some organisations can be said to be 'born global' from their inception.

As technology becomes more sophisticated and can deliver data and video links at increasing speeds within a mobile environment, marketers need to understand its capability in effective marketing implementation. At the same time they must understand and embrace the impact of globalisation in the marketplace. This chapter therefore seeks to integrate the organisational issues with the technological issues so that an integrated implementation system can be considered by marketers seeking to implement any given marketing strategy

Chapter questions

1 What are the key barriers to marketing implementation?

2 How can technology help to develop global organisations?

3 Why do marketers prefer to integrate marketing planning and implementation?

7 Organising for marketing

Introduction

Organising for marketing is a multifaceted undertaking. To implement successful marketing strategies, it is important to recognise and understand the visible and invisible elements surrounding organisations. The visible element of an organisation is often represented as its structure, or organisational chart, and shows its centralisation, formalisation and departmentalisation. For example, Figure 7.1 shows the visible elements of the marketing function within an organisation.

The invisible element consists of informal functions, actual communication flows and current cultural norms and behaviour patterns. These are much more subtle and are based on cultural patterns and norms (see Figure 7.2). The challenge, therefore, does not necessarily lie in organising the marketing department, but in organising an enterprise in such a way that the marketing section becomes an efficient function within the whole enterprise. At the same time, a favourable interaction needs to be set up between organisations to facilitate transactions.

The first section of this chapter describes what constitutes the visible and invisible parts of the organisation. This is followed by the basic concepts for organisational analysis and their implication for marketing practice. Then, there is discussion of the ways in which an organisation can develop a market culture, taking into account the invisible elements.

Figure 7.1 The visible elements of the marketing function

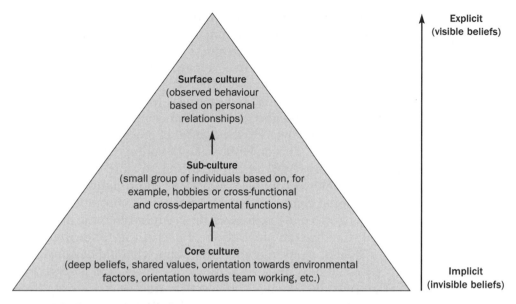

Figure 7.2 **Organisational culture**

The visible and invisible parts of the organisation

Basic concepts

Organisations are concerned with the way in which tasks are distributed and are understood by individuals. This encompasses several aspects (Mintzberg 1990, Helfer *et al.* 1998, Desreumaux 1998), shown in Figure 7.3:

- departmentalisation;
- specialisation;
- standardisation;
- coordination;
- formalisation;
- decentralisation/centralisation;
- control;
- differentiation/integration.

Figure 7.3 **Organising: a multifaceted undertaking**

Departmentalisation refers to the principles by which an enterprise is organised: departmentalisation by functions (marketing, accounting, human resources (HR) etc.), by markets or by products.

Specialisation refers to the extent to which tasks are defined and allocated to a specific person. There are two types of specialisation: vertical specialisation, which corresponds to the number of hierarchical levels, and horizontal specialisation, which corresponds to the number of different functions that have been identified.

Standardisation refers to the number of procedures that explain how tasks should be accomplished. This dimension can be conceptualised either as a characteristic of structure (Kalika 1995) or as one of the possible coordinating mechanisms (see Mintzberg 1990). According to Mintzberg, **coordination** (that is, the regulation of all organisational components) can be achieved through a variety of ways: mutual adjustment on a one-to-one basis, direct supervision that applies hierarchical authority and, finally, **standardisation** of one of the following elements: procedures, results, qualifications or norms. Here again, it should be noted that the coordinating process could be considered as part of the integration process, a concept introduced by Lawrence and Lorsch (1973), together with the concept of **differentiation**.

Formalisation relates to the use of written documents in communication and information processes.

The **decentralisation/centralisation** axis relates to the levels at which decisions are taken. The lower the decision level is, the more decentralised the organisation.

Control refers to the evaluative process by which tasks are judged. Results, or the implementation of control, can be evaluated.

Differentiation and **integration** can, and may, overlap (Lawrence and Lorsch 1973). Differentiation reflects the degree to which each department develops its own way of functioning, behaving and accomplishing tasks. For example, a marketing department will have to develop skills in marketing communications whereas a finance department will need to develop accounting skills. However, in order to develop coherent strategies, an organisation needs mechanisms for integration. These involve mutual adjustment, hierarchy (direct supervision), standardisation of procedures, committees, task groups, coordinating agents, project managers, product managers, common objectives, common norms and values, and training, etc. These are illustrated in Figure 7.4.

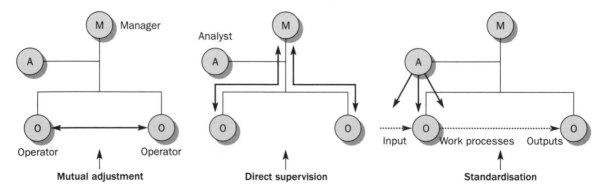

Figure 7.4 Mechanisms for integration

Structure and market-oriented culture in French franchise networks

Networking is a specific way to organise business activity. In franchise systems, the franchiser and the franchisees are legally independent but in functioning they are highly interdependent. Indeed, the franchiser provides the franchisee with a core concept, service or product, and guidelines to manage the business. Basically, the franchiser delivers a whole business formula and the franchisee agrees to respect the franchiser's rules.

France, in comparison with the rest of Europe, considers franchising to be most important (in terms of franchised units). As a franchise system could be considered as a decentralised yet formalised organisation, it is interesting to study their degree of market orientation.

In the field study conducted by Dubost *et al.* (2000), the decision structure is approached through the following dimensions:

- degree of participation;
- formalisation;
- control (through results or through behaviours).

Based on a sample of 71 franchise networks, three types of franchise structure are identified: (1) structured franchises, (2) informal franchises and (3) participative franchises. Structured franchises (30 networks) are characterised by a high degree of formalisation and a high degree of results' control. Informal franchises (21 networks) are characterised mainly by behaviours' control. Lastly, participative franchises (16 networks) allow a high degree of participation in decision making (see Figure 7.5). The rest showed a mixture of styles (4).

Figure 7.5 shows four axes: control, formalisation, behavioural control and participation. The different interconnecting webs show the degree to which each cluster exhibits these characteristics.

Statistical analysis demonstrates that informal franchise networks are clearly less market oriented than structured and participative ones. This is an important result as it illustrates that formalisation is not necessarily a barrier to market orientation. It also shows indirectly that a control system that is linked to a reward system is of foremost importance. Kohli and Jaworski suggested that a market-based reward system is important in enhancing market orientation. This is indirectly confirmed here, as result-based control seems more powerful than behaviour-based control. Lastly, a participative structure is also highly market oriented. This confirms the importance of the sharing, diffusing and coordination mechanisms in improving marketing functioning and effectiveness.

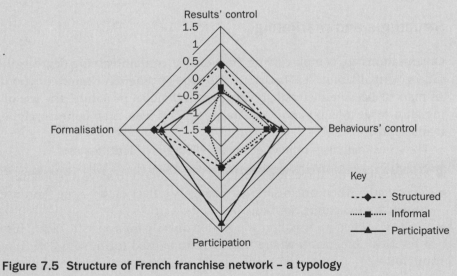

Figure 7.5 Structure of French franchise network – a typology

Source: Dubost *et al.* (2000) Franchise Research Committee, French Franchise Federation

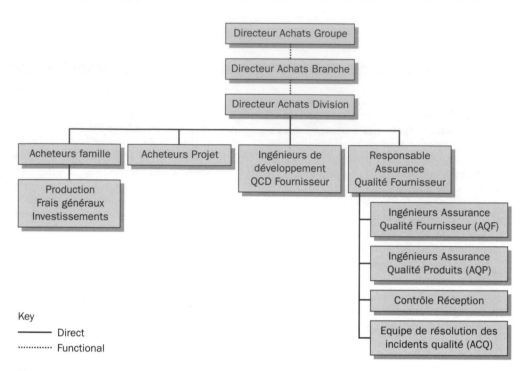

Figure 7.6 Supply department chart of the Valéo company

The overall structure of an organisation is often represented by a chart (Figure 7.6 is an example showing the Valéo company's supply department) representing areas of function and responsibility. This chart illustrates a section of a company that is basically hierarchical in nature.

Structures and marketing

Organisations are complex living entities that contain varying degrees of centralisation, formalisation, specialisation and require different degrees of coordination. As markets become increasingly complex and global in nature, the use of marketing knowledge (Menon and Varadarajan 1992) is seen as an increasingly important managerial area.

The three main uses of marketing knowledge are identified as:

- *instrumental* – the direct use of market information to solve a problem;
- *conceptual* – when organisations/managers reflect on an issue, and use market knowledge to define priorities;
- *symbolic* – when information is not used directly for a specific task. This involves a political dimension where information is used (or misused) with a specific intent.

The way marketing knowledge is used by organisations has implications for the way in which they could be structured. For example, for organisations using marketing knowledge symbolically, centralisation and formalisation can either stimulate or impede the transmission and use of market information. When information is used symbolically, there is a clear political dimension attached to it and it is used for specific purposes. High formalisation and centralisation can constitute a positive two-way channel of information but it can also impede this channel by instilling rigidity in the organisational system. However, in such circumstances, the instrumental use of marketing knowledge can be quite efficient. In some instances, a high degree of centralisation and formalisation may lead to political games. In most market-led organisations, there is often a high degree of formalisation of duties in order to respond quickly and efficiently to market needs. This is illustrated in Figures 7.7 , 7.8 and 7.9.

In the case study that follows on LGB consider how market analysis and the notion of adding value have changed the tangible and intangible parts of the LGB organisation. Also, consider the symbolic, instrumental and conceptual use of marketing knowledge.

Figure 7.7 The function-based marketing organisation

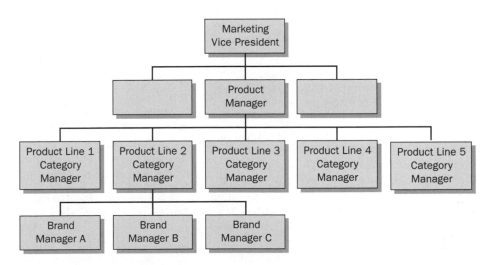

Figure 7.8 The product-based marketing organisation

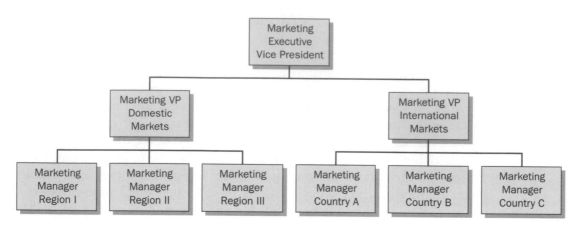

Figure 7.9 The geographic-based marketing organisation

CASE STUDY

Setting off a chain reaction

This company relied on identifying value-adding, non-value-adding and wasteful activities to strengthen the chain of processes and people. LG Balakrishnan & Brothers (LGB) had been through a recent business process restructuring (BPR) exercise. Speaking to a senior official at LGB, *eWorld* got the feeling that managing change – which is a natural fallout of any BPR initiative – must have come easily to LGB. The first promoters of the company could sense imminent change well enough. They managed to see the coming of nationalisation of bus services and prepared to exit the business of running a fleet of buses and enter into manufacturing of components for buses. Then, changing ever so slightly for the sake of a teeny-weeny BPR must have been child's play.

Satyam Computer Services helped LGB with the BPR, with the redesign of the order-generation process and of the product-engineering process. These components of the project took about six years from April 1995. BPR alone took some three years to implement with satisfaction. LGB is in a business that it calls the Transmissions business. It derives its revenues predominantly from chains required for automotives while it is also in the business of supplying industrial chains. With 14 lines of business, a group turnover of Rs 200 crore (of which the chains business contributed Rs 120

crore), and with manufacturing bases at five locations in South India and three regional offices across the country reporting to HQ at Coimbatore, LGB's BPR must have been quite a job.

Why did the company launch the BPR drive? Says S. Ramesh Kumar, senior consultant at Satyam, 'It had very little margins in its markets, the original equipment segment and in the replacement segment. Competition was gearing up for expansion, and its own productivity levels had to go up to become price competitive.' So it set about making up a vision plan calling it the P4 plan for BPR:

- a 270 per cent increase in productivity;
- a 100 per cent increase in production capacity in three years' time;
- reduce elongation of chains by 10 per cent (performance); and
- make the pricing ratio conducive to improving the marketability of the product.

A business process map helped define the whole business in six processes. Of these, the one that looked most like it could do with a change was the order-fulfilment process. Says Kumar, 'low overall equipment effectiveness was a concern. The long set-up time too was a concern. Employee involvement and skills had to be upgraded.' Adds the official, 'The quality of products was not a concern at all. But other parameters such as inventory turn ratio and other productivity norms had to be addressed.'

Satyam recommended the cellular design for the factory set-up. In other words, a factory within a factory model helped LGB improve in the areas causing concern. Here, IT played a role in setting up a *kanban* manufacturing system, order management system that integrated with the order-fulfilment process, the equipment effectiveness monitoring system and the measures of a performance monitoring system. The highlight of the project was the input–output analysis of the process. This helped define the activities of the organisation into three types: value adding (VA), non-value adding (NVA), and wasteful. Satyam helped LGB look at the number of activities making up a process and the man-hours required for those activities. It then divided these activities into those that worked for the customer (VA), those that worked for the company but did not directly affect the customer and those that worked for nobody (wasteful). Says Kumar, 'The idea here was to make sure that one maximised VA, by removing obstacles to performance, to minimise NVA and to eliminate waste.'

It is easy to see what VA processes are. But NVA?

Kumar just jumps at the query and says, 'Expediting or progress chasing are examples of NVA. Storing, warehousing, moving material in and out of the company, preparation of checks and controls documents and inspection also form part of the NVA.'

And waste? Pat comes the reply: 'Searching for a part or tool and reconciliation among documents is a classic case of wasteful activities. They add value to nobody.'

In the case of the OFP, it was found that VA contributed to about 68.2 per cent of the activities and NVA contributed to 31.7 per cent while the rest was wasteful. The official says that most of the objectives were met. The redesign of the order-generation process for industrial chains was as follows: the objective was to substantially increase the efficiency of the process. Satyam undertook market analysis to illustrate the actual position of LGB, to identify market needs, demands and customer expectations of LGB and to spot and analyse the gaps between customer expectation and delivery.

Satyam's analysis of the existing gaps indicated that there was no true standard operating procedure, several customer interfaces, not enough market intelligence, need for active business development, incorrect understanding of customer specifications and poor brand visibility.

Satyam came up with the following positioning strategy: based on market surveys, LGB had to have a solutions provider image that would help it best in the circumstances. The highlights of these were to have a single window for all chain-related requirements, strategic partnerships with customers and just-in-time deliveries. Action on these fronts resulted in a 184 per cent increase in the number of enquiries received, 169 per cent increase in enquiries quoted, 300 per cent increase in number of samples submitted and a 460 per cent increase in the number of approved samples.

For obvious reasons with regard to competition, neither the company nor the consultant was willing to reveal actual figures. The highlight of the redesign of the product engineering process (PEP) was the recommendation for concurrent engineering. The objective of the PEP redesign was to reduce the cycle-time of the enquiry process and to reduce new product development time each by half.

One of the issues the consultant cited as unproductive was the back and forth shunting of drawings from the sales force to research and development (R&D) for want of clear specifications.

The formation of a cross-functional team helped prevent unsuitable specifications creeping into the design at the concept stage itself. Industry-specific project leaders now came into the picture, thus helping the client himself decide what he wanted.

The Product Data Management component of the redesign used technology to reduce new product development time. LGB created a repository of design and related data that came in handy for re-use for future designs. A system that aided the online release of documents was also put in place. The company achieved its objectives on this front. Further, application engineers were brought in to ensure that accurate information was passed between the customer and the vendor.

Would LGB do this differently now? What were the lessons it learnt? Says the official, 'We would do it faster now, because of the learning that has

▶

accrued. Further, our priorities would be different now. For instance, we would look at new product development because that is crucial.'

Finally, why an external consultant? Would you do this again all by yourself?

The official feels, 'Satyam helped accelerate our progress. We might have been doing things on our own. Some were adequate, others not so. Further, bringing in Satyam helped us keep in touch with

modern management and manufacturing trends. It is easy being in a state capital. But in a place like Coimbatore, we have to consistently keep deputing people to attend seminars or conferences where new issues are discussed, at state capitals or the national capital. Having an external consultant helps.'

Source: Kumar (2002)

The role of intangible parts of the organisation

Intangible parts of the organisation are mainly differentiation and integration mechanisms, and culture. As mentioned previously, differentiation refers to the degree to which each department has its own way of functioning, behaving and accomplishing tasks. Hence the structure of a marketing department can be very different from that of a purchase department or from the accounting department. For example, the French company Sagem uses a geographic principle for the departmentalisation of its communication activity but it uses a product principle for departmentalising its defence activity (see Figure 7.10).

Conversely, a functional departmentalisation would, for instance, suggest that a marketing department could be organised around geographic markets while the production department could be organised around product or production processes. Sometimes, when a department is formally structured, as shown in Figures 7.7–7.9, it is possible that misunderstanding and misdirected communication between other functional departments will occur. Not only can the inner structure of each department be different but also their degree of standardisation, formalisation and decentralisation can vary. Ultimately this can generate interdepartmental conflict leading to inefficiency and sub-optimal performance. However, as organisations grow, size is often a critical factor leading to differentiation (Kalika 1995). These tangible aspects of organisations vary according to the needs of the markets and the need for organisations to be more customer oriented as we move into the twenty-first century. The development of the customer-centric organisation is discussed later.

Culture as an intangible dimension

Culture represents a problematic but extremely powerful integrating mechanism for organisations. Organisations function coherently as a result of the 'glue' provided by culture (Ouchi 1980). Weick (1987) argues that culture is a source of

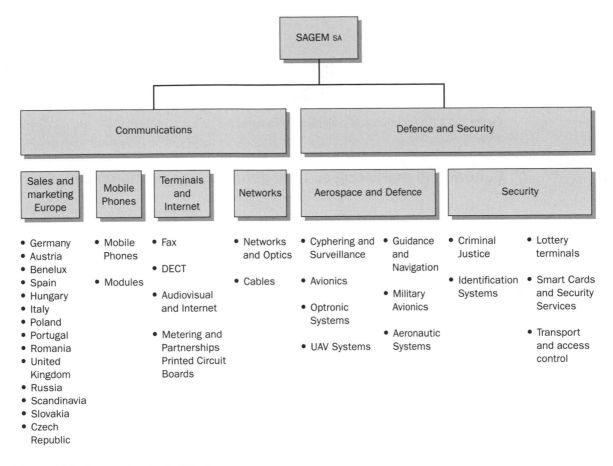

Figure 7.10 Corporate chart of Sagem
Source: http://www.sagem.com/en/

reliability. Cultures develop over time and become stable entities that can be relied upon to respond in specific ways to given stimuli.

Schein distinguishes three layers that comprise organisational culture. The first one is **basic assumptions** and relates to the fundamental beliefs that are shared within the organisation, such as: Is man good or evil? What is the right way to compete? What is reality? These basic assumptions will influence the second layer, **values**. Values are the principles that guide social interactions; they constitute a goal in themselves because of their intrinsic value. Lastly, historical **artefacts** are the most tangible or visible manifestation of the way the organisation has previously worked. These can be rituals, practices and discourses. Understanding culture, then, involves deciphering the historical artefacts and linking them with values and basic assumptions. These layers of culture are shown in Figure 7.11.

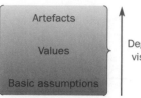

Figure 7.11 Components of organisational culture
Source: Schein (1992)

Culture and marketing culture: defining organisational culture

Although the scope of organisational culture is not completely established for organisational theorists, several common features have emerged which are encompassed in Schein's central work (1992). The pivotal idea is that culture serves as a framework for organisational actions and enhances external adaptation and internal coordination. Schein (1993) suggests organisational culture is:

> ... *a pattern of basic assumptions that a given group has invented, discovered, or developed in learning to cope with its problems of external adaptation and internal integration, a pattern of assumptions that has worked well enough to be considered valid and, therefore, to be taught to new members as the correct way to perceive, think, and feel in relation to those problems.*

Understanding culture is not easy and many different authors have different views as to its meaning and effectiveness within the organisational context. However, here we consider an idea of how culture (as an invisible element) impacts on an organisation.

From general organisational culture to marketing culture

Although many different authors have attempted to look at organisational culture and define it (Hofstede 1980, O'Reilly 1989, O'Reilly *et al.* 1989, 1991a, 1991b), very few have adapted this to a marketing context. Working within IBM, Hofstede initially identified four dimensions that can be used to analyse a culture:

- distance to power;
- risk avoidance;
- individualism versus collectivism;
- masculinity versus femininity.

Later this work became more detailed (Hofstede *et al.* 1990). In particular, principles and practices demonstrated that organisational values differed. Three types of values were identified:

- need for security;
- work centrality;
- need for authority.

These values concern the beliefs of an employee and the functioning of an organisation. For example, a typical statement representing the 'need for security' value is 'working in a well-defined job situation is important'; for the 'work centrality' value a typical statement is 'work is more important than leisure time'; for the 'need for authority' value a typical statement is 'it is not appropriate for management authority to be questioned'. Six types of practices that reflect values emerged, see Table 7.1.

O'Reilly (1989) and O'Reilly *et al.* (1991a, 1991b), on the other hand, assessed the fit between an individual and an organisation from a cultural standpoint. Hence, an analytical tool called the organisational culture profile (OCP) was developed. Various dimensions were used to describe organisational culture: innovative, attention to detail, results oriented, aggressive, supportive, reward emphasis, team oriented, and decisive. The advantage of this tool is that it provides a list of adjectives that can be used to assess the fit between a potential candidate and the proposed organisation. However, there is absolutely no mention of the *customer* and the *market*.

An analytical framework developed by Quinn and Rohrbaugh (1981) was initially designed to understand organisational performance, but was also found to be very useful in describing culture. This analytical framework functions on three axes: axis 1 concerns flexibility versus control; axis 2 concerns people versus organisation; and axis 3 concerns means versus goals. On this basis, the competing values model (CVM) establishes four organisational types: clan culture, adhocracy culture, hierarchical culture and market culture. Aspects of this model are discussed fully in Chapter 6.

An interesting analytical model incorporating culture within an organisational framework has also been formulated by Calori and Sarnin (1993). This model is the only one explicitly to describe a customer focus. The model differentiates values and practices and is shown in Figure 7.12. This model is the only one that integrates market-oriented values and cultural diagnosis. Given the complexities surrounding the notion of market and customer orientation, it is difficult to develop any formulaic stance for a market-led organisation. However, in marketing, as the emphasis changes from products and markets to *relationships and*

Table 7.1 Cultural practices

Dimension	Typical statement
1 Process oriented versus results oriented	Employees are told when a good job is done
2 Employee oriented versus job oriented	Organisation is only interested in work people do
3 Parochial versus professional	People's private life is their own business
4 Open system versus closed system	Only very special people fit into organisation
5 Loose control versus tight control	Everybody is cost-conscious
6 Normative versus pragmatic	Pragmatic, not dogmatic, in matters of ethics

Source: Hofstede *et al.* (1990) © Administrative Science Quarterly

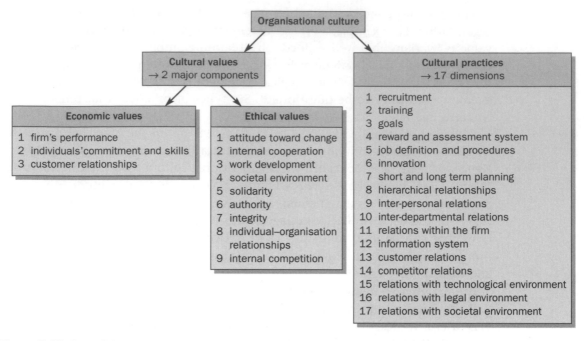

Figure 7.12 Describing organisational culture – the framework of Calori and Sarnin

Source: Calori and Sarnin (1993)

relationship building, a different focus is required for the future. Organisations need to be designed in such a way that they truly fulfill the marketing concept. In order to do this, they need to be customer oriented. This requires organisations to develop customer-focused business units and to develop cultures that are truly customer oriented (see Figure 7.13).

The transition from product focus to customer focus

There are several reasons for considering a customer-focused approach in designing organisations. These are:

- Production technologies allow mass customisation, resulting in a greater ability to service smaller segments with product features more appropriate to their needs. It is therefore no longer necessary to spend huge amounts on developing organisations that focus on products to the detriment of customers.
- Customer data warehouses and data-mining techniques make it possible to uncover previously unknown patterns of customer behaviour. These IT-based tools help marketers to make better decisions about their relationships with customers. The growing importance of IT means that marketers can concentrate more on developing a better knowledge of customers and their spending habits.
- Increasing numbers of products mean that resellers want product category level assistance. Organisations are therefore appointing product category managers. If

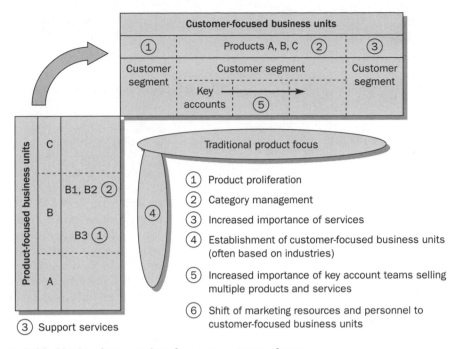

Figure 7.13 Moving from product focus to customer focus

Source: Adapted from Homburg *et al.* (2000)

a customer is regarded as a complex individual, then his or her needs and wants are likely to vary and it is also likely that retailers selling to them need to understand the category of goods (for example, electronics or hair care) that they are selling. Organisations manufacturing these goods therefore need category specialisation as opposed to product specialisation.

- Services are becoming increasingly important and many major organisations receive more profits from services than from products. Many organisations realise the importance of building relationships with customers on a long-term basis and offering better service level agreements. Better relationships lead to greater profitability. It is cheaper to retain customers than to attract new ones.

- Many organisations are beginning to reorganise their sales forces around customer groups (often industry based) to develop coherent solutions out of the products and services from multiple divisions.

- Following on from such an industry segmentation, many firms then assign key account managers to be the single point of contact with major accounts, selling the entire range of products and services produced by their firm.

The impact of technology and the movement towards relationships means that organisations must become more flexible and responsive to customer needs. Above all, organisations have to learn quickly and efficiently. How is this likely to develop in the future? A strong possibility is the development of the 'hypertext organisation', as discussed on page 148.

The client connection

There are three basic rules for sustainable success: customer retention, sales incentives and client knowledge

In most markets, there are one or two companies that outperform their rivals by staying closely connected to their customers. Prominent examples are: Enterprise Rent-A-Car, Pioneer Hi-Bred Seeds, Fidelity Investments, Lexus and Intuit. Their advantage, however, does not have much to do with customer relationship management (CRM) tools and technologies.

Information technology is a necessary, but not sufficient, component for achieving this advantage. On its own, IT contributes little to creating better relationships with customers. Rather, superior customer-relating capability is a function of how a business builds and manages its organisation.

Such relationships are the result of a clear focus on, and deft orchestration of, three components: an organizational orientation that makes customer retention a priority and gives employees wide latitude to satisfy them; a configuration that includes the structure of the organization, its processes for personalizing products or services and its incentives for building relationships; and information about customers that is in-depth, relevant and available through IT systems in all parts of the company.

Although each of these is straightforward, it is only when all three work in concert that a superior capability is created.

Research indicates the most successful companies – those with the best connections to their customers – are the ones able to create and maintain that integrated focus on orientation, configuration and information. This holds true for companies in all markets, whether they are growing fast or slow, are extremely or moderately competitive, have many customers or few, or are selling to businesses or consumers.

All companies can improve their customer relationships and, consequently, their performance by concentrating on these key components and developing a clearer sense of how they interrelate. To do so, managers must gain a greater understanding of each.

Orientation

The most important indicator of a firm's focus on customers is a shared belief customer retention is a high priority for everyone, not just to marketing or sales. Next is the openness of the company to sharing customer information. An orientation is counterproductive when one group, such as sales, believes it owns the customer. Potentially useful information is then held closely by one person or group who knows the customer and its history, vulnerabilities and requirements and is unlikely to convert that information into knowledge that can be shared by other teams and functions. Similarly, if the mindset and history of the business celebrates customer acquisitions through individual effort, little energy will be spent on assembling customer information all in one place.

A customer-relationship orientation is also shaped by the belief that different customers should be treated differently, on the basis of their long-run value. Most companies give lip service to this notion, but few have gone as far as International Business Machines Corp. did under Louis Gerstner, the chief executive from 1993 to 2002, who made it a company value to take on only the best customers and to do everything possible to cater to their needs.

That hard-nosed approach saved IBM from the worst of the problems that HewlettPackard Co., Cisco Systems Inc. and Compaq Computer Corp. encountered by chasing every Internet start-up without regard to their long-term ability to pay.

The kind of leadership and organisation-wide emphasis on customer retention shown by IBM sets leaders apart. In general, companies that embodied the attitudes and values of a true orientation toward customers – about 18% of those studied – enjoyed a significant advantage over their rivals.

Configuration

This refers to the incentives, metrics, accountabilities and structure that align a firm toward building customer relationships.

Configuration is the most influential component and best explains differences between businesses in their success with customers.

The use of incentives is an important means of keeping people in an organization focused on customers. Although this idea is well known, few companies act as though they believe it. One company that stays focused is Siebel Systems – not surprisingly, perhaps, since it is the leader in CRM software – which ties 50% of management's incentive compensation to measures of customer satisfaction.

In addition, 25% of its salesforce's compensation is based on those measures – and is paid a year after the signing of the sales contract, when the customer's level of satisfaction with the results can be determined. In most software companies, salespeople are paid when the contract is signed, a policy that fosters a one-time-transaction mindset.

Companies with superior configurations are structured to ensure their customers have a seamless interaction with all parts of the business. That prevents a customer from having to deal with different functional groups as separate entities within the same company.

A seamless connection is often best achieved when accountability for the overall quality of customer relationships is clear. Companies organized around customer groups and processes (rather than products, functions or geographies) are much better at providing clear accountability than those organized according to products, functions or geographies.

The real payoff comes when all the elements of a configuration – metrics, incentives and structures – are properly aligned. Achieving that alignment was the challenge facing General Electric's aircraft engine business group when it found that its jet engine customers were not happy with their service, even though the company's internal (six-sigma quality) metrics showed the opposite.

The group began a CRM project that was based on an in-depth study of what customers wanted in terms of responsiveness, reliability, value added by the services and help in improving their productivity. The project led the group to make wholesale changes in its configuration: New metrics based on customer requirements were added to traditional metrics (such as product reliability and compliance with standards), and the sales, marketing and product support groups were organized around customer-facing processes rather than functions. A corporate vice-president was assigned to each of the top 50 customers for the sole purpose of building the relationship, so each customer had a clear channel to the top of the organization.

To help customers improve their productivity – which was what they wanted most from the relationship – the engine group also put leaders of their six-sigma quality program on site with customers to provide training and work hand-in-hand on engine-service projects and parts inventory management.

Working and learning together, employees from GE and its customers found that the Internet was the best tool for personalizing the delivery of parts, and it became part of the CRM project. The technology was not the driver of the project, but it helped tighten the connections. The last step was to incorporate customer-service metrics into the employee evaluation criteria and provide rewards for superior service. Throughout the capability-building process, all aircraft-group employees were kept informed of new developments: For example, each morning employees received a summary of the group's performance on key customer requirements, as well as current engine-related problems such as delays or aborted takeoffs, so corrective action could be taken swiftly. As a result of its efforts, the aircraft-engine group now routinely earns high ratings on a range of customer-satisfaction metrics and is seen by its customers as an important contributor to their productivity.

Information

Most companies think of information technology first when they consider CRM capabilities, but in distinguishing leaders from followers, it is the least important piece of the puzzle. And yet executives confess to spending most of their resources on databases, software and data mining. They often do so reactively out of fear: 'Software vendors and consultants keep bringing us new solutions. We know they are making the same pitch to our competitors, and we don't want to fall behind,' is a comment often heard.

▶

However, most companies are not happy with the poor quality of their data and their continuing inability to obtain a full picture of their customers' history, activity, requirements and problems. It is the classic Red Queen syndrome: Although the companies are going faster and faster, they stay in the same place.

CRM technologies can help companies gain a coherent and comprehensive picture of customers, better organize internal data to cut service costs, help salespeople close deals faster, and improve the targeting of marketing programs, but only if the organization has begun to reconfigure and reorient itself toward customers.

Source: The client connection, *Financial Post Canada*, 2 June 2003

The hypertext organisation: a way forward for market-oriented learning organisations?

Based on the idea that learning (see Chapter 8) is of foremost importance for the organisation and for effective marketing development, a market-oriented learning organisation could be designed following the observations of organisational learning (OL) theorists.

According to Ingham (in Nonaka and Takeuchi 1995), certain types of structures seem to favour learning:

- decentralised structures;
- participative structures;
- flat structures;
- structures based on group projects or task forces;
- flexible structures.

Nonaka and Takeuchi (1995) propose an amalgamation of the effective elements of previous structures while suggesting a new way of seeing and designing organisational structure. This new model is the hypertext organisation. A hypertext organisation is made of multiple interconnected layers. Authors in market orientation have underlined the importance of interdepartmental connections for an effective market orientation.

The **central** layer is made up from the core activities of the organisation, which concentrate on routine functioning. In this scenario a hierarchical organisation is adequate. The **superior** layer entails multiple group projects where employees are expected to work creatively. Members of the group project come from different departments and are dedicated to a specific group until the project is completed. Lastly, a third invisible layer, called the **knowledge base**, which consists of sharing and recontextualising knowledge, is created in the first two layers. This layer is guided mainly by strategic vision and organisational culture. Nonaka and Konno (1993) propose the scheme shown in Figure 7.14 for the hypertext organisation.

This organisational design appears to have a lot of similarities with what is required for a good market orientation. Indeed, a market-oriented company needs a smooth and responsive organisation together with a large measure of innova-

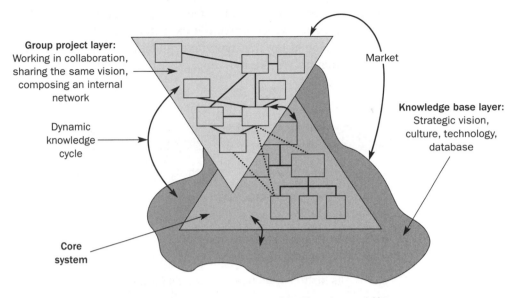

Figure 7.14 The hypertext organisation proposed by Nonaka and Konno
Source: Nonaka and Konno (1993)

tion. It takes advantage of traditional structure types such as bureaucracies, hierarchies, task forces, matrix structures, etc. and builds in responsiveness and innovation. An organisational design of this kind is not necessarily easy to describe and explain in annual reports, even though it may be one of the most effective ways to stimulate market orientation, learning and innovation, and may perhaps be the key to developing competitive advantage. Linking up core systems, knowledge systems and groups so they work in unison is perhaps the best way to develop customer-centric organisations capable of good relationship building.

Summary

Designing the structure of an organisation is an important component in developing competitive advantage. The structure helps to influence the functioning and adaptability of an organisation. Traditional concepts used for analysing the structure involve eight aspects: departmentalisation, specialisation, standardisation, coordination, formalisation, decentralisation/centralisation, control, and differentiation/integration. Assessing the degree to which an organisation incorporates these aspects helps to determine its tangible elements. On the other hand, differentiating and integrating mechanisms make up the less tangible aspects of an organisation.

Culture is also an important intangible aspect of organisations that needs to be considered. In an era where knowledge acquisition, transmission and use determine competitive advantage, it is important to consider how an organisation can effectively and efficiently build customer relationships. This has been shown by the move from a product to a customer focus. However, in the future it is likely that organisations will develop different layers that function effectively and coherently to meet and exceed customer expectations. These future organisations will probably develop along the hypertext model described above. Knowledge creation and dissemination will be dynamic, creating a virtuous circle of customer–organisation interactions.

Chapter questions

1 To what extent can we distinguish standardisation from coordination?

2 Does the organisational chart represent the whole structure of an organisation? Why/why not?

3 How can the role of differentiation mechanisms be conceptualised from a market-oriented point of view?

4 What is instrumental use of market information?

5 According to Schein (1992), how many components can be identified in organisational culture? What are the links between these components?

6 What types of change toward market-oriented culture can be identified? What are their respective benefits and drawbacks?

7 Is there a link between structure and the level of market orientation? If there is, is it a strong, established link?

8 Does an organisation's size matter when trying to create a market-oriented culture?

9 Outline the design of a hypertext organisation.

10 What are the benefits of hypertext organising with regard to market orientation?

8 The learning organisation

Introduction

Organisational learning can basically be defined as the process of improving action through better knowledge and understanding (Fiol and Lyles 1985). Yet several other descriptions have been suggested: adaptation, information processing patterns, development of organisational theory-in-use and institutionalisation of experience in the organisation (Shrivastava 1983). These descriptions demonstrate that organisational learning is a multifaceted phenomenon, which covers different degrees of learning and application. From a marketing point of view, the benefits of organisational learning can be reflected in faster and more efficient marketing processes. Indeed, several marketing authors (Day 1994, Sinkula 1994) suggest that it produces positive synergistic effects:

- Organisational learning is the development of new knowledge or insights that have the potential to influence behaviour.
- Learning facilitates behaviour changes that lead to improved performance.
- Dynamic and turbulent environments demand learning and behaviour changes that lead to improved performance.

In this chapter, the concept of organisational learning and its different facets will be discussed. The gap between individual and organisational learning is explored, as the mechanism that transfers individual learning to organisational learning cannot be taken for granted. Then we discuss how the benefits of a learning process can be maintained and developed. Lastly, the development of a learning orientation, hand in hand with a market orientation, is examined.

What are learning processes?

As suggested by Shrivastava (1983), organisational learning can have different meanings. In some instances, it can mean the ease with which an organisation can adapt to its environment. In others, it can mean the efficiency of utilisation of information

(information processing patterns). In both instances, learning takes place, but it is either a reactive process (adaptation) or a static process (information processing).

More recently, the learning organisation has been viewed as a continuously creative, innovative organisation (Senge 1990) and as a coherent, cohesive structure where each member is willingly active (Nonaka 1991). If an organisation is to be continuously creative and innovative, with each member willingly active, then we need to understand the learning processes that are involved.

In order to understand the processes, two types of learning have been defined. The first type is a lower-level learning, also called single-loop learning (Argyris and Schön 1978) or behavioural development. The second type is a higher-level learning, also known as double-loop learning or cognitive learning.

Single-loop learning

The first level of learning is limited to a section of an organisation. Often this section will have a defined set of behaviours designed to cope with particular problems. These are routine patterns and are triggered by particular stimuli within the environment. For example, if beer sales are low, a brewing company will launch its current advertisements. Any short-term problems are dealt with equally efficiently. This type of behaviour can also be described as reactive learning and is similar to mere behavioural adaptation. Single-loop learning does not stretch to questioning the phenomena that create the response (for example, why are the beer sales low?); it merely sets in motion conditioned responses to external stimuli.

Adaptive learning, or single-loop learning, often contains a 'learning boundary'. The way in which the business is conceptualised guides core capabilities. However, in many instances these could become 'core rigidities' that concentrate on the served market and foster a narrow perspective. Therefore an adaptive approach (single-loop) is usually sequential, incremental and focused on issues or opportunities within the traditional scope of the organisation's activities (see Figure 8.1).

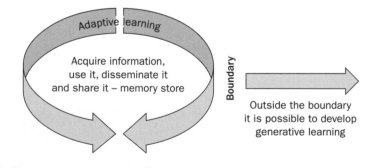

Figure 8.1 The process of organisational learning
Source: Adapted from Slater and Narver (1995)

Double-loop learning

This higher level of learning affects the whole organisation and is rarely contained within functional areas. It entails a deeper challenge to routine practices and rules. This type of generative learning shows a willingness to question long-held assumptions about mission, customers, capabilities and strategy. Often this is based on systems thinking and works through existing relationships, linking key issues and events. When an organisation begins to embrace double-loop learning, interrelationships and dynamic processes of change are important. Often a learning organisation that is adept at double-loop learning can take advantage of 'windows of opportunity' that may be available. Slower-moving organisations that have 'fixed' views of markets and their role within them may fail to take advantage of these opportunities.

Higher-level learning usually occurs during some types of crisis, for example a new strategy, new leader and significant changes in the market. It corresponds to the development of a new frame of reference. One of the consequences of double loop learning is the necessity to 'unlearn' an old process as old frames of reference are no longer efficient in coping with the new reality.

Which approach is best?

The ability to learn is, obviously, necessary for any organisation. However, trying to establish a hierarchy between lower- and higher-level learning is short-sighted. Single-loop learning, with its smaller reactive change, is necessary for everyday operational tasks. Some authors (Fiol and Lyles 1985) suggest defining lower-level learning as 'adaptation' and higher-level learning as 'learning', with learning being 'the development of insights, knowledge, and associations between past actions, the effectiveness of those actions and future actions'. Figure 8.2 contrasts the impacts of single- and double-loop learning on the organisation.

Although adaptation and learning are both important to managerial performance, there can sometimes be a conflict with adaptation routines that prevents an organisation from engaging in comprehensive learning. This is why the articula-

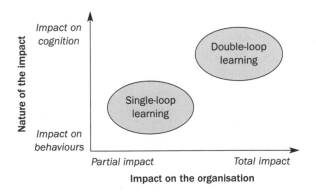

Figure 8.2 The impacts of single- and double-loop learning

tion between the different types of learning is important. An important aspect of this is to consider the impact of 'learning systems'.

Learning systems

Shrivastava (1983) distinguishes six types of learning systems (see Figure 8.3). These systems represent different ways of generating learning, which is another way of classifying learning processes. First the **one-man institution** refers to a system where only one man knows everything about the situation. In this learning process, the individual learns and then diffuses his knowledge to other members of the organisation. In the second approach, the **mythological learning system** functions through the exchange of stories and myths between members of the organisation. In these two learning systems, the knowledge is mainly, if not totally, subjective.

The third system is the **information seeking culture** where each member of the organisation is encouraged to be curious about the business and environment. The diffusion of knowledge is mainly by word of mouth and informality is its main characteristic.

The **participative learning system** is a system in which ad hoc committees and working groups are formed to solve certain managerial problems, hence knowledge is produced on a very specific basis and is decision oriented. Knowledge is formalised to facilitate the sharing of knowledge and expertise possessed by different participants in the ad hoc groups.

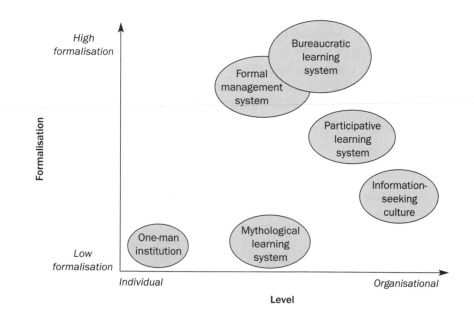

Figure 8.3 Types of learning systems

Source: Adapted from Shrivastava (1983)

The **formal management system** is the organisational solution for perpetuating the learning process. It corresponds to the planning, control and sharing of information. Virtually any organisational subsystem can take this approach: strategic planning, information system management, financial/budgetary control systems, etc.

Lastly, the **bureaucratic learning system** goes one step further and is the most formal way to organise knowledge. It entails procedures and regulations and aims to produce absolute, objective, impersonalised knowledge. One major danger of this type of system is that it concentrates on formal knowledge and is unable to deal with tacit knowledge.

From this review of learning systems, we can see that learning can be initiated, developed and framed in different ways.

One step further: deutero learning

Theorists recently identified another type of learning: deutero learning. This process enables the organisation to understand how knowledge is created and how learning is engaged. While double-loop learning refers to the ability to create new solutions (cognitive frame + behaviours), deutero learning is the process of learning itself. This is not an abstract way of thinking about learning; it is a contextualised, organisation-specific audit of how learning is achieved (see Figure 8.4).

The deutero learning idea suggests that, when reflecting on its current learning process, the organisation can foster its learning. This reflexive process can speed learning. For example, Moingeon and Edmondson (1996) show how Intel developed its 'carbon copy' learning system. This offered Intel the opportunity to quickly transfer its new research and development (R&D) technologies from one factory to another. Hence, once the organisation has understood its own learning process, it can systematise and replicate the most powerful learning process.

From individual to organisational learning

One big problem in organisational learning is the question of how learning is developed. The term 'learning' suggests that it begins at an individual level. Indeed, one could ask: How can an organisation learn? Is organisational learning more or less than the sum of individual learning? Several authors have explored this complex matter.

The knowledge base of individual learning has evolved from learning being considered within a stimulus–response paradigm, to notions such as memorising and forgetting (Shrivastava 1983). Recently, Kim (1993) explained that individual learning corresponds to both the acquisition of skills, or know-how, and know-why. This corresponds to two levels of learning: operational and conceptual. He suggests that learning is acquired through a four-step process, known as the OADI process, illustrated in Figure 8.5.

Learning Audit

First glance

1 Do we give the impression of learning from our business, activity, role, market and environment?

2 Do we feel there are changes in the environment? Do we respond to these changes? Do we anticipate them?

3 At what rate do we generate new ideas (products, new managerial tools, etc.)?

More in-depth analysis

1 Over the past five years, *how many* things did you learn?

2 What is *the scope* of the learning (better operations, new procedures, new ways of thinking, etc.)?

3 What *type of knowledge* was developed (subjective, mythological, objective, general, problem specific, task or area specific)?

4 Is this learning *shared* (at top-management level, at middle-management level, at employee level, in every department, in every SBU)?

5 Is this learning *stored* (degree of development of the information system, degree of interactivity, degree of utilisation; writs, notes, memos, internal newsletter, reports, word of mouth)?

6 Do you engage in formal meetings for *diffusing, sharing and discussing* the new things you discovered?

7 *Why* did you engage in the learning process (crisis, problems, periodic requirement, specific decision, ongoing process)?

8 *Who* initiates the learning process (individual or top management, informal network, department, task group)?

9 Do you *evaluate* the benefits of your learning process (in terms of economic performance, efficiency, organisational climate, members' motivation and satisfaction with their job)?

Figure 8.4 Learning audit – a proposal

Kim observes that there is a missing link between individual and organisational learning. The question is: If it is possible, how can individual learning be converted into organisational learning? This refers to knowledge, the product of learning. We could reformulate this question: How can the organisation integrate

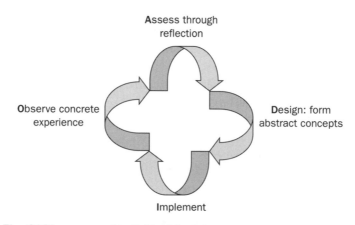

Figure 8.5 The OADI process of individual learning

and share knowledge that has been produced on an individual basis? Is it possible to generate knowledge that is not based on individual learning? This is especially important in marketing, as much of the marketing concept relies on intelligence dissemination and developing knowledge bases.

Shrivastava (1983) remarks that, whilst individual learning was originally studied by psychologists, several disciplines have tried to understand organisational learning. Consequently, the knowledge about organisational learning is more fragmented and this can explain the difficulty in building a comprehensive view of how organisational learning occurs.

Kim (1993) states that 'An organisation can learn only through its members, but learning is not dependent on any specific member'. Several models assume that organisational learning functions like individual learning. However, this premise is fraught with difficulty because individuals may learn in different ways. Kim indicates that one needs to understand the transfer mechanism from individual to organisational learning. The transfer lies in shared mental models. He suggests that mental models are the structure of organisational memory. The organisational learning cycle can be illustrated in the following manner:

1 It starts at the individual level: individual learning engaged through the OADI (Figure 8.5) process.
2 The result of learning is a change in individual mental models.
3 At this stage, organisational learning can occur with a change of shared mental models.
4 This leads to new organisational action.
5 Through individual actions and further learning, the cycle begins again (see Figure 8.6).

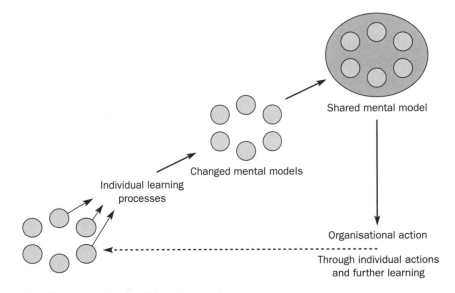

Figure 8.6 The organisational learning cycle

Nonaka and Takeuchi (1995) suggest that other types of process also exist through which knowledge creation can occur, which can also assist in linking individual and organisational learning. They identify two types of knowledge: **tacit** and **explicit**. Tacit knowledge is acquired by a process of diffusion resulting from social interaction, so a worker learns unconsciously from the experience of others. Tacit knowledge can be made explicit through analogies, metaphors, models and concepts. For example, the BCG model was initially developed and used by the Boston Consulting Group, which made the knowledge available to others through publication. Similarly, organisations can reflect ideas through models or analogies. In some instances, organisations resort to storytelling and metaphors. At its most basic level, tacit knowledge is shared through written rules and procedures. However, learning is not solely dependent on sharing and diffusing tacit knowledge. Learning processes also refer to explicit knowledge. It is possible for a *combination* of several pieces of explicit knowledge to create new explicit knowledge. This occurs when written models and procedures that exist in different parts of an organisation are brought together and new patterns or ideas emerge. The next section considers ways of 'trapping' the benefits of a learning organisation.

Retaining the benefits of learning: organisational memory and mental models

The role of memory is considered to be prevalent in learning processes. Kim (1993) states that 'learning has more to do with acquisition, whereas memory has more to do with retention of whatever is acquired'. Mental models are structures that organise the memory; this is true of both individuals and organisations. As noted before, the challenge is to build shared mental models so that individual learning is stored in people's memories and becomes part of the organisational memory.

Part of the problem lies in understanding the subsystems of memory. Memory subsystems are organised around two axes: the first axis is the level of memory (individual, collective and centralised) and the second axis is the nature of the memory (declarative, procedural and judgemental). Taking these subsystems into account is very important in order to audit the learning capabilities of the organisation. It is also crucial in order to develop the highest learning capability: the capacity for deutero learning.

Girod (1995) is a French researcher who identified the nine subsystems of organisational memory shown in Table 8.1.

The culture of learning

Although it is possible to give general guidelines for the development of learning, it is clear that, for organisations, learning is not only a matter of formalisation and the creation of a framework for learning. In fact, many organisations are aware that the culture and climate that exists within their environments can either facilitate or hinder learning.

Table 8.1 Organisational memory subsystems

		Nature		
		Declarative *(knowledge)*	*Procedural* *(know-how)*	*Judgemental* *(know-why)*
Level	*Individual*	**1** Individual knowledge (brain and documents) used within the organisation	**4** Individual skills used within the organisation	**7** Individual prospective memory, ability to interpret based on individual experience
	Collective non-centralised	**2** Acquisition of knowledge from others or knowledge creation through interaction	**5** Skills creation through collective action	**8** Creation of a shared interpretation
	Centralised	**3** Knowledge in centralised database	**6** Procedures described in manuals	**9** Official culture, formalised in documents

Source: Girod (1995)

CASE STUDY

Adapt or die...

Just as evolutionary history tells us that the fittest species survived because they were able to adapt to change, so should corporations in a changing business environment

In Darwin's theory, evolution was characterised as a gradual process in which all species went through changes at regular intervals. On examination of fossils, though, it was found that in reality evolution is punctuated. That is, crises in the environment, natural or self-imposed, demanded that species adapt or die.

Today, we are facing similar crises in business. Billions of dollars are being spent on change management. Yet most successful organisations cannot keep pace with their more nimble competitors. That which is targeted to change, remains unchanged. More is required by less. Organisations are required to cannibalise or be eaten...

These and several other paradoxes indicate that the business environment is demanding that corporations change their way of operating. Through evolutionary history, those species that

did survive did so because they were able to adapt to their environment. They proved to be complex adaptive systems. They thrived on disequilibrium and chaos, and changed themselves to enter a new relationship with the environment. There are lessons to be learned from behaving as complex adaptive systems.

If an organisation operates as a 'material' level complex adaptive system, then it is tied to the past, and to what may have once made it successful. Its world consists of known customers, known products, known markets, known processes and structure, and known strategies. Innovation is about 'tweaking' and about moving within the boundaries that have already established what it is. An organisation centred at this level has a limited number of options to choose from when confronted with change. Change itself is engineered as though the world is fixed, and

▶

therefore any efforts are only incremental, within the confines of the described world. Depending on the degree to which an organisation centred at this level can call on attitudes and strategies that are centred at the higher levels, it will likely be able to function far more successfully than an organisation that perceives and acts in the world solely from a material perspective.

An organisation operating as a 'financial' level complex adaptive system has more degrees of freedom. Being centred on financial results, whether ROI, sales, or market share, it is not necessarily bound to the world that has made it successful. It is not necessarily bound by past markets, customers, products, processes, structures or strategies. It has the added flexibility of changing any of these to ensure that it meets its specified financial goals. Yet, if it were required to go through a quantum change, as is being required of many organisations today, it runs the risk of becoming extinct so long as it remains insistently focused on meeting its imposed financial goals. It is to be noted that organisations operating at this level do embody all the positive capacities of the previous, material, level. At the same time, depending on the degree to which an organisation centred at this level can call on attitudes and strategies that are centred at the conceptual level, it will likely be able to function far more successfully than an organisation that perceives and acts in the world solely from a financial or a financial–material perspective.

An organisation operating as a 'conceptual' level complex adaptive system is not bound by its past. It has more degrees of freedom, and is in essence more fluid and adaptive than any form that precedes it. It seizes on ideas and will change its customers, products, markets, processes, structures and/or strategies to ensure that these ideas can be fulfilled. It, too, has the know-how and capability of all the previous levels embedded into it. Thus, material and financial capabilities are deeply embedded or easily available to it.

An organisation operating as an 'intuitional' level complex adaptive system is perhaps fulfilling some deep need, possibly far beyond that which it might even imagine. As such, it has opened to deep forces of formation, and is bound only by its ability to give the receiving intuition a form. At such a level of operation, old, accepted ways of organising may prove inadequate or incomplete, and the organisation may have to conduct its operations in new, virgin forms. Such an organisation is deeply creative and perhaps becomes the model by which many other organisations develop. Examples of organisations at each of these levels follow:

- An example of focused material-level operation, to the point where it becomes restrictive, is that exercised by the US rail industry. It wanted to continue to provide rail services, even though others had begun to provide transport services, and therefore signed its own death warrant.

- Another example of the material-level operation is that of a company in the 'typewriter' business. Computers now provide all the capabilities provided by a typewriter, and a lot more. Any company that insists on providing typewriters will soon be wiped out.

- An example of financial-level operation is that of Barnes & Noble. When Amazon.com actually began following through on its vision of becoming the largest bookstore on the planet, Barnes & Noble, threatened by its diminishing market share, spun off barnesandnoble.com. Its motivation was simply to regain lost market share. If, instead, it had moved to an ambition at the concept-based level, it may have been able to reinvent the retailing industry by being the first truly click-and-mortar type company.

- Another example of an enterprise operating at the financial level is Covisint, the e-marketplace joint effort between General Motors, Ford, and DaimlerChrysler. While Covisint had the possibility of being a concept-led play, in reality it has been motivated by a vision that is at a less-empowering financial level. Thus, to avoid the continuing costs of ongoing battles and pains associated with continuing to support their own auto-parts marketplaces against the efforts of other competitors in the same space, the Covisint principals decided to join forces to come up with a joint auto-parts marketplace. Since their motivation has been driven by the financial level, they have been unable to step up to the broader concept-led leadership required to bring such a venture to successful fruition. Thus, from the word 'Go', they have been attended by a host of problems, starting from the inability to come up with a mutually acceptable name for the project, to the ongoing difficulty in selecting the right technology platform, to the potentially crippling inability to really bring their suppliers along. These leadership problems were further compounded by the Federal Trade Commission's concern that the combined purchasing power of the automakers could be anti-competitive for suppliers.

■ An example of a concept-led company is that of Amazon.com. At its inception it sought to create the world's largest virtual bookstore. It sought to allow users to browse titles in the comfort of their home, while allowing them to view online reviews by other readers. It shipped books to buyers at prices comparable with, or less than, those available at its competitors. Its concept for selling books was so different from existing sellers of books that investors have allowed it to continue in operation for five years before it has even begun to show a profit. Further, it drew investors to its unique concepts, and through the funds that became available to it was able to quickly mobilise capabilities at the previous level – material and financial.

■ Another example of a concept-led organisation is that of Aravind Eye Care System. Note that this is not a business organisation, and therefore its inclusion in this category is tenuous, but done, nonetheless, to provide a rough indication of

what different levels of operation may mean. Aravind Eye Care System has grown organically in India, without upfront planning, and has assumed a unique practical shape, with a reach into villages unparalleled by any other organisation. This reach has assisted it in creating a unique culture through the young village girls who join Aravind to become its nurses, and the backbone of the organisation. This reach also allows Aravind to provide service to numerous blind people throughout southern India. It is driven by the vision and idea of its founder, and there is adhesion to this vision, even though circumstances change and time goes on. In this sense it remains concept-led.

To the best of the author's knowledge, companies at the intuitive level do not exist, though several may be in formation, driven by the vision of their leaders.

An organisation should thus be centred at the higher levels. This then provides it with the flexibility and living quality to become an effective organisation constantly fulfilling real needs. It thus becomes imperative to create a culture whereby there is always a push to the higher levels. As such, proactive actions and reactive measures need to be taken at every instance to ensure that every part of the organisation is operating with the highest degrees of freedom available to it.

Source: Malik (2002)

(Pravir Malik is a computer scientist and management consultant. Founder of Aurosoorya, he has consulted with several prominent organisations.)

How can the typology of organisations discussed in this case study help or hinder the formation of a learning organisation?

As culture has an important part to play in learning, it is useful to understand why (Baumard 1995):

■ An informed organisation is not necessarily more competitive; it is what the organisation makes out of the information that really counts;

■ Individual learning is usually dispersed into the organisation, with no real benefit at the collective level.

■ Learning from other managerial systems (for example, the USA trying to learn from Japanese management) is very difficult because one misses the details.

All of these observations indicate that the deeper capabilities of an organisation are very dependent on its culture. Surface-level learning, without the required cultural dimension, can lead to poor implementation of strategies.

Turning to the question of culture, it is important to re-emphasise that culture cannot be managed in the same way as other organisational dimensions because it is complex, socially constructed and always evolving. As Barney (1986 and 1996) demonstrated, culture is by definition unique, which means that each organisation has to find its own way. Often, mergers and acquisitions occur in the hope that the culture of the more successful organisation will dominate. However, the performance level of most organisations formed through mergers and acquisitions is poorer than that of the freestanding companies.

It is clear that top management has a lot of influence on the culture of an organisation (Schein 1983, 1992b, 1993) and that this can stimulate development. However, it is also clear that the expansion and integration of the changes initiated or desired by management will depend on every member of the organisation 'buying in' to the changes. Consequently, the ability to develop a learning culture will depend on the organisation's initial abilities and characteristics (see Figure 8.7). A particular organisation's potential is unique and cannot easily be compared with that of another organisation; each organisation has to develop its own capacities. While developing a learning culture, the organisation has to keep an eye on its environment (competitors, market, customers, suppliers and other salient stakeholders) because learning also occurs through external interaction. In such instances, benchmarking studies can be useful in assessing competitors' strengths and weaknesses. This learning can then be translated into specific actions that play to an organisation's strengths and its particular culture.

Developing a learning culture can be a problem for organisations that are not aware of their existing culture. In such cases, a cultural diagnosis can help the organisation to rethink, since organisational culture is the nervous system of the organisation.

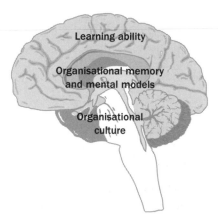

Figure 8.7 A brain metaphor of the links between culture, memory and learning

Learning is not straightforward

All preceding considerations suggest that learning is not necessarily straightforward. It may not be part of the initial culture or may be difficult to maintain as inertia impedes continuous learning. In line with this, at least three other factors should be noted. First, several authors indicate that unlearning is critical. Second, learning and cultural evolution require time. Lastly, the learning perspective can stand as a new approach to change processes and management.

The issue of **unlearning** is very important. This is linked to the different shortcomings of the learning process itself. Indeed, in their famous article 'The myopia of learning', Levinthal and March (1993) identified three pitfalls associated with myopic learning processes:

1 The tendency to ignore the long term, especially in first-level reactive learning.
2 The tendency to ignore the bigger picture; indeed the organisation's cognitive resources may be limited by the specialisation of the learning activities.
3 The tendency to overlook failures as they are considered irrelevant.

By unlearning, the organisation questions present and past knowledge that has been generated through learning. In fact, researchers (Spender and Baumard 1995) have witnessed the following phenomenon: organisations that made considerable efforts to learn are unwilling to change the core of the learning they gained through the hard learning phase. Hence, whilst learning should be an ongoing process, it can lead to learning rigidities because the process itself is so consuming (in terms of time, people, money) that the organisation is no longer in a position to reinvest in such efforts.

This is linked to what has been called the 'exploitation/exploration balance' by Levinthal and March. The idea is that higher-level learning consists of two phases: the exploration phase and the exploitation phase. A poor balance between exploration and exploitation can be described as follows: a learning organisation has spent a lot of resources in exploring a specific issue but it does not have enough resources to go further and elaborate on this, hence yielding a weak exploitation and leading to an incomplete learning (see Figure 8.8).

Organisations can encounter two different problems: either an excess of exploration or an excess of exploitation. In both cases, unlearning past behaviour patterns can contribute to a better balance between the two. For example, a company may be very good at market research and continually prides itself on this. However, when it comes to getting the goods on the shelves within the market, it invariably fails. In this instance, it has to 'unlearn' the previous behaviour pattern of relying on market research and balance this with a better learning of production capabilities.

In addition to this, an organisation also has to be able to assimilate learning over a period of time. Often key individuals within an organisation are so absorbed by day-to-day requirements that they fail to leave time for learning or reflection. Many researchers (Levinthal and March 1993, Baumard 1995) are finding that the time spent on reflection yields competitive advantage. Often too much emphasis is placed on speed of operations, especially by external agencies, yet time spent on reflection and understanding of organisational and market dynamics is time well spent.

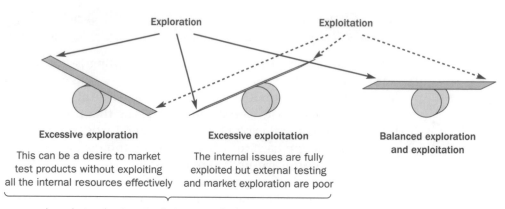

Figure 8.8 Exploration and exploitation

The organisation then can be seen as managing a **time paradox**. It has to be efficient in marketing, research and development (R&D), production, therefore necessitating a great deal of interdepartmental coordination, and even overlap in similar matrix organisations. However, it also has to take the time to integrate, digest and exploit the knowledge it has just produced through learning. In the long run, this paradox should be overcome as the learning process will, in time, help to speed up operations. A metaphor for this may be a travel agency learning to manage complex systems associated with ships and planes in its quest to offer the best possible holiday to a discerning traveller. Thus knowledge of both the aviation and cruise industries needs to be integrated and coordinated. This is depicted in Figure 8.9. Companies therefore need to see the holistic nature of their entities and try to overcome barriers that may seem insurmountable at times, taking the time to do this.

To overcome this paradox, the organisation can stimulate balanced learning through different means (Levinthal and March 1999). First, it can develop a whole

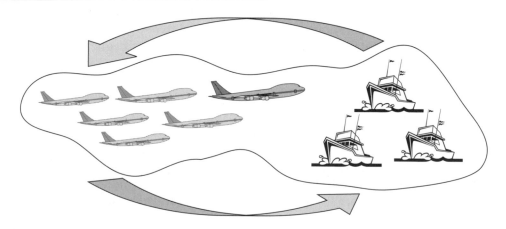

Figure 8.9 Managing planes and ships in the long run: overcoming the paradox

range of incentives. Classic economic responses can be considered for stimulating innovation (prime, property rights, etc.). However, human resource management tools should also be used, particularly career advancement, as a way of rewarding innovative people. Recruitment and the resulting selection process is also an important tool for integrating 'newness' into the organisation. Second, to avoid inertia, the organisational structure can also be used to maintain exploration. Instead of relying heavily on integration and socialisation, organisation can try to maintain diversity and individuality. Preserving individual 'deviance' can stimulate individual learning, which is the first step towards organisational learning. At the same time, top management can encourage risk taking and creativity, improving the organisation's ability to innovate (Kohli and Jaworski 1990). Learning also needs to be exploited and it is top management's role to try to integrate, digest, conceptualise and diffuse the results of learning.

Developing a learning, market-oriented organisation

In order to understand how marketing can benefit from a learning orientation, different types of marketing knowledge generated through the different levels of learning need to be harnessed.

Levels of learning and marketing knowledge

One of the most important issues in management practice (and consequently in academic research) is to use the knowledge that has been created through either learning processes or information gathering. Organisations often accumulate huge amounts of data without exploiting them: that is, data is not informed (*Latin informare*: to put into form). Creating marketing knowledge is *using* gathered data and information.

Menon and Varadarajan (1992) point out that there are three different types of knowledge utilisation: instrumental, conceptual, and symbolic.

1 *Instrumental* use of knowledge corresponds to the direct application of the findings in order to solve a problem. For example, when the decision to launch a new product is made, the instrumental use of information obtained from market research will be reflected in the packaging, the date of introduction, the communication campaign, etc. Here knowledge is generated with a direct link to a marketing problem: How should we package the product? When is the ideal time to launch it? What should be the communication mix? (Koenig 1990)

2 The *conceptual* use of marketing knowledge is when the knowledge is not directly applied to a specific problem. Rather, it is used to enhance the existing knowledge base of the organisation and its managers. It helps to modify the vision and add new concepts and perspectives for viewing traditional problems. For example, the study of the development of Internet technologies and the possibilities it offers can be used directly in proposing a new product or service

offering and can be used indirectly to rethink the process of product innovation. The generation of knowledge can either be problem specific or can be the result of strategic scanning (Koenig 1990).

3 Lastly, the *symbolic* use of knowledge corresponds to a distortion of the meaning of information in order to serve a managerial purpose. This amounts to a political use of information. Here, although knowledge is initially generated for a specific issue, its use is far removed from the initial intention. As already mentioned (see Chapter 7), Menon and Varadarajan (1992) suggest that the way an organisation is organised influences the way and the intensity with which marketing knowledge is used.

While Menon and Varadarajan (1992) focus their analysis on the use of marketing knowledge generated through research and studies, Sinkula (1994) provides a more comprehensive view by proposing a link between market information processes. He considers the use of market information in terms of acquiring, distributing, interpreting and storing market information and learning orientation. He finally proposes a model of market-based organisational learning.

Sinkula considers that market-based learning (MBL) is fundamentally different from classic organisational learning in five respects:

1 The external focus that underlies MBL leads to a more open perspective. It can also be considered as a prerequisite of internal-oriented learning because learning has to be nurtured by new, mainly external, data.

2 Sinkula stresses that MBL is a source of competitive advantage. The focus on the environment naturally leads to learning that will have an important impact on the competitiveness of the organisation.

3 MBL infers that the observation of other organisations is not necessarily a fruitful exercise.

4 Sinkula accepts that marketing information that resides within organisations is sometimes difficult to access because each individual has his or her own method of storing this information.

5 Sinkula argues that market information is much more important than other types of information (such as financial data, productivity results). Therefore, even if it might be more difficult, organisations that seek to gain a competitive advantage from their learning processes should focus on MBL.

Focusing on MBL demands that one understands the different types of marketing knowledge and how they can be generated through learning. Sinkula proposes the framework shown in Table 8.2.

Such a framework opens opportunities for an organisation to reassess its own MBL processes. Initially the diagnosis should focus on the amount and nature of market knowledge that is gathered in the organisation. Then further attention should be given to the progress of each type of market information within the organisation. Who produces or gathers it? What is done with this information? Who are the other people who access this information? What is the sequence of dissemination? Do the people affected by the information use it and in what way? This can assist in understanding what is done with market information and what are the potential discrepancies (see Figure 8.10).

Table 8.2 Levels of MBL, manifestation and examples

Types of knowledge and learning process	Manifestation	Example
Dictionary	Labelling and description of things	Description of market segments, product movement
Episodic	Development of historical databases	Description of past sales, past phenomena and cause–effect relationships
Endorsed	Development of systems of norms and strategies	Development of an 'espoused' way of doing market research
Procedural	Actual practices that may deviate from the endorsed knowledge	Actual practices and tacit rules that are involved in market research
Axiomatic	Development of fundamental organisational beliefs	The fundamental reason why market research is conducted the way it is and why it continues to be conducted this way
Augmented	Response to gaps detected between espoused and actual way of doing things	Renewed ways of organising the acquisition of market information
Deutero	Development of consciousness about how to learn	Understanding of how market information is developed and used within the organisation and of its impacts

Source: Adapted from Sinkula (1994)

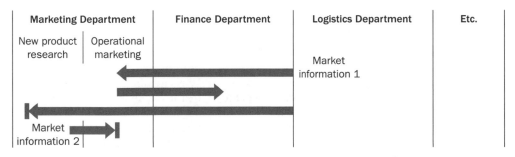

Figure 8.10 Tracking market information throughout the organisation

Synergistic effects of learning orientation and market orientation

Day (1994) was one of the first authors to underline the potential virtuous circle between learning and market orientation. For him, learning corresponds to the ability to ask the right question at the right time. Organisations that are market oriented share assumptions about how their markets behave and evolve. To support their view and keep contact with their customers, they have to implement market-driven learning.

Developing continuous learning about markets supposes that the necessary skills for carrying out the following activities have to be acquired:

- scanning with peripheral vision;
- ensuring sensible decisions through market research;
- activating the sensors at the point of customer contact;
- learning from benchmarking;
- continuously experimenting.

Creativity and innovation are clearly developed through a learning process that entails peripheral vision and experimentation. In order to foster this within individuals, top management needs to be open and not fazed by risk taking. In other words, management has to have the ability to create an environment which facilitates learning and sharing information. Baker and Sinkula (1999) state that this can have a profound impact on developing an organisation that is market oriented. They suggest that, in general, organisations with high levels of learning orientation are strongly market oriented and perform well in the marketplace.

When you have read the case study on Powderject, answer the following questions:

1 *What are the long-term sacrifices that Powderject had to make in order to become market oriented?*
2 *How is this orientation likely to impact on its organisation structure?*
3 *What aspects of Market Based Learning (MBL) are important to consider in this case?*

CASE STUDY

Powderject

Powderject Pharmaceuticals, the Oxford-based biotech firm, has announced plans to sell off its flagship needle-free injection business and focus on a number of vaccine products. The announcement comes as the first powder-based needleless product approaches final stage trials before being released on the market. Analysts welcomed this bold restructuring in the light of mounting evidence that, in most cases, drug delivery via rival liquid-based devices was likely to prove quicker and cheaper to bring to market than the powder technology.

Julie Simmonds, an analyst at Beeson Gregory, said Powderject's decision to spin off its non-vaccine interests was tacit recognition of the limits of its needleless injection device. 'If it is going to be the next big thing in drug delivery, they would not be selling it,' she said.

The company has declined to put a value on its non-vaccine business, but analysts said it is likely to be less than Powderject would have hoped some months ago. Chairman and chief executive Paul Drayson said the divestment would be completed by the end of 2001. 'We will have a better handle on the likely terms round about September,' he said, adding: 'We could be looking at a joint venture or a full divestment.'

Asked if the radical refocusing was likely to prompt a company name change, Mr Drayson said there were no plans to do so. He added that about 80% of the restructured company's vaccine portfolio was deliverable through the powder-based device. Powderject will also retain the intellectual property rights to the technology.

As part of the restructuring programme, Powderject has also revealed it is to buy Swedish vaccine firm SBL Vaccin for $50m, plus $40m conditional on product approvals and projected sales. The sale is to be funded by a mixture of cash and shares. SBL, which makes vaccines against diarrhoea for long-haul travellers as well as vaccines against cholera and polio, had sales last year of £16m. It is expected to contribute to profits in its first full year under Powderject ownership.

Mr Drayson said SBL's anti-diarrhoea vaccine had considerable potential for applications in the third world. At present 2m children die every year from diarrhoea, making it the second biggest killer of under five-year-olds. 'If funding in the developing world can be sorted out this could be a promising market,' Mr Drayson said.

Powderject sales for the year to April 2001 were £40m, up from £2.8m the previous year and at the top end of analysts' expectations. Growth was largely driven by continuing strong sales in its flu vaccine. Meanwhile, losses for the year were £19.6m, in line with expectations. Yesterday, shares in Powderject closed unchanged at 485p.

Source: Simon Bowers, *The Guardian*, 4 July 2001

Summary

This chapter covers a range of issues related to the ways in which organisations develop learning capacities which, in turn, enhance their ability to become market oriented. Organisational learning can basically be defined as the process of improving action through better knowledge and understanding. Two types of learning levels can be distinguished: single-loop learning that relates to a reactive type of learning and double-loop learning that corresponds to a more profound conceptual and proactive learning. A third type that has been identified is deutero learning that corresponds to the ability of learners to learn.

Different types of organisational systems will generate different types of learning. For example, a one-man institution will generate individual-based knowledge, whereas a bureaucratic system will generate organised, formalised knowledge. The development of shared mental models helps to form the link between organisational and individual learning. At the same time, top management's ability to foster an environment conducive to creative thinking and risk taking appears to develop better learning organisations, capable of being market oriented and better positioned in the increasingly competitive marketplace of the twenty-first century.

Chapter questions

1 What is organisational learning? What are its consequences?

2 What types of learning are traditionally identified? Is there a better type of learning?

3 How can individual learning be transferred at organisational level?

4 What is the role of organisational culture in the learning processes?

5 How is organisational memory organised? What is its role in organisational learning?

6 Why is unlearning so important?

7 Why is learning not straightforward?

8 What distinguishes market-based learning from organisational learning?

9 What are the links between organisational learning and market orientation (refer also to Chapter 1)?

9 Measuring marketing performance

Introduction

There is currently much debate in marketing about the measurement of perform-ance. Marketers are being pressurised by top management to become more accountable for their expenditures and activities. Accountancy has always been pre-eminent in assessing organisational performance, using well-developed and well-used financial performance measures. It is now becoming increasingly impor-tant that marketers develop measures of effectiveness that will sit side by side with financial performance measures. Authors such as Doyle (2000) and Highson *et al.* (2001) are beginning to address this growing area of concern for marketers and businesses in general.

One of the most controversial areas in marketing is understanding how market-ing actions affect performance. With the opening of the debate on measuring levels of market orientation in the last two decades, the focus on the effects of such orientation on organisational performance has sharpened. Unlike accounting, marketing does not have standardised techniques for measuring performance. For this reason, in many organisations, marketing expenditure and budgets tend to have arbitrary allocations, relegating the importance of marketing to a lower level. Marketing expenditures often do not produce direct results that can be measured within a short space of time; for example, an advertising campaign may result in better sales performance after a ten-month time lag. However, an organisation's accounts are presented annually and generally fail to reflect such time lags.

Marketing measures that are commonly used include market share, return on investment and brand equity, although organisations are now using many more measures and these vary according to the sectors in which the organisation is oper-ating. This chapter will begin by looking at the role of financial analysis and will then look at the role of marketing metrics. As the area of marketing metrics is wide and not fully developed, there are still likely to be more questions than answers. However, some comprehensive measurement models are presented.

The role of financial analysis

For the purposes of disseminating information to shareholders and stakeholders, organisations produce annual accounts that include financial flows, profits and losses and balance sheets. Many accounts also contain information on market shares, geographic segmentation and regional segmentation. Recently there has been considerable interest in understanding the use of particular sets of data pertaining to marketing. These can be the measurement of brand equity, customer satisfaction, customer loyalty and retention, share of voice and marketing spend. Some of these measures are discussed later in this chapter.

Interestingly, not many organisations utilise the full range of marketing metrics for measuring their marketing performance, but stick to traditional financial measures. These measures do help in understanding the position of an organisation. Senior managers can use previous years' data to project possible trends (particularly if the results are all available in the same format). In most cases, the analyses are based on financial ratios. These accounting ratios are used in the interpretation of financial statements and are most useful when comparing different time periods, which can be helpful in identifying trends and understanding strengths and weaknesses. If, for example, inventory levels are high in a balance sheet, does this imply that there is a peak where the organisation is anticipating a surge in demand for products, or does it imply falling sales? Financial ratios are often the backbone of organisational reporting and have been used for a very long time. Some of the ratios most commonly used are outlined below.

Profit ratios

Profit ratios measure management's overall effectiveness in generating profits from the available resources. If an organisation is highly efficient in its markets, it should exhibit a high level of profitability. It is useful to compare an organisation's profitability against that of its major competitors in its industry. Such a comparison shows whether the organisation is operating more or less efficiently than its rivals. Over a period of time, any changes in profitability will indicate whether the organisation is improving its performance or not. A variety of ratios are used to measure profitability:

Gross profit margin

This is calculated by first deducting production expenses from the sales revenue, to determine the gross profit. The gross profit is then divided by the sales revenue. The amount remaining can then be allocated to cover overheads.

$$\text{Gross profit margin} = \frac{\text{Sales revenue} - \text{cost of goods sold}}{\text{Sales revenue}}$$

Net profit margin

This is calculated by dividing the net profit by the sales revenue. Net profit is the profit after production costs and overheads have been deducted, but before the deduction of tax. (Note that this is normally known as PBIT – profit before interest and taxes; some companies may also calculate PAIT – profit after interest and taxes.) The net profit margin is important because organisations need to make profits to survive and for future investment to develop and grow markets. They also need profits to pay dividends to shareholders who support the company.

$$\text{Net profit margin} = \frac{\text{Net profit}}{\text{Sales revenue}}$$

Return on total assets

This ratio measures the profit earned on the employment of the organisation's assets. It is calculated by dividing the net income by total assets. Net income is the profit after preferred dividends (those set by contract) have been paid. Total assets includes both current and fixed assets.

$$\text{Return on total assets} = \frac{\text{Net income}}{\text{Total assets}}$$

Return on shareholders' equity

This ratio measures the percentage of profit earned on the shares held in the organisation. Organisations that are attractive to shareholders are those that can maximise this ratio. The greater the return, the greater the amount of money that can be distributed to individual shareholders:

$$\text{Return on shareholders' equity} = \frac{\text{Profits after taxes}}{\text{Total equity}}$$

Liquidity ratios

Liquidity refers to cash and realisable assets that are available to an organisation for immediate use. The lower the liquidity, the greater the danger of an organisation not being able to meet its immediate cash commitments or tactical marketing requirements. It is important to note that the Quick ratio is more useful in determining the ready realisable assets and cash available to an organisation as quite often it is difficult for an organisation to speedily dispose of stocks (included in the current ratio). The ratios used to calculate liquidity are:

$$\text{Current ratio} = \frac{\text{Current assets}}{\text{Current liabilities}}$$

$$\text{Quick ratio} = \frac{\text{Current assets – stock}}{\text{Current liabilities}}$$

$$\text{Inventory to net working capital} = \frac{\text{Inventory}}{\text{Current assets} - \text{current liabilities}}$$

Leverage ratios

Leverage ratios, also known as gearing, show the level of an organisation's debt in relation to its assets. This ratio is of interest to shareholders and potential investors since the level of gearing affects shareholder returns. Efficient use of debt can often enhance returns, whereas inefficient use of loans and debt can seriously reduce shareholder returns. An example of this is the recent demise of Enron.

Organisations often need to raise money, or increase existing borowings, to fund further investments in marketing or new product development. They can raise funds in the marketplace either through loans or share issues. Leverage ratios include:

$$\text{Debt to assets} = \frac{\text{Total debt}}{\text{Total assets}}$$

$$\text{Long-term debt to equity} = \frac{\text{Long-term debt}}{\text{Total equity}}$$

Activity ratios

These ratios reflect the efficiency with which the organisation is dealing in the marketplace. High inventory levels could signify flagging sales, which could indicate poor distribution or lack of advertising or sales efforts. Activity ratios include:

$$\text{Inventory turnover} = \frac{\text{Sales}}{\text{Inventory}}$$

$$\text{Fixed asset turnover} = \frac{\text{Sales}}{\text{Fixed assets}}$$

$$\text{Average collection period} = \frac{\text{Accounts receivable}}{\text{Average daily sales}}$$

As you can see, many of these measures incorporate sales data, so the performance of marketing may be assessed to some degree. Measures related to marketing, however, are complex and varied and the next section will look at some of the measures that can be used for assessing marketing performance.

Marketing metrics

As the marketplace gets more turbulent and competitive, organisations are forced to balance their books and therefore marketing expenditure tends to increase or decrease depending on revenue streams (McCullough 2000). Marketing budgets are based on perceptions that marketing is an expense and it is difficult to assess its impact on profitability. There are a number of drawbacks if only accounting measures are used for measuring performance:

- Accounts can be difficult to interpret, even if accurate financial data are reported.
- The performance ratios outlined above are affected by industry-related factors (Miller and Toulouse 1986).
- Accounting measures can vary from organisation to organisation, depending on the protocols adopted.
- Organisations can and do either overestimate or underestimate earnings for tax purposes and for other reasons.
- Even large accounting firms have been known to cross the fine line between honest and dishonest reporting of accounts.

Financial performance measures are clearly important for organisations, but they tend only to show the economic dimensions of performance and perhaps neglect the organisation's other, more important goals (Venkatramen and Ramanujam 1986).

An organisation's performance measurement system strongly affects the behaviour of people both inside and outside the organisation. Organisations need to use measures derived from their strategies and capabilities. Unfortunately, many organisations espouse strategies about customer relationships, core competencies and organisational capabilities, but only measure performance using financial measures. Financial measures are valuable in summarising the easily measurable economic consequences of actions already taken. Performance measures indicate whether an organisation's strategy and its implementation and execution are contributing to bottom-line improvement. Moreover, performance measurements provide managers with better insights into planning, control, and improving organisational performance. Not all organisations are able to translate improvement in customer satisfaction or quality, for example, into bottom-line financial results. Although financial measures have shortcomings, they are still important to all stakeholders (Kaplan and Norton 1996). The most commonly used performance measures include financial measures such as return on investment, net profit, liquidity and leverage ratios, gross and net contribution margins, market share, sales growth and turnover. There are three major marketing attributes that performance measures should include:

1 *The adaptability or innovativeness of an organisation* (Bhargava *et al.* 1994, Walker and Ruekert 1987). Measuring adaptability reflects an organisation's understanding of the changing environment and its ability to create and market new products or innovations.

2 *The effectiveness of particular marketing strategies.* This analysis helps to foster a clearer understanding of the competitive stances adopted by the organisation.

3 *Efficiency in the execution of particular strategies.* The efficiency with which an organisation executes particular strategies needs to be understood and measured (Bonoma and Clark 1988, Walker and Ruekert 1987, Drucker 1974).

It is clear that marketing performance measures will differ in the services and manufacturing sectors and from one industry sector to another. Each of the key measurement areas is illustrated in Figure 9.1 and explored below.

Adaptability

An organisation must demonstrate adaptability to the changing environment to be continually successful in the marketplace. Changes in the environment could include:

■ changing customer preferences and tastes;
■ demographic shifts;
■ new offerings from competitors;
■ changing cultural and social dimensions;
■ changing technology;
■ changing service expectations.

To respond to such changes, an organisation needs to measure its successes in the following areas:

■ new product success rates;
■ new service delivery success rates;

Figure 9.1 Key performance measures

- the number of patents registered;
- the number of trademarks registered;
- percentage of income derived from new products or services in the last five years;
- success of new products and services compared with the competition;
- the number of research and development projects under way;
- the number of new brands acquired;
- assessment of changing pricing levels.

Efficiency

Efficiency measures in marketing reflect whether an organisation is using its asset base to the best of its ability. Efficiency may have different meanings for different organisations. A fast-food restaurant, for example, may find that it measures its efficiency in terms of service levels and rate of turnover of clients, whereas a manufacturing company may look at its research and development activities and capacity utilisation. The range of measures is therefore quite wide, as this list shows:

- capacity utilisation;
- research and development productivity;
- percentage employee turnover;
- turnover per employee;
- distribution levels and efficiency;
- inventory levels;
- speed of service delivery;
- IT efficiency;
- productivity per employee;
- return on investment (ROI);
- product availability (in different geographic locations).

Effectiveness

Every organisation needs to assess the effectiveness of its marketing strategies. Again, measures of effectiveness vary from industry to industry and from organisation to organisation. However, some broad measures can be put forward. These are:

- unit sales;
- market shares by unit and volume;
- market share by segment;
- number of customers;
- customer loyalty;
- customer complaints;
- relative quality;
- relative value.

In addition to these measures of effectiveness, it is also important to understand branding equity measures, such as:

- customer preferences;
- purchase intent;
- brand value;
- brand strength;
- level of trust in the brand;
- brand image.

Brand equity

Brand equity is the 'added value endowed by the brand to the product' (Farquhar 1989). The quality of information about a brand, its perceived value and its general standing within a local or global marketplace help to determine its strength (see Chapter 5). The success of a particular brand provides an organisation with profits and the potential to gain future profits, thereby creating an asset which has a value. The degree of success that can be achieved can be assessed by understanding the level of brand equity achieved, taking into consideration the effect of advertising (Ambler 1997). As advertising effects are rarely immediate, advertising expenditure may show a poor performance level in terms of sales in the short term. However, the marketing activity could boost the brand equity, resulting in a *future* growth in sales and profits. These future profits could be generated by the level of memory and positive image created in the mind of the consumer. The issue of building equity is further complicated by the growth of the Internet and mobile communications. Boulding *et al.* (1993) consider that the level of trust associated with a brand is also important and may be regarded as:

- part of the brand–consumer relationship and therefore brand equity;
- dynamic and non-linear, slow to build and fast to destroy;
- both an antecedent and a consequence of success (this needs to be considered carefully when assessing performance levels);
- a habit?

Towards an integrated model

All the measures discussed above are useful in analysing an organisation's performance. Organisations may be better or worse than their competitors in some areas of performance. The changing nature of measuring performance as a result of the development of the Internet and mobile technologies also needs to be taken into account as the Internet often augments the marketing strategies adopted by an organisation. Specific measures here include **customer retention**, which is closely associated with customer satisfaction; **sales improvement**, which is closely associated with profitability of online marketing development; and **image enhancement**, which is the focus of current Internet marketing development. These measures are based on the understanding that effective marketing activities are characterised by a service orientation, a drive towards innovation, a focus on quality and a reasonable achievement in return on investment (ROI). If an organisation's presence on the Internet is effective, it will encourage consumers to visit and explore its website until they find what they need. Website visits and repeat visits can be encouraged in a number of ways, including sponsoring online contests, offering free sample products and providing value-added, Internet-based customer services.

Given that measuring marketing performance is generally fraught with difficulties and that there are few general standards to which to adhere, it may be useful to try to integrate financial and non-financial measures. This will eventually lead to a greater understanding of why an organisation may be able to achieve a good return on investment (Lenskold 2002). The general argument underlying the model for maximising resources shown in Figure 9.2 is that the ROI measure can account for all costs and complete customer value can be analysed, which enables

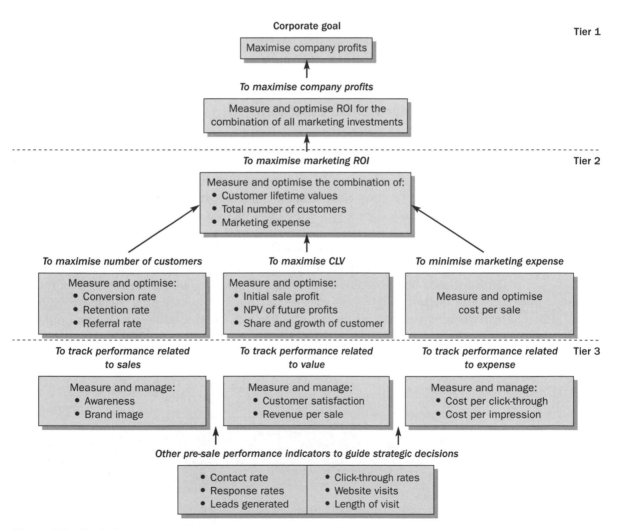

Figure 9.2 Maximising resources

the organisation to prioritise marketing investments and maximise profits. The measures in the model are divided into three tiers, as shown in Figure 9.2. It is important for organisations to assess the returns that marketing investments can provide in terms of profit. These investments could be in advertising, customer retention or public relations.

The three key measures used in the model are as follows:

- *Customer lifetime value (CLV).* This indicates the profits that accrue from customer transactions as a result of marketing investments. Increasing transactions have a positive impact on the ROI. This measure also helps with allocation of resources for target marketing and with the development of customer retention and new customer procurement strategies. The use of technology and customer relationship management (CRM) software helps to determine the value of each customer, both currently and in the future. Figure 9.3 shows a process for measuring CLV.
- *The total number of customers acquired through marketing investments.* The ROI will continue to improve unless the costs of acquiring new customers exceed the costs of retaining old ones.
- *The marketing expense incurred to generate returns.* As profits grow and the expenditure ratio lessens, the ROI will improve.

Three-tier performance indicators

These indicators are discussed at length above, and the list can be quite varied, depending on the sector in which an organisation is operating. By monitoring how these indicators eventually lead to greater sales, the links between Tier 3 and Tier 1 in Figure 9.2 can be ascertained. It is important to note that measures such as customer satisfaction or the number of hits on a website do not automatically translate into profit generation. Marketing managers therefore need to be cautious and use them for improving and modifying marketing strategies rather than using them as performance indicators per se. The incorrect use of indicators was amply demonstrated by the recent burst of the dot.com bubble. Online measures such as hits and click-through rates were used to justify pushing up the share prices of many companies which subsequently failed to provide adequate returns on investment. For this reason, marketing measures should be carefully evaluated to see

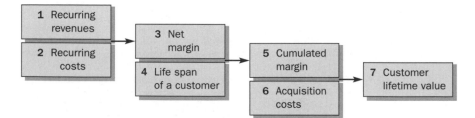

Figure 9.3 Seven-step process to measure customer lifetime value
Source: Bacuvier *et al.* (2001)

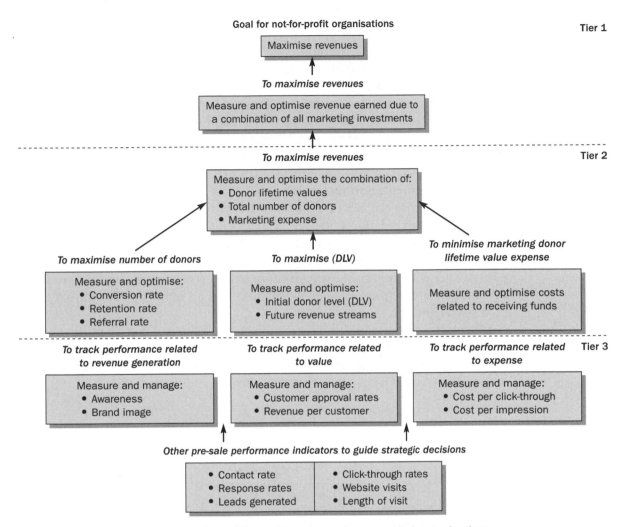

Figure 9.4 Maximising revenues for not-for-profit and non-governmental organisations

how effectively they contribute to the organisation's goal of generating profits. It may be perfectly acceptable for not-for-profit and non-governmental organisations to use the model and replace certain measures, as shown in Figure 9.4.

The discussion so far shows that the use of marketing measures is becoming an essential component in understanding the effectiveness of marketing strategies. However, it is always difficult to separate cause and effect in marketing as marketing strategies often have effects in the longer term. It is also difficult to devise a composite set of measures for any organisation. The measures depend on the sector in which the organisation operates and on its particular characteristics in terms of operations management and customer retention strategies. Often organisations utilise different types of software for gauging customer contact. As technology develops, it is likely that the use of marketing measures will become more complex, rather than simpler.

Recent research into consumers' perceptions of e-service quality (Yang and Jun 2002) showed that Internet purchasers valued reliability, access, ease of use, personalisation, security and credibility, in this order. On the other hand, Internet non-purchasers valued (again in order) security, responsiveness, ease of use, reliability, availability and personalisation. This demonstrates the need to interweave technology-based measures with the standard measures used by organisations. Measures may also need to be tailored to the customer segments being addressed.

The key to fully understanding the lifetime value of a specific customer and to applying the most appropriate customer management strategy is segmentation (Bacuvier *et al.* 2001). Business organisations should aim to adopt a simple and operational segmentation methodology that can be readily used by operational managers and that can discriminate sufficiently by customer value (Doyle 2000). The selected segmentation dimensions should discriminate either on the revenue side (for example, usage intensity and behaviour) or on the cost side (for example, products purchased, channel used, intensity of customer care usage and service levels). This will provide the organisation with a complete map of the 'wells' of value creation and 'pits' of value destruction and an understanding of why they exist (see Figure 9.5).

Making clear connections between customer behaviour and customer demographic profiles is critical to organisations interested in keeping customers and increasing their profitability. The implementation of an efficient profiling/segmentation methodology must address the following issues (Thearling 1999, Wundermann 2001):

Figure 9.5 Using customer segmentation and customer satisfaction measures for designing and implementing targeted marketing mix strategies

- robust transaction data, properly collected and updated;
- data-warehousing capabilities for capturing and storing the data (databases);
- an associated retrieval and data delivery system;
- data-mining tools that reflect the unique nature of the business;
- detailed costing information, including the process cost and the physical product or service cost;
- a meaningful business model that clearly represents the company–customer interaction and the fluctuations in the life cycles of both customers and businesses.

The satisfaction measurement has to be specific to each of the organisation's targeted customer segments because the needs and wants of each customer segment are usually different, as are the quality standards they expect of the offered products and services.

Not only do organisations need to benchmark their results after the completion of the customer survey, but they must also evaluate the process they used to obtain these results. Such data must be as accurate as possible, especially if staff bonuses or other incentives are triggered by achieving satisfaction improvement targets (Chambers 2000). It is also important to disseminate the results of customer satisfaction measurement to all organisational levels. Little action will be taken to improve customer satisfaction if employees do not know enough about these results or their implications (Hill 2001). The amount of feedback provided to employees will also send messages about how important the customer survey is to the organisation.

Thorough research of the specific sources of customer satisfaction and dissatisfaction and of the importance attached to these by customers will indicate areas of excellence and areas where improvement is necessary in the organisation's strategy (Figure 9.2). On the basis of this research, a marketing mix strategy targeted to specific customer segments can be designed and implemented. The issue of customer value and equity (Rust *et al*. 2000) is discussed in Chapter 2. The key components are:

- *Value equity*. This is customers' perceptions of value based on perceptions of quality, price and convenience.
- *Brand equity*. This is based on customers' perceptions of a brand that are not explained by an organisation's objectives. These perceptions can be emotional, subjective and irrational.
- *Retention equity*. This results from customers choosing to do business with an organisation. Retention-building activities and repeat purchases help to build retention equity.

The essential elements here are the various components driving customer equity. However, it is clear that creation of value, development of a brand and creation of retention equity have associated costs and these costs have to be recouped from the customer base, which contributes to satisfaction levels for a product or service.

Understanding measurement within the global context

Organisations operating globally must be aware of a range of measurements that relate to their product or service offering. Organisations often measure their level of success in different countries through their relative market share in each country or the levels of distribution achieved. In some cases, the measures will include profit levels per product or service category. There is an argument that organisations ought to look at their global market share as a performance measure (Usinier 1999) so that competition is seen as being global right from the outset. This helps to prevent an organisation being too absorbed in its own market and helps it to be more aware of its position in relation to the competition. Performance measures can also be improved as a result of experience effects, in which case effective measures of performance could be as follows:

- *Scale effects*. Larger production scales on a global basis can result in decreased costs. The consequent increase in profits could help to improve research and development expenditure. An example of this is the rapid growth of the Samsung brand on a global basis (see also the next case study on Chupa Chups, a global brand).
- *A build-up of brand equity*. Brand image can be measured using a very wide range of variables, depending on the type of research carried out. For example, when Philips began its new campaign, 'Let's Make Things Better', it relied on measuring the impact of the advertisement by measuring the 'share of voice' it had gained in various countries around the world. Share of voice basically measures how easily the slogan can be recalled and awareness of the brand vis-à-vis Philips' main competitor, Sony. The measure of success in this instance is the growth of brand awareness through the slogan associated with the brand. The use of a standard brand slogan is being utilised by Philips to create a global brand which is easily recognised. In the middle of the 1990s Philips had a disparate brand image in different countries. The brand was associated with products ranging from light bulbs to televisions. The slogan is now being used to promote an image of innovation and quality.

CASE STUDY

FT

Sweet ambitions to tempt more takers

Branding a boiled sugar sweet on a stick takes an unusual amount of marketing imagination. The makers of Chupa Chups, the world's best-selling lollipop, have responded to the challenge recently by packaging the product in toys, in plastic dynamite sticks and hand grenades, in make-up kits and paint cans and in something called 'Jaws Pop' – described by the company magazine as a collection of 'cranky

crocodiles and shady sharks that reveal a Chupa Chups lollipop when the lever on their backs is moved'.

The family-owned Catalan company has had merchandising deals with Barbie dolls, the Simpsons, Pokémon and the Spice Girls. It has become adept at cheeky publicity stunts, such as sending 'the first lollipop into space' with Russian astronauts in 1995.

Its efforts have helped the brand spread to 170 countries. Now the company's goal is to transform Chupa Chups into 'the Coca-Cola of lollipops' – as ubiquitous, and as ingrained in the dietary habits of teenagers, as the sugary, carbonated drink.

For a while, a strategy built around a flawless distribution system, international expansion and zany marketing seemed to work: Chupa Chups' consolidated sales during the 1990s grew at an annual compound rate of 27 per cent, to €424m (¥271m) in 2000, when the sugar confectionery industry as a whole was growing at a mere 2–3 per cent a year.

Last year, however, sales fell for the first time in more than a decade, to €414m. The company's vertiginous expansion came to a halt after a merchandising deal with Pokémon went sour. Children tired of the Japanese cartoons, leaving Chupa Chups with a lot of unsold Pokémon lollies.

Some executives also believe that the prolific marketing department was out of control. 'Lollipops in [plastic] hand grenades was completely over the top,' one executive confides. Had Chupa Chups, a household name in Spain, with its flowery, red and yellow logo designed by Salvador Dali, mistaken its impressive sales abroad for the belief that it had established a powerful inter-national brand?

David Hensley, a consultant with Futurebrand in the UK, says companies that are expanding rapidly often confuse strong sales with brand recognition. 'Chupa Chups has a great distribution network. It has been the key to its international success. But what youngsters are buying are lollipops. They are not necessarily choosing Chupa Chups over other lollipops. It takes a lot of time and advertising to elevate a commodity into a brand.'

Xavier Bernat, the current chairman, whose father founded Chupa Chups 44 years ago, rejects this judgment. Mr Bernat believes he has built Chupa Chups into an internationally recognised brand. By marketing in the club scene and in clothes stores, he says, he has expanded his 'target market' of seven to 12-year-olds in the past three years to include teenagers, who now buy more than half of his lollipops. In Russia, where Chupa Chups set up a factory 10 years ago, the company sells 1bn lollipops a year.

Mr Bernat is also stretching the brand through licensing agreements with Unilever, which is producing Chupa Chups toothpaste and ice-cream, and with perfume and clothes manufacturers. 'Chupa Chups is not a passing fad,' he says. 'It is a growing business.' Nevertheless, Mr Bernat concedes that most of his efforts have been devoted to building the distribution network and expanding overseas. Licensing deals bring in only marginal income. Distribution, he says, must precede brand recognition. 'Chupa Chups has to be everywhere. In clubs, petrol stations, cinemas, kiosks and all kinds of stores. It must be instantly available, like Coca-Cola, always an arm's length away from desire.'

The question is whether Mr Bernat will succeed in making Chupa Chups as desirable as Coke. Breakthroughs come from the most unexpected quarters. When Johan Cruyff, former coach of Barcelona football club, was told to stop smoking after a heart attack, Chupa Chups sent him lollipops to help combat his craving for cigarettes. Photos of Mr Cruyff sucking lollies on the trainer's bench sent Chupa Chups sales soaring in Catalonia. Since then, they have become popular among football players. Zinedine Zidane likes to chew them after training sessions. David Beckham was spotted with one during last month's World Cup in Japan.

'Celebrity suckers', as Chupa Chups likes to call them, have made it acceptable for adults to buy lollipops. But Chupa Chups' main customers remain children and teenagers, whose fickleness poses a particular challenge for a company intent on building an enduring brand.

Mary Peterkin, a brand consultant at Enterprise IG in London, says the key to success is to remain relevant to your customers. 'Competition from other confectioners and changes in fashion trends pose particular difficulties for companies that market to teenagers. Levi Strauss is an example of a company that lost sight of its customers' needs. Drinks and cosmetics companies are constantly reinventing themselves to keep abreast of fashion trends. Chupa Chups will also have to reinvent its product to remain relevant to each new generation of teenagers.'

She thinks that Chupa Chups has a fighting chance. 'The company is in tune with the way young people think,' Ms Peterkin says. 'That is a good platform to build on.'

Source: Crawford 2002

Consider the key measures of performance that could be useful for Chupa Chups as it endeavours to become a global brand.

Measuring the impact of promotions

Shorter-term performance measures depend on understanding the impact of promotions on customers. Promotions can be based on:

- *Price differentiation* – either raising or lowering prices and considering the impact on sales.
- *Offering gifts or two products for the price of one* – this has now become a common strategy for promoting products ranging from magazines to vitamin tablets.
- *Trial and sampling* – where small samples of a product are distributed so that consumers can try them. This type of activity is more suitable for items such as perfumes and food.
- *Competitions* – promotions can be undertaken through quizzes or other competitions. Increasingly, promotions are being offered via the Internet through 'pop-ups' and banner advertising.

The types of measures which can be used to ascertain the impact of these promotional activities are shown in Table 9.1.

Table 9.1 Objectives by types of promotion

Consumer promotions	*Commercial promotions*
Trial	Visit to new outlets
First purchase	Customer retention
Repurchase	Visit frequency increase
Loyalty	First purchase growth
Reduced prices	Increases in average basket price
Increase of quantity consumed	
Purchase frequency increase	
Trial of a new variety	
Distribution promotions	*Network promotions*
List of new products	Increase of quantity sold
Stock	Gain in distribution presence
Facing increase	Introduction of new products
Point of purchase display	Increase in size or range
Participation to advertising	Reselling actions

Source: Ingold (1995)

Measuring environmental performance

Many organisations, either through choice or coercion as a result of legislation, are now beginning to measure their environmental performance and incorporate good environmental practices in their marketing strategies. They measure environmental performance using environmental performance indicators (EPIs). In many cases, organisations go through crisis orientation, then move towards process orientation and then on to chain orientation (Scherpereel *et al.* 2001). During the crisis-oriented stage, organisations tend to be penalised for non-compliance with environmental legislation through a system of fines and penalties. They then try to demonstrate improvement in legal compliance to their shareholders by avoiding such penalties. In the process-oriented stage, control of environmental risks and cost-efficient reduction of pollution and waste go beyond legislative requirements. Organisations at this stage have comprehensive and systematic environmental management systems, which are measured and reported in the organisation's accounts. In the chain-oriented stage, environmental performance measures are extended along the value chain and social performance measures are also included. Some of these are (Spencer-Cooke 1998):

- human rights;
- labour conditions (including forced and child labour, collective bargaining);
- supply chain and overseas suppliers (including fair trade and factory monitoring);
- technology transfer and investments in emerging economies;
- trade with oppressive regimes;
- defence and weapons;
- alcohol, tobacco, gambling and pornography;
- animal testing;
- philanthropy and volunteerism;
- downsizing and restructuring.

Comprehensive guidelines for adopting environmental measures are shown in Table 9.2.

Table 9.3 shows the indicators of performance outlined by the World Business Council for Sustainable Development (WBCSD) (Lehni 1998). The seven elements defining eco-efficient improvement are:

- reduced material intensity;
- reduced energy intensity;
- reduced dispersion of toxic substances;
- enhanced recyclability;
- maximised use of renewables;
- extended product life;
- increased service intensity.

Table 9.2 Measuring environmental effects

Environmental orientation	Related EPIs	Examples of indicators
Crisis-oriented stage	Output indicators directed at compliance	Environmental discharges to air and water, efficiency of pollution treatment equipment, quantity and disposal conditions of waste per type
	Environmental management indicators directed at compliance	Number and frequency of complaints, fines and penalties, their nature and impact intensity, extent and effectiveness of corresponding corrective programmes
Process-oriented stage	Eco-efficiency indicators at the company level for inputs (resource conservation)	Energy, water, material (raw material/packaging) consumption efficiency related to product volume, number of employees or financial returns per category
	Eco-efficiency indicators at the company level for outputs (impact minimisation, pollution prevention, valorisation)	Emissions per substance/effect/media concerned, waste by type/originating activity/production quantity
	Environmental accounting indicators directed at the environmental management system	Environmental expenditures, costs resulting from environmental non-compliance and litigation, environmental costs and savings avoidance of the current year and previous years
		Degree of specific codes, internal policies or standards, number of training programmes and participants, improvements achieved, return on investment for environmental improvement projects, number of levels of management with specific environmental responsibilities, community relations (complaints, negative press reports, formal reports)
Chain-orientated stage	Output indicators on a product chain level	Environmentally harmful substances in the product chain (toxic dispersion) using life-cycle assessment (LCA)
	Input indicators on a product chain level	Materials intensity with the idea of closing material loops through re-use, recycling, product durability, resource conservation and energy intensity along the chain (including extraction/supply and use phases)
	Social performance indicators	
		Employment generated, labour productivity (value added to the national GDP/number of employees), relationship between employee and company (personnel fluctuation rate, average duration of contract), education to build and maintain human capital (time invested for education and training), disabling illness, income level and distribution, investments made outside the company in benefit for the community, sustainable metrics

Source: Scherpereel *et al.* (2001)

Table 9.3 Gathering environmental information

Indicator	Unit	Measurement method	Potential data source
Greenhouse gas (GHG) emissions Amount of GHG emissions to air from fuel combustion, process reactions and treatment processes including CO_2, CH_4, N_2O, HFCs, PFCs and SF_6 (excluding CHG emissions released in generation of purchased electricity)	in metric tons of CO_2 equivalents	– List of greenhouse gases: Kyoto Protocol, Annex A – Global warming potentials: IPCC, Climate Change 1995, Second Assessment Report – Transformation factors for fuels: from fuel carbon content e.g. Responsible Care: Health Safety and Environmental Reporting Guidelines, CEFIC November 1998, page 311. GHG emissions from process reactions and treatment processes are calculated/ estimated using specific knowledge of processes, waste composition and treatment efficiency	Cost reports Fuel invoices Plant survey EHS records Estimation or calculation

Note: Businesses and their stakeholders may find it useful to provide additional information for some generally applicable indicators (e.g. Energy Consumption indicator for total energy consumption and energy consumption by specific sources such as electricity, fuel-based, and non-fuel based consumption; Greenhouse Gas Emissions in total CO_2 equivalents and specific CO_2, CH_4, N_2O, HFCs, PFCs and SF_6 emissions).

POTENTIAL GENERALLY APPLICABLE INDICATORS
In this table we list indicators that might soon become generally applicable indicators if current efforts to develop common global agreement on measurement methods are successful.

VALUE INDICATORS

Indicator	Unit	Potential measurement method	Potential data source

Net profit/earnings/income	in USD, Euro, Yen or company's usual reporting currency	Net sales minus all expenses for the period including: cost of goods sold; selling; general and administrative expenses; technology expenses; R&D costs; amortisation and adjustment of intangible assets; restructuring and special charges; interest expenses; other expenses; income tax
		  International Accounting Standards Committee (IASC)
		  Generally Accepted Accounting Principles (GAAP)
			Financial reports

ENVIRONMENTAL INFLUENCE INDICATORS

Indicator	Unit	Potential measurement method	Potential data source
Acidification emissions to air Amount of acid gases and acid mists emitted to air (including NH_3, HCl, HF, NO_2, SO_2 and sulfuric acid mists) from fuel combustion, process reactions and treatment processes	in metric tons SO_2 equivalents	– List of acids: ICI: Environmental Burden The ICI Approach, 1997 – Acidification Potentials: Heijungs et al., CML University of Leiden, 1992; and Hauschild and Wenzel, Chapman & Hall, London, 1997	Plant surveys EHS reports Estimation or calculation
Total waste Total amount of substances or objects destined for disposal	in metric tons	Definitions of waste and disposal: Basel Convention, 1992: Definitions and Annex IV	Plant surveys EHS reports Estimation or calculation

Source: Lehni (1998)

Eco-efficiency calls for business to achieve more value from lower inputs of materials and energy and to reduce emissions. It involves all areas of a business and is as relevant to marketing and product development as it is to manufacturing or distribution. The range of possibilities outlined here demonstrates the pervasive nature of eco-efficiency. The WBCSD also recommends that the indicators should:

■ be relevant and meaningful with respect to protecting the environment and human health and/or improving the quality of life;
■ inform decision making to improve the performance of the organisation;
■ recognise the inherent diversity of business;
■ support benchmarking and monitoring over time;
■ be clearly defined, measurable, transparent and verifiable;
■ be understandable and meaningful to identified stakeholders;
■ be based on an overall evaluation of an organisation's operations, products and services, especially focusing on all those areas that are under direct management control;
■ recognise relevant and meaningful issues related to upstream (for example, suppliers) and downstream (for example, product use) aspects of an organisation's activities.

Developing appropriate measures

The discussion so far shows the range and scope of measures that can be adopted in marketing. As technology evolves and as even the smaller companies begin to compete in world markets, the range of measures that can be adopted can seem quite complex and bewildering. This section therefore tries to assess what are the best types of measures for different businesses to adopt.

When choosing appropriate performance measures for an organisation, they should be divided into the following categories:

■ *Strategic*. These are used to measure the overall performance of an organisation. They could be key measures such as market share and return on investment, and could include market share in geographic regions and the overall effectiveness of branding strategies. They should also include measures of the eco-efficiency of the organisation's products as this is becoming increasingly important in advertising the 'green' credentials of an organisation.
■ *Tactical*. These could include short-term measures to improve customer satisfaction, loyalty rates and promotional effects.

The measures adopted for each area of an organisation may vary according to the type of business activity undertaken. When selecting and developing measures, it is useful to adopt a screening procedure to assess the acceptability, suitability and feasibility of the proposed measures (Johnson and Scholes 2002) – see Figure 9.6.

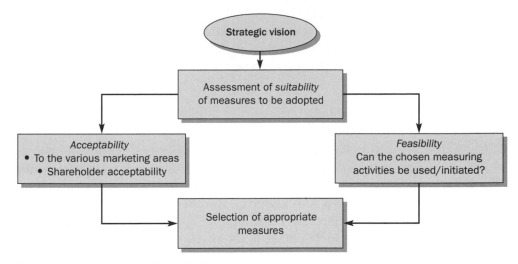

Figure 9.6 A framework for selecting marketing measures

Source: Adapted from Johnson and Scholes (2002)

Suitability

An assessment of the most suitable performance measures that could be adopted for a particular organisation is likely to be based on the following factors:

- The industry sector in which the organisation operates.
- The service or product orientation of the organisation.
- Whether the organisation is a commercial enterprise, or a not-for-profit or non-governmental organisation.
- The level of technology used for automatic measurement. For example, transactions can be recorded automatically on the Internet and customer transactions are recorded in a database when loyalty cards are used. These records can subsequently be used for data mining.
- The strategic vision of the organisation. For some organisations rates of return may be paramount whereas for others, such as NGOs, the emphasis could be on the rates of consumer awareness or the level of funds generated.
- Whether the measure chosen is likely to be valuable in the long run and whether trends can be ascertained.
- Whether the measures chosen can be used to benchmark against competitors.

Once suitability has been assessed, the proposed measures can then be screened by considering acceptability and feasibility.

Acceptability

Are these measures acceptable to the various stakeholders? Do they make sense and do they actually measure the right areas and issues? If measures are adopted that really are not acceptable to the individuals developing the strategies, the outcome will be fudged or anomalous results will occur. The measures adopted must also demonstrate something tangible to the various stakeholders and be in line with their expectations. Measures such as brand equity are often undertaken by advertising agencies and these must be acceptable and meaningful to marketing personnel.

Feasibility

This tests whether it is practical and useful to adopt the chosen measures. For example, an organisation must have the correct software for automatic measurement of customer contact, especially if it is introducing customer relationship management (CRM) strategies. Has the organisation enough resources to carry out brand equity research through an agency? Does it have systems in place with retailers to obtain details of revenues generated at point of sale through electronic point of sale (EPOS) systems?

The grid shown in Figure 9.7 is a useful tool for carrying out the screening process when selecting marketing measures.

Chosen measure	*Suitability* of measure for the required purposes	*Acceptability* to key functions and stakeholders	*Feasibility* and resource availability	Can the chosen measure be used for *benchmarking*?

Figure 9.7 Grid for assessing marketing measures

Summary

This chapter outlines some of the key measures that can be used in marketing. The use of measures is as much an art as it is science. Organisations are obliged to publish some measures, such as financial measures, according to the standards laid down by accounting authorities and to fulfill the legal requirements of the countries in which they operate. Organisations are not, as yet, obliged to publish measures of marketing performance; however many are now beginning to show these in their reports. The chapter offers some practical guidelines on adopting measures and on assessing their possible effectiveness through a better return on investment. However, other measures may be more appropriate for NGOs and not-for-profit enterprises. It is impossible to list all the measures that could be adopted as each organisation has its own systems and idiosyncracies. However, all organisations need to be aware of their ecological efficiency and its impact on lowering costs and promoting sustainable development. Given that measures are likely to vary from organisation to organisation, some systematic appraisal is necessary to determine the best possible and, above all, valuable and sensible outcomes for each organisation since these measures are important in determining strategy development and the vision for the organisation. In the twenty-first century, it is likely that marketing measures will become increasingly important in determining company performance and its strategic, ethical and environmental health.

Chapter questions

1 Why are marketing measures now considered to be an important aspect of an organisation's performance?

2 Assess the complexity of developing marketing measures for:
   – a manufacturing company;
   – a financial services company.

3 Why should marketers be concerned with using environmental measures of performance?

10 New perspectives in developing marketing strategies

Introduction: Coping with uncertainty

Over the last century, marketing has undergone many changes and is now a more complex discipline. When all the issues discussed in the previous chapters are taken into account, it is clear that marketing in the twenty-first century will need to incorporate many changes resulting from changes in demographics, values, technology, ethics and a more globalised society. Many marketing managers have to be able to deal with uncertainty and are beginning to find that the old paradigm of working through the marketing mix and the four Ps, although helpful when developing strategies, is no longer a sufficient framework for addressing the new challenges posed by changing markets and changing technologies. This chapter consolidates the material discussed in previous chapters within some new frameworks and perspectives proposed by eminent marketing authorities.

Moving away from the 4Ps

The product, price, promotion and place concept has helped, and continues to help, marketers to develop appropriate strategies for their products by taking into account the various elements of the marketing mix. However, with the recent changes in society and the changes created by the use of technology, it is becoming apparent that this is a somewhat limited view of the scope and nature of marketing. There is an argument that marketing needs to have a much higher profile in organisations and needs to embrace a much more holistic view. In order to do this successfully, organisations have to embrace the marketing concept more closely and to become more 'customer-centric' (Deshpande 1999). Figure 10.1 shows the gradual evolution in marketing towards customer orientation. Being customer oriented has never been as easy, or as difficult, as it is now. On the one hand, the growth of better information systems and the rapidity of data transfer

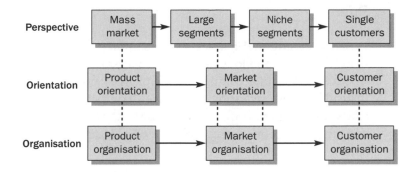

Figure 10.1 Growth of customer-centric marketing
Source: Sheth *et al*. (2000)

means that the range and breadth of customer information can be made available at any place, at any time, in a split second. On the other hand, even with this availability, being customer oriented is posing difficulties for many organisations. These difficulties are related to the development of better processes and organisational structures, as discussed in Chapters 5, 6, 7 and 8.

The marketing mix is no longer static and 'place' is no longer a fixed location. Similarly, promotion is no longer confined to a product but goes beyond to the brand that is being communicated. Pricing structures may vary according to time (seasonal and other factors) and global locations. There is even potential to tailor products to suit individuals. Given these factors, the 4Ps seem to be a straitjacket from which marketing needs to break free.

The advent of the Internet and wireless communications technologies offers a different perspective on the 4Ps. One of the key features of the new electronic communication media is consumers' ability to control both contact and content (Peters 1998, Kitchen 1999). Early research into the willingness of consumers to utilise technology in shopping behaviour reveals that the ability to control the presentation of product information has a strong influence on the involvement of computer mediated environment (CME) activities (Carson and Ogle 1996). This development emphasises the need for marketers to develop a proper online environment to allow their consumers to interface with their online presence. Within the virtual environment, both experiential (such as 'surfing') and goal-directed (such as 'searching') behaviours compete for consumers' attention (Hoffman and Novak 1996). Consumer surfing behaviour normally has different information needs from searching behaviour. Moreover, surfers and searchers tend to follow different navigation routes, which reflect their online behaviour patterns. Marketers need to possess some core competences in understanding these new patterns of consumer behaviour so that online marketing activities result in a degree of success.

Because of these new technological features, normal marketing practices need to be revisited and revised effectively (Hoffman and Novak 1996, Kitchen 1999). Information-intensive activities are transforming marketing and handing more power to consumers (Clark 1997, Griffith 1998). The possible impact on the 4Ps is shown below.

Price

Unlike conventional marketing development, Internet marketing can no longer focus solely on previous pricing mechanisms since the transparent nature of the Internet makes price comparison simple (Davenport 1995). It could be argued that, instead of the conventional strategies, competition should be based on the 'specialty axis' where online pricing reflects the degree of *added value* to online consumers (Hoffman and Novak 1996). It should not be based on a cost-plus approach to pricing.

Product

In the digital marketing environment, consumers can be intimately involved in online marketing processes (Clark 1997). In other words, the conventional concept of product development is no longer appropriate in the new environment. Instead, marketers should focus on developing *capabilities* to allow customers to mediate with online marketing processes (Bishop 1996). An example of this is the website Myski, where customers can interact with the company and request specific styles and sizes, or specify requirements in ski design (www.myski.com). Other companies allow choices in virtual dressing, where a customer's 'avatar' is used to try on clothes and ask for design modifications. This allows customer interaction on a global basis, not just on a localised basis such as going to the nearest shoe designer or tailor. It also augments the idea of co-creation in marketing (Sheth *et al.* 2000). Co-creation marketing involves both the marketer and the customer interacting in aspects of design, production and consumption of the product or service.

Place

As shown, the constraints of geographic location no longer exist on the Internet (Kitchen 1999). Rather, Internet marketers should focus on building a user-friendly online environment to enhance customer *experience* on the Internet (Peters 1998).

Promotion

With the advancement of telecommunications, large quantities of information can be transmitted inexpensively, multimedia objects can be transported efficiently and isolated computers can be networked globally. Consequently, the development of marketing communications needs to change from a traditional information-poor, emotional-rich focus to an information-rich, multidimensional focus. The educational, personal and entertainment aspects of marketing communications become useful catalysts to enable this transformation (Rohner 1998).

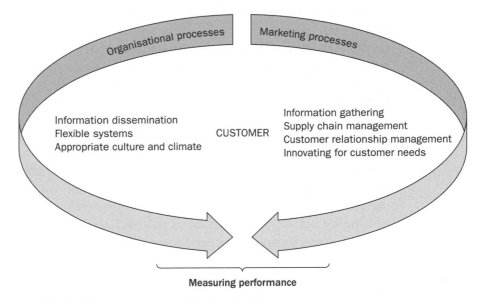

Information dissemination
Flexible systems
Appropriate culture and climate

CUSTOMER

Information gathering
Supply chain management
Customer relationship management
Innovating for customer needs

Measuring performance

Figure 10.2 Building customer-centric organisations
Source: Deshpande (1999)

These developments are all leading towards a more relational rather than trans-actional approach to marketing. The customer is part of the transactional process, not an idle recipient of a product augmented by promotion, price and directed to a location for purchase. There is now considerable interest in trying to understand how organisations can become customer-centric. Every organisation, whether it is profit oriented or not, has to be able to satisfy its customers. To become customer-centric, marketers need to be able to assess each customer individually and satisfy their needs either directly or through a third party. To develop a customer centric focus within organisations, a number of issues must be taken into account (see Figure 10.2).

Consumer behaviour

How do consumers really behave? The consumer is now faced with a wider range of services and products than at any other time. These services and products are not only available globally and locally, but they are also available on the Internet. Marketing is moving from a process of transactions with the consumer to relation-ship building with the consumer. Relationship building has implications for understanding brand loyalty and consumer behaviour. Are customers loyal or not? What are their behaviour patterns and how can consumer groups be categorised? How are segments really behaving, both globally and locally?

The life cycle concept has been built on understanding the gradual evolution and growth of mass markets. Markets are now increasingly fragmented, but fragments may have similarities across the globe. Organisations have to be aware, when carrying out market research, that they must understand consumer behaviour and product diffusion characteristics within globally fragmented markets. The consumer is not a simple, static demographic profile; the consumer changes and evolves over time, exhibiting a range of attitudes, behaviours, experiences and economic factors (Wyner 2002). Each variable offers marketers a chance to ascertain market behaviour that may translate into purchase of a particular product or service. In order to track this behaviour and understand the product or service purchasing propensity of a customer, an organisation must develop relationship marketing skills and needs to become customer-centric. This can be done through developing comprehensive databases and tracking changing behaviour patterns. At the same time, organisations need to be effective and efficient in their approaches to customers to ensure increased sales and better profits. Marketing productivity depends on efficiency (doing the right things) and effectiveness (doing things right), as shown in Figure 10.3.

The marketing function needs to create loyal and committed customers at low cost. If loyal customers are created at unacceptably high costs through loyalty programmes or promotional offers, organisations could create costly and ineffective customer bases (Seth *et al.* 2000). Family norms are changing (one parent families, extended families, second families, same gender families, singles, etc.) and gender roles are changing so the segmentation process becomes ever more complex. To add to the complexity, individuals may be able to straddle different professions. Lawyers in patenting law may be biochemists and doctors could specialise in medical law. Individuals also find that the distinction between home life and work life is blurring as the use of technology becomes prevalent. All this demands flexibility and a dynamic view of segmentation (Karin and Preiss 2002) – see Figure 10.4.

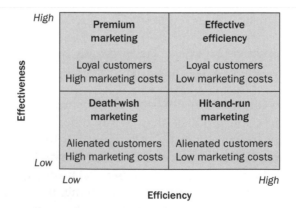

Figure 10.3 Marketing efficiency and effectiveness
Source: Sheth and Sisodia (1995)

TRADITIONAL APPROACH (Discrete variables)	NEW APPROACH (continuous variables)
Geographic	
Density (urban, suburban, rural)	Intensity and nature of activity
Climate (northern, southern)	Natural and artificial conditions
Demographic	
Chronological age (young/old)	Psychological age
Marital status (single/married)	Household arrangement
Gender (male/female)	Sexual self-image
Income (all major currencies)	Buying ability
Profession	Capability
Nationality	Communal affiliation
Religious affiliation	Level of orthodoxy
Home–work separation	Home–work combination
Psychographic	
Choice of lifestyle (hippy, swinger, straight)	Spectrum of lifestyle preferences
Pigeon-hole definition of personality (compulsive, gregarious, authoritarian, ambitious)	Apparent personality changes with circumstances
Behavioural	
Occasions (regular or special)	Perception of the occasion
Benefit (quality, service, economy, speed)	Benefit mix
User status (non, ex, potential, first time, regular)	Degree of user experience
Usage rate (light, medium, heavy)	Degree of usage rate
Loyalty status (non, medium, strong, absolute)	Satisfaction level
Readiness stage (unaware...intending to buy)	Ripeness level
Attitude toward product (enthusiastic...hostile)	Degree of openness toward offer

Figure 10.4 Modified segmentation model

Source: Karin and Preiss (2002)

As the case study on page 200 illustrates, understanding consumers is a complex process, especially when cultural aspects are included in the equation. In addition to this, there is currently much interest in ascertaining the role of emotions in marketing. Research on emotion and its role in consumer behaviour is in its infancy, yet emotions govern the way in which advertising content is developed and the motivations behind consumers' purchase decisions. Questions that arise concern the role of emotions in marketing exchanges and relationships, and their role in developing, maintaining or severing marketing relationships (Bagozzi *et al*. 1999). There are even bigger questions regarding the role of emotions in satisfaction levels and customer loyalty. In the twenty-first century, real progress in marketing will be made by customer-centric organisations that can truly understand how and why consumers behave in the way they do. At the same time, exploring how better-performing organisations behave is likely to be crucial to developing successful marketing strategies.

CASE STUDY

The cultural melting pot

As first generation immigrants are nearing retirement, subsequent generations are living in a multicultural and diverse environment. These second and third generation immigrants cannot be neatly categorised into clear-cut segments, but instead possess a wide range of beliefs, values and interests that have been influenced by both an Eastern and Western upbringing, with a predominantly Western backdrop.

So how do marketers segment this group or even individuals? This group comprises those who are native-born British–Asian or Asian–British (however patriotic one feels), who may be second, third or even fourth generation and have been raised within a British culture but have both Eastern and Western mindsets. Their affiliation can be strongly linked with mainstream Britain rather than with those who have emigrated from their country of origin.

Their views and beliefs are often a mixture of host and home country loyalties, and peers, family members, work colleagues and other relevant groups can influence their purchase decisions. However, a confusion or conflict may arise for marketers as they realise that the concept of 'situational identity' is very relevant to these segments.

This 'chameleon' behaviour of British Asians, being able to switch back and forth between roles in an ethnic culture and British mainstream culture, leads marketers to either reassess their generic marketing communications strategies or completely ignore these groups because of the perceived complications of segmenting this group.

Thus marketing activity is often targeted in a somewhat stereotypical way that makes a mockery of segmentation and doesn't really relate to the group's 'needs and wants' as marketing purports to do. Individuals who find their social identities at the intersections of at least two salient subcultures use their bi-cultural skills to bridge those worlds.

So where does the future lie for marketers? Can they continue merely to pay 'lip service' to this group's needs by segmenting in a manner that doesn't scratch the surface of the cultural diversity within the group? Or can they move away from the 'generic marketing and cultural melting pot' and dig deeper to find differences and similarities, and perhaps even an element of 'man-made culture', to develop more relevant segmentation systems that will foster truly customer-oriented marketing activities?

Source: Adapted from Sekhon (2002)

The dynamic environment

The marketplace has never been as dynamic and muddled as we enter the twenty-first century. This dynamism is a result of great changes in the following:

- *The structure of markets.* Markets are becoming global and, as a result of deregulation and technological changes, there is a blurring between sectors and of the boundaries that define them.
- *The mobility of individuals and the great increase in global travel.* With global travel come global offerings and familiarity. At the same time, markets are also beginning to fragment into different mosaics and niches.
- *The growth of information technology and its impact on marketing.* The Internet heralded great changes in the growth and globalisation of information exchange in the 1990s and this is becoming embedded into organisational systems and procedures. Hot on the heels of the Internet is the growth of wireless communications, leading to faster customer communications both on a local and global scale.

- *The nature of marketing segments.* Market segments are no longer static. There are fundamental shifts in family structures, ethnic mixes and segments that straddle global boundaries.
- *Strategic alliances and networks between organisations.* Many more organisations now work on a collaborative basis, sharing research and development and new product development. Collaboration leads to a greater emphasis on branding.

The structure of markets

In the twenty-first century, organisations collaborate, compete or even act as customers and almost every organisation has these multiple roles. This is illustrated by the rise in the number of alliances taking place globally and the term 'cooptition' is now often used in marketing. The new economy is moving towards networks, partnerships and joint ventures. According to one study (Fountain and Atkinson 1998), social capital (networks, shared norms and trust that are fostered in collaboration and alliances) may be as important as physical capital (plant, equipment and technology) and human capital (intellect, character, education and training) in driving innovation and growth. These relationships not only create value but can also drive innovation.

As competition intensifies and markets become more complex, organisations are now beginning to embrace partnerships with suppliers, customers, universities, government bodies, research laboratories and other competitors in order to source new technologies and to innovate. The USA has led the way in this with a rapid growth in networks of organisations, through the creation of partnerships or consortiums. This has led to revolution within the US economy by the creation of technological innovations. While Europe and the USA had approximately the same number of industry technology alliances in 1985, alliances in the USA have since boomed, especially in the 1990s, while they have declined significantly in Europe and Japan (Figure 10.5).

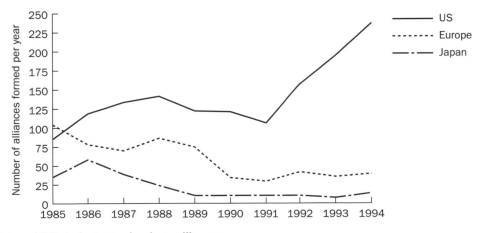

Figure 10.5 Industry technology alliances

Source: Fountain and Atkinson (1998)

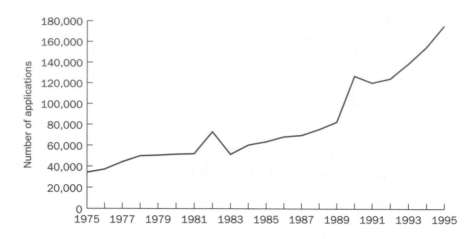

Figure 10.6 Trademark applications in the USA between 1975 and 1995

Source: Fountain and Atkinson (1998)

As already discussed, consumer segmentation patterns are changing and consumer choices are increasing. An important indicator of consumer choice is the number of trademarks that are registered. In the USA particularly, trademark applications have soared to their highest ever levels (see Figure 10.6). The public is informed of approximately 50,000 new products annually in the USA (McKenna 1997).

Intense competition means that technology-based products and services face increasingly short product cycles as new and better products come on stream regularly. The speed with which information can be transmitted and global competition have led to compressed product development cycles. According to a recent study, new US products now take 23 months to produce, on average, compared with 35.5 months in 1990. This is the much-heralded productivity revolution which shortens product development cycles. Information technology is a great driver of increasing efficiency, customisation of products and services, and speed of undertaking business. At the same time there is a blurring of industry sectors and services and examples of this are shown in Table 10.1.

Table 10.1 The blurring of industry boundaries

Old sectors	New sectors
Publishing (print)	Print/media/Internet/digital/information/TV
Telephony (land lines)	Wireless applications/Internet digital downloads/data transmission
Education (fixed locations)	Globalisation/Web-based interactive
Brewing	Leisure/entertainment/inns serving food

The future impact of technology

As the price of data transmission drops to very low levels, it is likely that most devices will contain data-transmission devices. Fridges will be able to transmit faults directly to the company so that repairs can be effected with the minimum of inconvenience to the consumer. Figure 10.7 illustrates how the price of data transmission is dropping dramatically as the price of transmission devices falls to a fraction of a cent, which is shown in Figure 10.8. This creates instantaneous global communication and means that organisations can track consumers and understand how and why they purchase certain goods. Companies such as Gillette have begun experimenting by creating 'smart shelves' in supermarkets and putting 'smart tags' on razors. The purpose of this is to speed up supply chains and to pre-

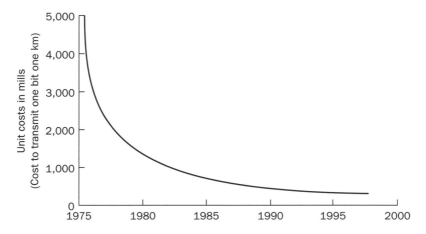

Figure 10. 7 Data transmission cost curve

Source: Fountain and Atkinson (1998)

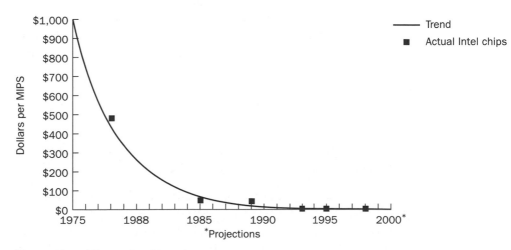

Figure 10.8 Microprocessor price curve

Source: Fountain and Atkinson (1998)

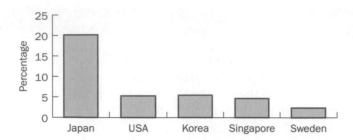

Figure 10.9 Percentage of mobile telephone users accessing the Internet
Source: National Research Institute, Japan (2002)

vent theft. Other benefits centre around customers, offering them better warranty, returned-goods services and enhanced customer relationships. In the end, the success of such developments (which would have been inconceivable even two years ago) will depend on consumer acceptance of an intrusion into their privacy (*Economist* 2003). In anticipation of this, Gillette will offer the option to disable the tags at the checkout counter. Currently the cost of 'smart' tags is estimated to be between 20 cents and 10 cents. If larger volumes are produced, the cost could drop to around 5 cents, which is a small additional cost on products ranging from luxury handbags to razor blades.

The rapidity with which mobile communications have been embraced by people all over the world indicates that humans wish to communicate continuously. This also creates many opportunities for marketers. The trends in Japan indicate how both the European and the American markets are likely to evolve. Figure 10.9 charts the percentage of mobile telephone users accessing the Internet in various countries in the world. Again the Japanese model leads the way – other countries are likely to follow.

As consumers are able to access information from anywhere, at any time, the ubiquitous consumer is beginning to emerge. Where technology was once the preserve of sophisticated consumers and business people, it is now firmly within the public domain. This change has major repercussions for marketers, as speed of communication and agility in providing goods and services at different locations become important. Figure 10.10 illustrates the changing nature of the Internet. The speed of communications and the ease with which consumers can be located and addressed create problems of security and ethics. It could be argued that ethics are likely to play an increasingly important part in marketing.

Ethics as a source of competitive advantage

Marketing practice is now integrating the potential of information and communication technologies through the utilisation of databases and Internet marketing. Billions of potential consumers can be reached this way. The discussion above on the use of smart tags also indicates the way customers could be located wherever they live. A brief observation of the practices of marketing on the Internet shows that

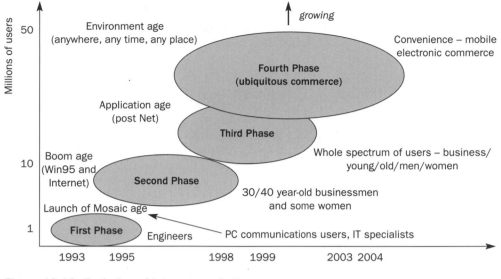

Figure 10.10 Evolution of Internet marketing

Source: Adapted from the National Research Institute, Japan (2002)

some organisations implement aggressive actions such as pop-ups, deceiving banners and hyperlinks, and other forms of intrusive mechanisms which impinge on personal privacy. As technology moves from desk-based PC applications to mobile communications, it has the potential to become even more intrusive, with the possibility of local tracking (within a 50-metre radius of a food or retail outlet, for example). Given that such powerful devices will become the norm within two to five years, organisations that wish to differentiate themselves from their competitors will have to adopt marketing ethics in order to gain and keep consumers. Short-term thinking will push organisations towards ever shorter campaigns and advertising plans, which will push them towards an unethical stance. This danger can be averted by organisations adopting a proactive ethical attitude towards consumers within their e-marketing strategies. To adopt such a proactive stance, organisations need to develop a model of ethical interactivity with consumers. Figure 10.11 illustrates the problems associated with intrusiveness when using different communication media.

Consumer information and privacy

Internet technology provides opportunities to gather consumer information 'on an unprecedented scale' (Kelly 2000). Some aspects of information gathering are visible (such as voluntary disclosure of information when purchasing a product, accessing a website and obtaining free merchandise) and some are less visible (such as anonymous profile data, Information Protocol, cookies). Many consumers remain hesitant about Internet purchasing because of possible uses and abuses of this information. The development of software facilitating a 'private Internet experience' and 'completely undetected surfing' is an indication of consumer concern about the invasion of privacy.

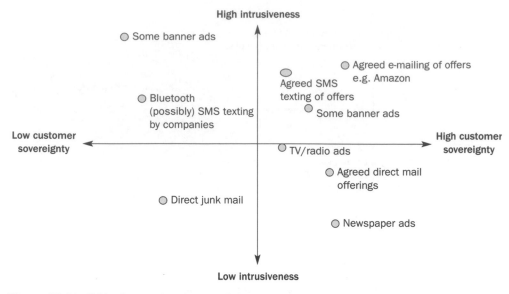

Figure 10.11 Ethical perceptual map of the current range of advertisements

Source: Gauzente and Ranchhod (2001) © Academy of Marketing Science

A survey of the top 100 commercial websites shows that only 20 per cent of organisations apply a full ethical policy. This shows that there is room for the development of competitive advantage (Culnan 1999a and 1999b). The reports show that five aspects can be used to assess a website's position concerning privacy:

1 *Notice*: are consumers notified about what information is collected, how it will be used and whether it will be disclosed to third parties, and about whether cookies are used or not?
2 *Choice*: are consumers asked if they agree with all aspects of the information being gathered?
3 *Access*: do consumers have access to the information gathered? Are they given the opportunity to review and correct the information?
4 *Security*: do the organisation's systems for information transfer and subsequent storage protect consumers' privacy?
5 *Contact*: are consumers provided with contact details so they can ask questions or register complaints regarding privacy?

Using information – the issue of marketing tools

Internet advertising is an important marketing tool which presents a range of possibilities for customer interactivity and involvement (Ranchhod 1998). Marketing professionals try to understand how individuals surf through websites so that they can attempt to increase the click-through ratio (CTR). Banner advertising has become an important vehicle for many Internet-based advertisements and much research is dedicated to its design elements. Researchers and practitioners try to identify key variables: type and size of banners, animation, use of colour, sounds, images, incentives, etc. (see www.bannertips.com). Certain features can be observed and are recommended as efficient, such as pop-ups, deceiving banners (computer-like messages with an 'OK' button). Here are some excerpts from advice given for designing an efficient banner:

- *Feature a call to action.*
- *Create urgency.*
- *Use the word 'FREE'.*
- *Certain truisms remain true – intrigue and sex sell.*

Parallel to Internet advertising, the development of e-mail marketing and spam are features of aggressive e-marketing. Organisations can, however, choose other paths and inform consumers that the organisation takes an ethical stance by creating and diffusing Internet ethical charts. The lack of ethical guidelines on marketing practices is deplorable (Chonko and Hunt 2000) but such a development and its diffusion to consumers will be critical in the future. Ethics can play a large part in the design of websites. Whether any practices should be banned on the Internet within a free society is, however, a moot point. Nonetheless, it is possible for organisations to exercise self-restraint and to develop personalised sites that depend on individuals' tolerance levels.

As Internet software becomes more sophisticated, it will be increasingly possible to tailor sites for individual ethical preferences. The seven criteria shown in Figure 10.12 could form the basis of creating and sustaining competitive advantage. This figure clearly illustrates that ethical marketing is critically associated with an

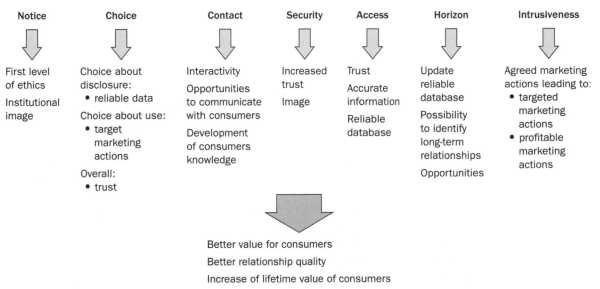

Figure 10.12 Ethical marketing criteria and competitive advantage

Source: Gauzente and Ranchhod (2001) © Academy of Marketing Science

organisation's long-term orientation. Advantages like image, trust, relationship quality and reliable and up-to-date database are representative of the goals of organisations with a long-term market orientation. An organisation that has a short-term orientation is likely to lose its competitive advantages in the long run to organisations that develop ethics as a marketing weapon for the consumer's benefit (Gauzente and Ranchhod 2001).

Social marketing

Social marketing means using social change-management mechanisms that involve the design, implementation and control of marketing communications aimed at increasing the acceptability of a social idea or practice to one or more groups of target adopters. It utilises concepts of market segmentation, consumer research, product concept development and testing, directed communication, facilitation, incentives and exchange theory to maximise the targeted adopter's response. These target groups may need to be advised about healthy living or the importance of being active in saving the environment. In the long run, this type of marketing communication needs to create a change of behaviour in individuals (Andreasen 2002). The social marketing approach should therefore entail :

- behaviour-change in the individuals who are targeted, for example stopping smoking;
- continuous market research, with market testing of intervention strategies and the monitoring of the success of these interventions;
- careful segmentation of target audiences to ensure maximum efficiency and effectiveness in the use of scarce resources;
- the creation of attractive and motivational exchanges with target audiences;
- an attempt to use all four Ps of the traditional marketing mix; for example, rather than just advertising or communications it should create attractive bene-fit packages (products) while minimising costs (price) wherever possible, making the exchange convenient and easy (place) and communicating powerful messages through media relevant to, and preferred by, target audiences (promotion);
- careful attention to the competition faced by the desired behaviour; for example, healthy eating may face challenges from fast foods and processed foods or from social behaviour within a particular group (see Table 10.2).

Marketers are also becoming aware of the positive impact that marketing actions involving a social dimension can have on organisations (Handelman and Arnold 1999). Increasingly, therefore, companies such as the Body Shop engage in 'enlightened capitalism' as they promote social causes through their brands, thereby enhancing brand image (Richards 1995).

Social marketing issues are likely to explode as issues surrounding health, the environment and other social aspects such as rural migration grow in importance

Table 10. 2 Possible collaboration of approaches to social marketing given the sources acting as barriers to action

Problem	Barrier	Role for social marketing	Role for community mobilisation	Role for structured change Approaches
Motivation	Individual	Creating awareness Promoting great benefits at a low cost	Urging media cooperation	Building web links to hard-to-reach individuals
	Community	Urging opinion leaders to motivate others	Creating awareness Raising public concern	Creating incentives for group organisation
	Structural	Urging change in structural rewards/penalties (e.g. taxes)	Holding briefings	Changing structural rewards/ penalties (e.g. taxes)
Opportunity	Individual	Creating awareness of behavioural opportunities	Urging business and political cooperation	Changing economic barriers to individual action
	Community	Urging businesses to provide access to change agents	Changing repressive social norms	Eliminating antitrust restriction on business cooperation
	Structural	Urging use of government facilities for programmes	Bringing pressure to bear on legislators	Providing government subsidies
				Changing physical environments
Ability	Individual	Providing modelling of ideal behaviour	Pointing group members to individualised change tools	Allowing government agencies to provide training
	Community	Providing communication tools for outreach	Conducting group training	Allowing government premises (e.g. schools) for group training
	Structural	Urging removal of public disincentives	Changing community structures	Removing public disincentives

Source: Andreasen (2002)

in the twenty-first century. Currently in Europe and the USA, the problems of over-consumption of food and the quality of food consumed by individuals are major social issues, as an overweight population places increasing burdens on health services. The case study below illustrates the possible impact that social marketing could have on behaviour patterns, mitigating the enormous marketing impact of major food companies.

When you have read the case study on page 210 answer the following questions:

1 *What are the key barriers to developing social marketing strategies for increasing healthy eating patterns within communities?*
2 *How could success be measured?*

Diet industry will be winner in battle of the bulge as Europe goes to fat

A tide of obesity will sweep Europe over the next four years and cause a boom in the diet industry as consumers try to get back into shape, market analysts said yesterday. The most serious weight problems will be seen in Germany where the proportion of people who are overweight or obese will increase from 57% last year to 71% in 2006. Problems of excess weight will affect 69% of adults in Spain and the Netherlands, 60% of Swedes and 59% of Italians. Although Britain and France will have weight problems, they will have more people who are underweight than obese. In Britain the proportion who are overweight or obese will increase from 48% last year to 52% in 2006. In France it will rise from 37% to 50%.

The forecasts were prepared by the market analysts Datamonitor on the basis of trends since 1996. Obesity was measured using a body mass index (BMI) to measure excess fat. The index divides the person's weight in kilograms by their height in metres squared. A BMI of 20–25 is normal, 25–30 is overweight and more than 30 is obese. Andrew Russell, the company's consumer market analyst, said the trend to excess weight followed 20 years of convenience foods and unconventional mealtimes. 'Modern diets are more calorific, yet people expend less energy during the day…Those who find themselves overweight and those who are keen to avoid being in that position are increasingly interested in using both exercise and diet to manage their shape,' he said.

The diet food and drinks market would increase from £51bn in 1996 to £61bn in 2006. The underweight were the least likely to take exercise, but people of normal weight were 'a good market segment as they display a strong desire to manage their shape and more willpower to apply the necessary changes to their lifestyle,' he said.

The overweight were the second most profitable group. They would continually try to make small changes to their lifestyle and diet without ever removing the underlying need to do so. This made them 'potentially lifelong customers. While both the normal weight and overweight consumer can oscillate between a desire for health and a desire for indulgence, the overweight consumer will do so with greater frequency – possibly even between lunchtime and dinner.' Mr Russell said people abstaining from alcohol because they were concerned about their weight or shape would cost the European drinks industry £3.2bn by 2006.

Children are 'eating themselves sick' with poor diets and unhealthy lifestyles, nutritionists warned yesterday during a conference at the Royal College of Paediatrics and Child Health in London. They suggested that postwar rationing was better for children than the 21st century snack culture. Youngsters today were experiencing the nutritional equivalent of the Victorian age when rickets and scurvy were commonplace.

Source: Carvel (2002)

Rural marketing

Allied to the interest in social marketing, rural marketing is also likely to play an important role in developing rural markets for the benefit of rural communities in the twenty-first century. A major proportion of the world's population lives in rural areas. However, with the advent of satellites (both mobile communication and television) it is possible to market goods and services to rural locations. At the same time, it is possible for individuals within rural communities to market their own products and services more easily.

Table 10. 3 Population breakdown by continent/region

Continent	1999 (millions)	2025 (millions)
Asia	3,588	4,725
Africa	778	1,454
Europe	729	701
USA and Canada	304	369
Australasia, South Pacific	29	41
Latin America, Caribbean	449	690

As populations increase around the globe, more consumers will enter the marketplace. A large proportion of these individuals will be living in isolated rural locations throughout the world. According to traditional marketing views, this market is generally regarded as being invisible and not very profitable (Mahajan *et al.* 2000). However, rural markets in countries such as India and China are huge and, as Table 10.3 shows, they are estimated to be even greater by 2025 as roughly 70 per cent of the population will live in rural locations.

These invisible markets are becoming increasingly significant to both small and large organisations. In spite of very low per capita income in large swathes of rural Asia, South America and Africa, the large numbers represent growing buying power, especially when families or groups of people team together to purchase large items such as televisions or computers. In addition, people from rural locations often migrate to cities and other countries to work and introduce new ideas and new consumption patterns to the rural locations when they return.

As the world increasingly shrinks in terms of communications, more and more products can be sold universally. At the same time, films set in rural China or India are important catalysts for change. Many multinationals are now beginning to see that the major growth area for consumption lies within the rural regions of the main continents. They are therefore developing different and more localised branding strategies for their products. In developing such strategies, it is useful to consider different approaches to marketing such as the following:

1 Developing products that meet market needs

Many rural markets need products which improve efficiency. For example, simple vehicles or scooters may be more appropriate in rural locations than large commercial vehicles to speed up the transport of goods or services. A rotovator rather than a tractor may be more appropriate for small farms in remote locations when factors such as cost and distance in relation to operation and maintenance are taken into consideration.

2 Understanding the 'informal' economy

Many rural transactions are undertaken informally and are therefore not included in a country's gross domestic product (GDP). This transaction method and the amounts involved need to be understood by marketers who are attempting to sell to rural markets. For example, the economist Friedrich Schneider estimates that the 'shadow' or informal economy may account for one-seventh of the output of the world's wealthiest nations and a much higher proportion of that of developing nations. According to these estimates, the shadow economy has been growing three times as fast as the formal economy since the 1960s. In India, in 1998, only 12,000 of the nation's estimated 900 million citizens admitted to earning an income of more than $28,000 per year – and only one in 77 people filed a tax return. Others estimate that India's unofficial economy may be as large as its national income (Mahajan *et al.* 2000).

3 Understanding the role of second-generation émigrés

In many countries in the world, particularly the USA, Canada and Japan and countries in Europe, there are large numbers of émigrés from the major rural areas of the world. The figures provided here show the differing population mixes in some of the major world economies: Figure 10.13 shows the percentage of the population of the USA by race and Hispanic origin (but not by country or origin); Table 10.4 shows the breakdown of the populations of the UK, France and Germany by ethnic group. This data indicates the growing significance of other races within the major Western economies. It also opens the door for developing marketing strategies for ethnic populations related to their countries of origin. For example, individuals of Hispanic origin in the USA are very likely to have close links with Mexico and other South American countries.

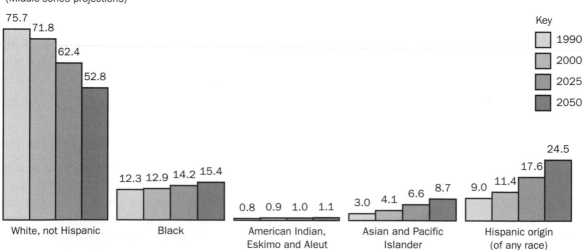

Figure 10.13 Percentage of the US population by race and Hispanic origin

Source: US Bureau of the Census (1998)

Table 10.4 Population of the UK, France and Germany by ethnic group

UK	Population (July 2000 estimate)		59,778,000
	Ethnic groups %	English	81.5
		Scottish	9.6
		Irish	2.4
		Welsh	1.9
		Ulster	1.8
		West Indian, Indian, Pakistani and other	2.8
France	Population (July 2000 estimate)		59,766,000
	Ethnic groups	Celtic and Latin with Teutonic, Slavic, North African, Indochinese, Basque minorities	
Germany	Population (July 2000 estimate)		83,251,000
	Ethnic groups %	German	91.5
		Turkish	2.4
		Other, made up largely of Serbo-Croation, Italian, Russian, Greek, Polish, Spanish	6.1

Source: Based on Central Intelligence Agency (2002)

The following case study illustrates that companies such as Unilever already understand the importance of rural markets and are beginning to blaze a trail in the adoption of new marketing strategies.

When you have read the case study, answer the following questions:

1 What are the key lessons for companies wishing to enter rural markets?
2 What segmentation techniques could be applied to rural markets?

CASE STUDY

Act local, think global

Hindustan Lever's strategic and marketing innovations have the potential to transform its business in India and to improve the quality of life of the country's rural citizens. Now the company is exporting those ideas to other parts of the world – from Indonesia to the Congo.

'Necessity is the mother invention.' That may be the most basic lesson behind Hindustan Lever's remarkable track record of innovation in rural India. When a giant company with a 30-year track record of growth suddenly confronts flat sales, it has two choices: Cut costs to stay profitable, or work harder to discover new ways to grow. The leaders at Hindustan Lever have opted for the second choice – and have identified India's hundreds of millions of rural consumers as a high-priority market. That's why every management trainee at Hindustan Lever begins his or her career by spending six to eight weeks in a rural village, eating, sleeping, and talking with the locals.

▶

Marketing executives make frequent two-day visits to low-income and rural areas. Managers at every level are trained in techniques for talking and listening to consumers. And scientists apply time and energy figuring out how to do more with less.

'We need to apply top-class science to solve simple problems at a reduced cost for the consumer,' says Dr. V.M. Naik, deputy head of Hindustan Lever's Research Laboratory in Bangalore, India. Naik, who spends about 70% of his time in the lab, was the primary scientist behind recent mass-market products, such as low-cost ice creams and low-cost soaps. The success of the soap process and others – like Hindustan Lever's marketing campaigns – started with a fundamental insight into consumers. Both researchers and marketers recognized that Indian women who wash clothes at a public tap or river often use the same laundry soap to wash their body. But the laundry soaps were typically too harsh for both skin and water. So researchers developed a lightweight laundry soap to double as a personal soap. Behind the product-concept innovation are manufacturing innovations. Lever labs and pilot plants are replete with manufacturing machines that its scientists built themselves – either because existing machines cost too much, or because the technology didn't exist to make products in the cost-efficient way that Hindustan Lever had designed. The new laundry soap, for example, uses a simple process to cast the soap immediately in the shape of a plastic package. The manufacturing process is an energy saver, too, because it doesn't convert the soap as many times – from liquid to tablet to bar – as other soap-making processes do. Lever built a machine for less, saved energy costs, and plans to pass on the savings to consumers.

Because Naik identified a different consumer need, he was able to develop a different process to meet that need. 'Technology that once liberated consumers can be a constraint for new innovation,' says Naik. 'New products require new principles.' His new principle: Reduce the load on the environment. That means using less detergent and fewer hydrogenated oils. The result? The company uses less than half of the current agricultural land usually required to raise oil seeds to produce soap. And fewer active ingredients mean less harm to the water supply. What's next on the innovation agenda, both for Hindustan Lever and its global parent, Unilever? To export the ideas and techniques that are unleashing growth in rural India to other parts of the world with similar strategic hurdles: language barriers, limited water and electricity, political instability, financial upheaval, barely motorable roads. Here are some examples of Lever's ongoing strategic ingenuity from around the world.

Nice product, but can you get it to market?

In the Philippines, a country composed of more than 7,000 islands, physical distribution can get expensive – when it's possible at all. And Unilever faces an additional market hurdle in that country, a former U.S. colony: a historical preference for buying American (read: Procter & Gamble). Unilever's response? Change the game. To lower the overhead cost of Surf laundry detergent, compared to P&G's Tide, sachets of Surf were distributed in jute rice sacks. The sacks were cheaper than cardboard and were more flexible for storage, and they kept the product dry. The company's local affiliate then focused on bicycle brigades as an inexpensive method of distribution. It designed a bicycle that could carry the heavy load of the bags and still be lightweight enough for someone to pedal to remote areas.

In tumultuous times, focus on fundamentals

The Congo is not anyone's idea of a stable, comfortable place to do business. But even in the midst of political upheaval in the Congo, 'people still need to wash their clothes and eat staple foods,' says John Miller, senior vice president for home and personal care for Unilever South Africa. Of course, people may eat only once every two days instead of every day, and they may well use detergent bars for both their clothes and their dishes. So instead of trying to move consumers into new or higher-margin products, Miller and his colleagues in the Congo focused on the fundamentals with radio ads that featured pitches for the most basic elements in Unilever's product line.

Want profits? Sell lots of small things

Nihal Kaviratne, the chairman of Unilever Indonesia who cut his teeth in India with

Hindustan Lever, wasn't shocked to find that 63% of Indonesia's 204 million people live in rural areas. So he borrowed from the company's prior success with sachets. 'Our whole business is built on low-dose sizes,' he says. But how could the company keep the sachets profitable? Although it's expensive to produce so many small units, the sachet material used in Indonesia is less expensive than elsewhere.

That means Indonesia gets the same profit margin on a plastic 6-milliliter sachet of shampoo as it does from a 50-milliliter bottle.

Source: Rekha Balu, Act Local, Think Global, *Fast Company*

(Rekha Balu is a Fast Company senior writer.)

Companies such as Coca-Cola are also vigorously embracing the rural markets by developing and selling smaller-sized bottles (Kripalani 2002). Apart from consumer goods, services like cellular phones and insurance are also growing. Cell-phone operators like Escotel Mobile Communications Ltd, a joint venture between Hong Kong investment company First Pacific and New Delhi-based Escorts Ltd, are finding new customers all over rural India. Fishermen in coastal Kerala in the south use the phone service to find the best prices for their catch, a practice that can earn them up to 50 per cent more. Escotel now controls 14 per cent of India's non-metro cellular market, providing service to 500,000 subscribers in 3,240 towns and villages. This enables local producers to market goods locally, adding to the growth of rural economies. In the twenty-first century, rural marketing is going to play an important role in the development of the world's poor communities. However, marketers will be walking a thin line between meeting real local marketing needs and the marketing needs of large multinationals wishing to expand their market base. A quote from the International Forum on Globalization underlines the position quite clearly:

> ... *roughly half of the world's people still live directly on the land, growing their own staple foods, feeding families and communities. They use indigenous seed varieties developed over centuries. They have perfected their own organic fertilizers, crop rotations and natural pesticide management. Their communities have traditionally shared all elements of the local commons, including water, labor and seeds. They have been exemplary in preserving the biodiversity necessary for community survival, and have fed local communities for centuries. But they are all under assault from the corporate industrial agricultural system.* (http://www.ifg.org/alt_eng.pdf)

In this respect, companies such as Hindustan Lever have tried to benefit both communities and corporate profits by working closely with rural self-help groups (SHGs). With the help of their project *Shakti*, SHGs have the option of distributing the organisation's products as a sustainable income-generating activity. The model hinges on a win-win relationship, with the SHGs engaging in an activity that brings sustainable income, while Hindustan Lever gets an interface for interaction with its customers (Kaul and Lobo 2002).

An alternative to this is the marketing model developed by Vandana Shiva (Mehta 2002). She has formed an organisation called Navdanya (Nine Seeds), based in Delhi. This organisation encourages farmers to produce hardy native varieties of crops that can be grown organically. The produce is then marketed through the farmers' own network. In this manner, local needs are met and marketing of the produce takes place through the network. Consumers benefit from a greater variety of produce. This initiative reflects the continuing battle between the globalisation and localisation of products and services in marketing.

Towards a new strategic marketing model

As explained in Chapter 1, organisations can adopt a number of marketing models. In this book, we have attempted to understand some of the key drivers of marketing in the twenty-first century. As a result of this, a new marketing model that takes account of the new realities is proposed (see Figure 10.14). This model takes into account the various points discussed in the preceding chapters. The model considers each of the elements discussed in this book, before developing organisation-specific strategies. The key issues to consider are as follows:

■ Understanding the role of strategic planning in delivering the marketing concept and the need to adopt a wider view of marketing strategy as discussed in Chapter 1. Organisations also need to consider various stakeholders and the key issues in developing mission statements.

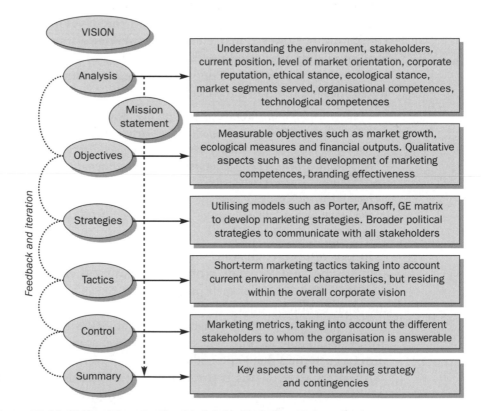

Figure 10.14 Strategic marketing model for the twenty-first century

- No strategies can be developed without a strategic analysis of an organisation's current position. In this respect, Chapters 2 and 5 contain important elements: Chapter 2 gives a comprehensive account of analytical techniques; Chapter 5 discusses the importance of brands and advertising strategies.
- In developing the overall strategy, an organisation needs to understand the nature of its stakeholders and its own approach towards them. Ethical and environmental issues need to be taken into account, as discussed in Chapters 3 and 4.
- The values and the learning abilities of organisations determine their ability to deliver customer-oriented strategies. In the twenty-first century, competitive ability is often determined by the speed with which organisations can learn and implement strategies. These issues are discussed at length in Chapters 6, 7 and 8.
- For most organisations, strategic success depends on the ability to measure performance in different directions. As there are differences from organisation to organisation, it is important that these measures are tailor-made for each, as discussed in Chapter 9. Measures should also take into account the ethical and environmental dimensions of marketing, which links back to Chapters 3 and 4.
- Finally, as technology changes and evolves, all marketers need to be able to make informed judgements about new and developing areas in marketing. Some of these aspects are covered in this chapter.

Each of these issues is covered within the boxes in the model shown in Figure 10.14. The model is not prescriptive as different organisations will have different emphases in terms of the markets they target and serve. It also incorporates the ethical and ecological stances that ought to become important aspects of an organisation's reputation and marketing communications strategy.

Summary and final observations

This and the preceding chapters lay the groundwork for understanding how marketing is likely to evolve in the twenty-first century. The world is changing fast and this must be reflected in marketing strategies. Technology, particularly the Internet, is playing a crucial role in bringing markets closer and mobile communications are making it easier for distant communities and individuals to communicate easily. Transparency in managing organisations means that greater emphasis needs to be placed on corporate governance and the role of stakeholders. Organisations must become increasingly concerned about the fragility of the planet and its eco-systems and develop products and services that minimise pollution and conserve energy.

At the same time, the profile of consumers is changing. In the rich nations, consumers are becoming more sophisticated and concerned about global issues; in poorer countries, consumers still have to be reached, but their marketing needs are very different, as illustrated in this chapter. Organisations have to consider how they develop relationships with their consumers and ensure that the way they are organised internally is effective. In marketing terms, organisations should not be judged by return on investment alone but by a wide range of measures, including ecological measures.

The old models of marketing need to be revisited and adapted to the needs of this century. Marketers must understand that pushing consumption is only one aspect of marketing and that meeting social and ecological needs is going to become more important as resources dwindle. Products and services with new localised marketing strategies are likely to benefit the consumer more than global standardisation. The era of responsible, customer-oriented marketing is dawning and marketers must embrace this. They have a range of tools available to them as a result of technological advances that have taken place.

There is great concern among most consumers about the degradation of the environment and the ethical stances taken by organisations. NGOs and consumers themselves are voicing these concerns openly. To work within this new order and to become truly customer oriented, this book attempts to show the wider context in which marketing operates and the ways in which customer orientation can be implemented.

Chapter questions

1 What role is technology likely to play in developing consumer tastes?

2 Discuss how flexible and responsive marketing strategies must be in the light of social and environmental changes.

References

Abell, D. F. (1978) 'Strategic Windows', *Journal of Marketing*. 42(3), 21–27.

Abell, D. F. (1979) *Strategic Marketing Planning: Problems and Analytical Approaches*. Prentice-Hall.

Ackoff, R. L. (1981) *Creating the Corporate Future*. London: Wiley.

ACNielsen (2001) 'ACNielsen finds 43 brands have a billion dollar global presence', http://acnielsen.com/news/european/2001/20011031.htm.

Alba, J. W. and Hutchinson, J. W. (1987) 'Dimensions of Consumer Expertise', *Journal of Consumer Research*. 13, March, 411–54.

Allenby, B. (1994) 'Industrial Ecology gets down to earth', *IEEE Circuits and Devices*. 10(1), 20–24.

Ambler, T. (1997) 'How much of brand equity is explained by trust?', *Management Decision*. 35(3–4), 283–92.

Ambler, T. (1998) 'Advertising and Profit Growth', *Admap*. May.

Anderson, S. and Cavanagh, J. (1996) *Top 200: The Rise of Global Corporate Power*, Washington DC: Institute for Policy Studies.

Andreasen, A. R. (1984) 'Life Status Change and Changes in Consumer Preferences and Satisfaction', *Journal of Consumer Research*. 2, December, 784–94.

Andreasen, A. R. (2002) 'Marketing social marketing in the social change marketplace', *Journal of Public Policy and Marketing*. 21(1), 3–13.

Andreasen, A. R. and Drumwright, M. E. (2001) 'Alliances and Ethics in Social Marketing' in Andreasen, A. R. and Drumwright, M. E. (eds) *Ethics in Social Marketing*. Washington DC: Georgetown University Press.

Anonymous (2000). The State of the World, Worldwatch Institute.

Argyris, C. and Schön D. A. (1978) *Organizational learning*. Reading, MA: Addison-Wesley.

Armstrong, A. and Hagel, J. (1996) 'The Real Value of Online Communities', *Harvard Business Review*. 74(3), 134–41.

Bacuvier, G., Peladeau, P., Trichet, A. and Zerbib, P. (2001) 'Customer Lifetime Value: Powerful Insights into a Company's Business and Activities', Booz Allen Hamilton. http://www.bah.com.

Bagozzi, R. P., Gopinath, M. and Nyer, P. U. (1999) 'The role of emotions in marketing' *Journal of the Academy of Marketing Science*. 27(2), 184–206.

Bailey, D. and Clancey, J. (1997) 'Stakeholder Capitalism via Socialism', *Renewal*. 5(2), 49–60.

Baker, W. E. and Sinkula, J. M. (1999) 'The synergistic effect of market orientation and learning orientation on organizational performance', *Academy of Marketing Science Journal*. 27(4), 411–27.

Barney, J. B. (1986) 'Organizational culture: can it be a source of sustained competitive advantage?', *Academy of Management Review*. 11(3), 656–65.

Barney, J. B. (1996) *Gaining and sustaining competitive advantage*. Reading, MA: Addison-Wesley.

Bart, C. and Baetz, M. (1998) 'The Relationship Between Mission Statements and Firm Performance: An Exploratory Study', *Journal of Management Studies*. 35.

Bartlett, C. A. and Ghoshal, S. (1992) Managing Across Borders: *The Transnational Solution*. London: Century Business.

Baumard, P. (1995) 'Des organisations apprenantes? Les dangers de la "consensualité"', *Revue Française de Gestion*. Septembre–Octobre, 49–57.

BBC News (2002) 'Black Tower Targets Comeback', http://news.bbc.co.uk/1/hi/business/1908934.

Bennet, M. and James, P. (1999) *Sustainable Measures: Evaluating and Reporting of Environment and Social Performance*. Sheffield, UK: Greenleaf Publishing.

Bergeron, F. and Raymond, L. (1995) 'The Contribution of Information Technology to the Bottom Line: a Contingency Perspective of Strategic Dimensions'. *Proceedings of the International Conference on Information Systems*, Amsterdam, 167–81.

Bergeron, F., Buteau, C. and Raymond, L. (1991) 'Identification of Strategic Information Systems Opportunities: Applying and Comparing Two Methodologies', *MIS Quarterly*. 15 (1) 89–103.

Berman, S. L., Wicks, A. C., Kotha, S. and Jones, T. M. (1999) 'Does Stakeholder Orientation Matter? The Relationship Between Stakeholder Management Models and Firm Financial Performance', *Academy of Management Journal*. 42, 488–506.

Berry, L. L. (2000) 'Cultivating Service Brand Equity', *Academy of Marketing Science Journal*. 28(1), 128–37.

Berthon, P., Pitt, L. and Watson, R. (1996) 'The World Wide Web as an Advertising Medium', *Journal of Advertising Research*. 36(1), 43–54.

Bhargava, M., Dubelaar, C. and Ramaswami, S. (1994) 'Reconciling diverse measures of performance: A conceptual framework and test of a methodology', *Journal of Business Research*. 31, 235–46

Bien, M. (2001) 'Ethical Investing, Even a Blue Chip Share Can be Green', *The Independent*. 25 February (Foreign Edition). UK.

Bishop, B. (1996) *Strategic Marketing for the Digital Age*. Toronto: Harper Business.

Boeker, W. (1989) 'Strategic Change: the Effects of Founding and History', *Academy of Management Journal*. 32(3), 489.

Bonoma, T. V. (1984) *Managing Marketing*. New York: The Free Press.

Bonoma, T. V. (1985) *The Marketing Edge: Making Strategies Work*. New York: The Free Press.

Bonoma, T. V. and Clark, B. H. (1988) *Marketing performance assessment*. Boston: Harvard Business School Press.

Boulding, W., Kalra, A., Staelin, R. and Zeithaml, V. (1993) 'A dynamic process model of service quality: from expectations to behavioural intentions', *Journal of Marketing Research*. 30, February, 7–27.

Bower, J. (1970) *Managing the Resource Allocation Process*. Homewood, IL: Irwin.

Brady, M., Saren, M. and Tzokas, N. (1999) 'The Impact of IT on Marketing: an Evaluation', *Management Decision*. 37(10), 758.

Bridges, S., Lane Keller, K. and Sood, S. (2000) 'Communication Strategies for Brand Extensions: Enhancing Perceived Fit by Establishing Explanatory Links', *Journal of Advertising*, Winter, 29(4).

Brown, J. (2001) 'Losses cut as Martin wins back M&S deals', *Daily Express*. 29 September.

Bruce, M., Leverick, F., Little, D. and Wilson, D. (1996) 'The Changing Scope and Substance of Marketing: the Impact of IT' in Beracs, J., Bauer, A. and Simon, S., (eds), *Proceedings of the European Academy of Marketing Conference: Marketing for an Expanding Europe*. 1, Budapest University of Economic Science, 185–204.

Buckley, P. J. and Casson, M. (1979) 'Going International: The Foreign Direct Investment Behaviour of Smaller UK Firms', in Mattsson, L. G. and Wiedersheim P. (eds) *Recent Research on the Internationalisation of Business*. Uppsala: *Proceedings of the Annual Meeting of the European International Business Association*.

Burgelman, R. A. (1983) 'Corporate Entrepreneurship and Strategic Management: Insights from a Process Study', *Management Science*. 29(12), 1349–64.

Burgelman, R. A. (1991) 'Intraorganisational Ecology of Strategy Making and Organisational Adaptation: Theory and Field Research', *Organisational Science*. 2, 239–62.

Cahill, D. J. (1997) *How Consumers Pick a Hotel – Strategic Segmentation and Target Marketing*. The Haworth Press.

Calori, R. and Sarnin, P. (1993) 'Les facteurs de complexité des schémas cognitifs des dirigeants', *Revue Française de Gestion*. Mars-Mai, 86–93.

Cameron, K. and Freeman, S. (1991) 'Cultural Congruence, Strength and Types: Relationship to Effectiveness', *Research in Organisational Change and Development*. 5, 23–58.

Cameron, K. and Quinn, R. E. (1983) 'Organisational Life Cycle and Shifting Criteria of Effectiveness: Some Preliminary Evidence' *Management Science*. 29, 33–51.

Campbell, A. and Yeung, S. (1991) 'Creating A Sense of Mission', *Long Range Planning*. 24(4), 10–20.

Carstairs, R. T and Welch, L. S. (1982) 'Licensing and Internationalisation of Smaller Companies: Some Australian Evidence', *Management International Review*. 22, 33–44.

Carson, C. and Ogle, V. E. (1996) 'Storage and Retrieval of Feature Data for a Very Large Online Image Collection', *Data Engineering Bulletin*, 19(4), 19–27.

Carvel, J. (2002) 'Diet industry will be a winner in battle of the bulge as Europe goes to fat', *The Guardian*. 31 May.

Central Intelligence Agency (2002) *The World Factbook 2002*. Washington, DC: U.S. Government Printing Office.

Cespedes, F. V. (1991) *Organizing and Implementing the Marketing Effort*. Reading, MA: Addison-Wesley

Chambers, J. (2000) 'Customer satisfaction at Cisco Systems', td Marketing Research, Inc. www.tdmktg.com/resources.html.

Chang, T. and Grub, P. D. (1992) 'Competitive Strategies of Taiwanese PC Firms in the Internationalisation Process', *Journal of Global Marketing*. 6(3), 5–27.

Charter, M. and Polonsky, M. J. (1999) *Greener Marketing: A Global Perspective on Greening Marketing Practice*. Sheffield, UK: Greenleaf Publishing.

Chonko, L. B. and Hunt, S. D. (2000) 'Ethics and Marketing Management – A Retrospective and Prospective Commentary', *Journal of Business Research*. 50, 235–44

Clark, B. H. (1997) 'Welcome to My Parlor', *Marketing Management*. Winter, 11–25.

Clark, N. et al. (1997) 'The Process of Internationalisation in the Operating Firms', *International Business Review*. 6(6), 605–23.

Clarkson, M. B. E. (1995) 'A Stakeholder Framework for Analyzing and Evaluating Corporate Social Performance', *Academy of Management Review*. 20(1) 92–117.

Clegg, S. R. (1991) *Modern Organisations: Organization Studies in the Post Modern World*. London: Sage Publications.

Clift, R. (1995) 'Clean Technology: an Introduction', *Journal of Chemical Technology and Biotechnology*. 62 321–26.

Coffey, J. J. and Palm, G. (1999) 'Fixing It in the Measurement Mix', *Bank Marketing*. 31(6), 24–29.

Cottrill, K. (1998) 'Out of the Lab and Onto the Table', *Journal of Business Strategy*. 19(2), 38–39.

Cova, B. (1996) 'What Postmodernism Means to Marketing Managers?' *European Management Journal*. 14(5), 494–99.

Coviello, N. and Munro, H. (1997) 'Network Relationships and the Internationalisation Process of the Small Software Firms', *International Business Review*. 6(4), 361–86.

Crawford, L. (2002) 'Sweet ambitions to tempt more takers', *Financial Times*. 16 July.

Crittenden, V. L. and Bonoma, T. V. (1988) 'Managing Marketing Implementation', *Sloan Management Review*. Winter.

Cronin, M. J. (1996) *Global Advantage on the Internet*. New York: Van Nostrand Reinhold.

Crosbie, L. and Knight, K. (1995) *Strategy for Sustainable Business: environmental opportunity and strategic choice*. Maidenhead, UK: McGraw-Hill Book Company Europe.

Croteau, A. and Bergeron, F. (1991/1998/2001) 'An Information Technology Trilogy: Business Strategy, Technological Deployment and Organisational Performance', *Journal of Strategic Information Systems*. 10, 77–99.

Culnan, M. J. (1999a) 'Privacy and the Top 100 Web Sites: Report to the Federal Trade Commission', McDonough School of Business, Georgetown University, http://www.msb.edu/faculty/culnanm/gippshome.html

Culnan, M. J. (1999b) 'Georgetown Internet Privacy Policy Survey: Report to the Federal Trade Commission', McDonough School of Business, Georgetown University, http://www.msb.edu/faculty/culnanm/gippshome.html

Czinkota, M. R. and Ronkainen, I. (1995) *International Marketing*. 4th edn. Fort Worth: The Dryden Press.

Das, S. R., Warkentin, M. E. and Zahra, S. A. (1991) 'Integrating the Content and Process of Strategic MIS Planning with Competitive Strategy', *Decision Sciences*, 22, 953–84.

Datamonitor (1999) 'Organic Trade Association and Datamonitor', Datamonitor's 1999 U.S. Organics Report.

Davenport, T. H. (1995) 'Marketing on the Internet. Journal of Targeting', *Measurement and Analysis for Marketing*. 261–69.

David, F. R. and David, F. R. (2003) 'It's time to redraft your mission statement', *Journal of Business Strategy*. 24(1), 11–16.

Davis, D., Morris, M. and Allen, J. (1991) 'Perceived Environmental Turbulence and its Effects on Selected Entrepreneurship and Organisational Characteristics in Industrial Firms', *Journal of Academy of Marketing Science*. 19, 43–51.

Day, G. S. (1994) 'Continuous learning about markets', *California Management Review*. Summer, 9–31

Day, S. G. (1986) 'The Evolving Role of Strategy Analysis Methods', in King, W. R. and Cleland, D. I. (eds) *Strategic Planning and Management Handbook*. NY: Van Nostrand-Reinhold.

Deloitte Research (2003) Creating Digital Loyalty Networks, http://www.dc.com/obx/

Deng, S. and Dart, J. (1994) 'Measuring Market Orientation: A Multi-factor, Multi-item Approach', *Journal of Marketing Management*, 10, 725–42.

Denis, J. and Depelteau, D. (1985) 'Market Knowledge, Diversification and Export Expansion', *Journal of International Business Studies*. 16(3), 77–89.

Deshpande, R. (1999) 'Foreseeing marketing', *Journal of Marketing*. 63(164), 164–70.

Deshpande, R. and Webster, F. E. (1989) 'Organisational Culture and Marketing: Defining the Research Agenda', *Journal of Marketing*. 53, 3–25.

Deshpande, R., Farley, J. and Webster, F. E. (1993) 'Corporate Culture, Customer Orientation, and Innovativeness in Japanese Firms: a Quadrad Analysis', *Journal of Marketing*, 57, 23–37.

Desreumaux, A. (1998) Théorie des organisations, Editions Management et Société Eds., Caen.

Dibb, S. (1998) 'Market Segmentation: Strategies for Success', *Marketing Intelligence & Planning*. 16(7), 394–406.

Dick, A. and Basu, K. (1994) 'Customer Loyalty: Toward an Integrated Conceptual Framework', *Journal of the Academy of Marketing Science*. 22 (April), 99–113.

Dickson, P. R. (1992) 'Toward a General Theory of Competitive Rationality', *Journal of Marketing*. 56, 69–83.

Dillon, W. R., Madden, T. M., Kirmani, A. and Mukherjee, S. (2001) 'Understanding what's in a brand rating: A model for assessing brand and attribute effects and their relationship to brand equity', *Journal of Marketing Research*. 38(4), pp. 415–29.

Dinjens, J. F. J. and Ligthart, J. M. (1982) *Revision of the Social Class Concept: Classifying Consumers: a Need to Rethink*. European Society for Opinion and Marketing, Brugge, Belgium: Research (ESOMAR). June 9–11.

Donaldson, T. and Preston, L. E. (1995) 'The Stakeholder Theory of the Corporation: Concepts, Evidence and Implications', *Academy of Management Review*. 20(1), 65–91.

Doyle, P. (2000) *Value-Based Marketing: Marketing Strategies for Corporate Growth and Shareholder Value*. Chichester: John Wiley & Sons.

Dru, J. M. (1997) *Disruption: Overturning Conventions and Shaking Up the Market Place*. New York: Wiley.

Drucker, P. (1974) *Management: Tasks, Responsibilities, Practices*. New York: Harper and Row.

Drummond, G. and Ensor, J. (2000) *Strategic Marketing: Planning & Control*. Oxford: Butterworth-Heinemann.

Dubost, N., Gauzente, C., Guilloux, V., Roussel, P. and Kalika, M. (2000) 'Franchise et culture managériale', Research Report to the French Franchise Federation, Paris. October.

Dyer, J. H. and Singh, H. (1998) 'The Rational View: Cooperative Strategy and Sources of Interorganisational Competitive Advantage', *Academy of Management Review*. 23(4), 660–680.

Economist (1993) 'America's Little Fellows Surge Ahead', 3 July. 59–60.

Economist (2003) 'The IT Revolution: The Best Thing Since the Bar-Code', 366(8310), 71–72.

EPA (1992) *Life Cycle Design Guidance Manual*. Environmental Protection Agency, EPA 600 1R-92/226, Cincinnati, USA, http//www.epa.gov

Farquhar, P. H. (1989), 'Managing brand equity', *Marketing Research*. 1, September, 24–33.

Farrell, O. C. and Lucas, G. H. (1987) 'An Evaluation of Progress in the Development of a Definition of Marketing', *Journal of Academy of Marketing Science*. 15, 12–33.

Fiol, C. M. and Lyles, M. A. (1985) 'Organizational learning', *Academy of Management Review*. 10(4), 803–13.

Firat, A. F. and Schultz II, C. J. (1997) 'From Segmentation to Fragmentation', *European Journal of Marketing*. 31(3/4), 183–207.

Flohr, T. (2000) 'IT: Know Thyself', *Intelligent Enterprise*, 3(8), http://www.intelligententerprise.com/000515/feat2.shtml.

Fomburn, C. (1996) *Reputation: Realising Value from the Corporate Image*. Cambridge, MA: Harvard Business School Press.

Fountain, J. E. and Atkinson, R. D. (1998) *Innovation, Social Capital, and the New Economy: New Federal Policies to Support Collaborative Research*. Washington, DC: Progressive Policy Institute, July, http://www.ppionline.org.

Frank, R. E. (1972) *Market Segmentation*. New Jersey: Prentice Hall.

Freeman, E. (1984) *Strategic Management: A Stakeholder Approach*. London: Pitman.

French, H. (2000) 'Coping with Ecological Globalization', *The State of the World*. Worldwatch Institute. New York and London: W.W. Norfton and Company. 184–211.

Frooman, J. (1999) 'Stakeholder Influence Strategies', *Academy of Management Review*. 24, 191–205.

Fuller, D. A. (1999) *Sustainable Marketing: Managerial-Ecological Issues, Industrial Examples*. Sage Publications Ltd.

Garnier, G. (1982) 'Competitive Export Behaviour of Small Canadian Firms in the Printing and Electrical Industries', in Czinkota, R. and Tesar, G. (eds) *Export Management*. NY: Praeger.

Gauzente, C. and Ranchhod, A. (2001) 'Ethical Marketing for Competitive Advantage on the Internet', *Academy of Marketing Science Review*. http://www.amsreview.org/articles/gauzente10-2001.pdf.

GEMI – Global Environmental Management Initiative (1993) *Total Quality Environmental Management*. Washington: GEMI.

Girod, M. (1995) 'La mémoire organisationnelle', *Revue Française de Gestion*, September–October, 30–42.

Grant, R. M. (2002) *Contemporary Strategy Analysis: Concepts, Techniques, Applications*. 4th edn. Malden, MA: Blackwell.

Greenley, E. G. and Foxall, G. R. (1997) 'Multiple Stakeholder Orientation in UK Companies and the Implications for Company Performance', *Journal of Management Studies*. 34(2), 259–84.

Griffith, D. A. (1998) 'Making the Web Strategically Accountable', *Marketing Management*. Summer. 41–49.

Groenewegen, J. (2000) 'European Integration and Changing Corporate Governance Structures: the Case of France', *Journal of Economic Issues*. 34(2), 471–79.

Gunter, B. and Furnham, A. (1992) *Consumer Profiles: An Introduction to Psychographics*. International Thomson Business Press.

Hakansson, H. (1982) *International Marketing and Purchasing of Industrial Goods: an Interaction Approach*. New York: John Wiley.

Hamel, G. (2000) *Leading the Revolution*. Boston, Mass: Harvard Business School.

Hamel, G. and Prahalad, C. K. (1989) 'Strategic Intent', *Harvard Business Review*. 67(3), 63–77.

Handelman, J. M. and Arnold, S. J. (1999) 'The Role of Marketing Actions With a Social Dimension: Appeals to the Institutional Environment', *Journal of Marketing*, 63(3), 33–48

Hannan, M. T. and Freeman, J. (1984) 'Structural Inertia and Organizational Change', *American Sociological Review*, 49, 149–64.

Hannis, M. (1998) *The Myth of Green Consumerism: Consumption, Community and Free Markets*, Lancaster University Mave Programme.

Hart, S. L. (2000) *Beyond Greening: Strategies for a Sustainable World. Business and the Environment*. Boston, MA: Harvard Business School Publishing.

Hatch, M. J. (1993) 'The dynamics of organizational culture', *Academy of Management Review*. 18(4), 657–93.

Hax, A. C. and Majluf, N. S. (1984) *Strategic Management: an Integrative Perspective*. Englewood Cliffs, NJ: Prentice Hall.

Helfer, J. P., Kalika, M. and Orsoni, J. (1998) *Management, stratégie et organisation*. 2nd edn. Paris: Vuibert Gestion.

Henderson, J. C. and Venkatraman, N. (1999) 'Strategic Alignment: Leveraging Information Technology for Transforming Organizations', *IBM Systems Journal*. 38(2/3), 472–84.

Highson, C. J., Ambler, T. and Barwise, T. P. (2001) 'Marketing Metrics: What should we tell shareholders?' *Market Leader*, Winter, 10–11.

Hill, N., Roche, G. and Self, B. (2001) Customer Satisfaction Measurement for ISO 9000: 2000. Butterworth, Heinemann. http://www.leadershipfactor.com.

Hof, D. R., Browder, S. and Elstrom, P. (1997) 'Internet Communities', *Business Week*. 5 May, 38–45.

Hoffman, D. L. and Novak, T. P. (1996) 'Marketing in Hypermedia Computer-Mediated Environment: Conceptual Foundations', *Journal of Marketing*. July, 50–68.

Hofstede, G. (1980) *Culture's consequences*. Newbury Park, CA: Sage.

Hofstede, G., Neuijen B. and Ohayv, D. D. (1990) 'Measuring organizational cultures: a qualitative and quantitative study across twenty cases', *Administrative Science Quarterly*, 35, 286–316.

Holstein, W. J. (1992) 'Little Companies, Big Exports.', *BusinessWeek*. 13 April, 70–72.

Homburg, C. H., Workman, J. P. and Jensen, O. (2000) 'Fundamental changes in marketing organization: the movement toward a customer-focused organizational structure', *Journal of the Academy of Marketing Science*. 28(4), 459–78.

Hooper, R. (2000) 'Internet Banking: Quick to Adapt to Technology', *Financial Times*. 20 December.

Hughes, G. D. (1981) *Marketing Management: a Planning Approach*. Reading, MA: Addison-Wesley.

Hutton, W. (1996) 'The 30/30/40 Society: the Economic and Fiscal Implications', Third Cantor Lecture on the Future of Work, *RSA Journal*. March, 32–6.

Ingold, P. (1995) *Promotion des ventes et action commerciale*. Paris: Vuibert.

Jawahar, I. M. and McLaughlin, G. L. (2001) 'Toward a Descriptive Stakeholder Theory: an Organisational Life Cycle Approach', *Academy of Management*, 26(3), 397–414.

Jaworski, B. J. and Kohli, A. K. (1993) 'Market Orientation: Antecedents and Consequences', *Journal of Marketing*, 57, July, 53–70.

Jenkinson, A. (2001) 'APRIL Takes a leaf out of the green book', *Pulp and Paper International*. 42(8), 19–21.

Johnson, G. and Scholes, K. (2000) *Exploring Corporate Strategy*. 5th edn. London: Prentice Hall.

Johnson, G. and Scholes, K. (2002) *Exploring corporate strategy: Text and cases*. London: Prentice Hall.

Jones, T. M. (1995) 'Instrumental Stakeholder Theory: A Synthesis of Ethics and Economics', *Academy of Management Review*. 20(2), 404–37.

Jones, T. M. and Wicks, A. C. (1999) 'Convergent Stakeholder Theory', *Academy of Management Review*. 24, 206–21.

Jung, C. (1923) *Psychological Archetypes*. London: Routledge and Kegan Paul.

Kalakota, R. and Robinson, M. (1999) *e-Business Roadmap for Success*. Canada: Addison Wesley Longman.

Kalika, M. (1995) *Structure d'entreprise – Réalités, déterminants, performance*. Paris: Economica.

Kaplan, R. S. and Norton, D. P. (1996) *Balanced Scorecard: Translating Strategy into Action*. Boston: Harvard Business School Press.

Karhammar, A. (2002) 'Knowledge: the holy grail?' Knowledge Management Special Report. Callan Publishing. http://www.connectweb.co.uk/special reports/knowledge/1/the_holy_grail.shtml

Karin, I. and Preiss, K. (2002) 'Strategic marketing models for a dynamic competitive environment', *Journal of General Management*, 24(4), 63–78.

Kassaye, N. (1999) 'Sorting Out the Practical Concerns in World Wide Web Advertising', *International Journal of Advertising*. 18, 339–61.

Kaul, S. and Lobo, A. (2002) 'Rural Thrust: Sluggish sales push FMCG firms to take new initiatives', *Business India*, 2–15 September, 88–89.

Keeler, L. (1995) *Cybermarketing*. New York: Amacall.

Kelly, E. P. (2000) 'Ethical and Online Privacy in Electronic Commerce,' *Business Horizons*. May.

Kerin, R. A., Mahajan, V. and Varadarajan, P. R. (1990) *Contemporary Perspectives on Strategic Market Planning*. Boston: Allyn and Bacon.

Kim, D. H. (1993) 'The link between individual and organizational learning', *Sloan Management Review*, Fall, 37–49.

Kitchen, P. J. (1999) *Marketing Communications: Principles and Practice*. London: Thomson Business Press.

Knapp, D. E. (1999) 'Brand Equity', *Risk Management*. New York, September, 46(9), 71–4.

Knight, G. A. and Cavusgil, S. T. (1996) 'The Born Global Firm: A Challenge to Traditional Internationalisation Theory' in Cavusgil, S. T. (ed) *Advances in International Marketing*. 8. London: Jai Press.

Knox, S. and Walker, D. (2001) 'Measuring and Managing Brand Loyalty', *Journal of Strategic Marketing*. 9(2), 1–18.

Koenig G. (1990) *Management stratégique – Vision, Manœuvres et Tactiques*. Paris: Nathan.

Kohli, A. K. and Jaworski, B. J. (1990) 'Market Orientation: the Construct, Research Propositions, and Managerial Implications', *Journal of Marketing*, 54, 1–18.

Komenar, M. (1997) *Electronic Marketing*. NY: Wiley Computer Publishing.

Kotler, P. (1998) *Marketing Management: Analysis, Planning, Implementation and Control*. (6th edn). Englewood Cliffs, NJ: Prentice Hall.

Kotler, P. (2000) *Marketing Management*. 10th edn. NJ: Prentice Hall.

Kotler, P. (2001) A *Framework for Marketing Management*. NJ: Prentice Hall.

Kotler, P., Armstrong, G., Saunders, J. and Wong, V. (2001) *Principles of Marketing*. 3rd European edn. Harlow, England: Prentice Hall.

Krantz, M. (1999) 'Online workers windfall could flatten investors', *USA Today*. 26 October.

Kreiner, P. and Bhambri, A. (1991) 'Influence and Information in Organisation-Stakeholder Relationships', in Preston, L. E. (ed), *Research in Corporate Social Performance and Policy*. 12, 3–36. Greenwich, CT: JAI Press.

Kripalani, M. (2002) 'Rural India, Have a Coke', *International Asian Business*. 27 May.

Kumar, B. (2002) 'Setting off a Chain Reaction', *Business Line–India*. 2 October.

Lannoo, K. (1995) 'Corporate Governance in Europe', *Working Party Report No. 14*. Centre for European Policy Studies.

Lawrence, P. R. and Lorsch, J. W. (1973) 'Adapter les structures des entreprises', *Les Editions d'Organisation*. Paris: Economie d'Enterprise.

Lawson, M. (2002) 'The life and death of a brand', *The Guardian*. July 1.

Lehni, M. (1998) *WBCSD project on Eco-efficiency Metrics and Reporting: State-of-play Report*. Geneva: World Business Council for Sustainable Development.

Lenskold, J. D. (2002) 'Marketing ROI: Playing to win', *Marketing Management*. 11(3), 30–34.

Levinthal, D. A. and March, J. G. (1993) 'The myopia of learning', *Strategic Management Journal*, 14, 95–112.

Levitt, T. (1960) 'Marketing Myopia', *Harvard Business Review*. 38(4), 45–56.

Lunn, A. (1982) 'Some Basic Principles and Recent Development', *Seminar on Classifying Consumers: a Need to Rethink*. Brugge, Belgium: European Society.

MacDougall, A. (1995) 'Tomorrow's Company? Feedback', *Renewal*. 3(2).

MacMillan, A. (2000) 'Genetically Modified Foods: the British Debate', http://cbc.ca/news/viewpoint/correspondents/macmillan_gmf.html.

Madsen, T. K. and Servais, P. (1997) 'The Internationalisation of Born Globals: an Evolutionary Process.', *International Business Review*. 6(6), 561–83.

Mahajan, V., Pratini De Moraes and Wind, J. (2000) 'The Invisible Global Market', *Marketing Management*, Winter, 9(4), 30.

Makower, J. (1994) *Beyond the bottom line:putting social responsibility to work for your business and the world*. Simon & Schuster.

Malhotra, S. and Mangrulkar, S. (2001) 'Branding in the last of unsaturated markets', *Design Management Journal*. Fall, 12(4), 53–58.

Malik, P. (2002) 'Adapt or Die', *Business Line–India*. 3 October.

Mazur, L. (2000a) 'Internet spin-offs show crisis within traditional brands', *Marketing*. 23 March, London, 20–21.

Mazur, L. (2000b) 'Meddling with a brand does not help manage it', *Marketing*. 24 February. London, 20–21.

McCullough, R. (2000) 'Marketing Metrics', *Marketing Management*, 9(1), 64–65.

McDonald, M. H. B. (1993) *Strategic Marketing Planning*. London: Kogan Page.

McKean, J. (2002) *Information Masters: Secrets of customer race*. John Wiley and Sons.

McKenna, R. (1997) *Real Time: Preparing for the Age of the Never Satisfied Customer*. Boston: Harvard Business School Press.

McKinsey and Co. (1993) *Emerging Exporters: Australia's High Value-Added Manufacturing Exporters*. Melbourne: Australian Manufacturing Council.

Mehta, D. (2002). Heroes: 'Vandana Shiva – Seeds of self-reliance', *Time*. 60(10) 32, 2 September.

Menon, A. and Varadarajan, P. R. (1992) 'A model of marketing knowledge use within firms', *Journal of Marketing*, 56, October, 53–71.

Miller, D. and Toulouse, J. M. (1986) 'Chief executive personality and corporate structure in small firms', *Management Science*. 32(11), 1389–409.

Miller, R. L and Lewis, W. F. (1991) 'A Stakeholder Approach to Marketing Management Using the Value Exchange Models', *European Journal of Marketing*. 25(8), 55–68.

Mintzberg, H. (1979) 'Patterns in Strategy Formation.', *Management Science*, 24, 934–48.

Mintzberg, H. (1987) 'The Strategic Concept 1: Five Ps for Strategy', *California Management Review*. 30, Fall, 11–24.

Mintzberg, H. (1990) *Le management*. Paris: Les Éditions d'Organisations.

Mintzberg, H. (1994) *The Rise and Fall of Strategic Planning*. NY: Free Press.

Mintzberg, H. and Waters, J. A. (1985) 'Of Strategies, Deliberate and Emergent', *Strategic Management Journal*, 6, 257–72.

Mitchell, R. K., Agle, B. R. and Wood, D. J. (1997) 'Toward a Theory of Stakeholder Identification and Salience: Defining the Principles of Who and What Really Counts', *Academy of Management Review*. 22, 853–86.

Mitroff, I. L. (1983) *Stakeholders of the Organisational Mind*. London: Jossey-Bass.

Moingeon, B. and Emondson, A. (eds) (1996) *Organizational learning and competitive advantage*. London: Sage.

Moorman, C. (1995) 'Organizational Market Information Processes: Cultural Antecedents and New Product Outcomes', *Journal of Marketing Research*. XXXII, 318–35

Müller-Heumann, G. (1992) 'Market and Technology Shifts in the 1990s: Market Fragmentation and Mass Customisation', *Journal of Marketing Management*. 8, 303–14.

Narver, J. C. and Slater, S. N. (1990) 'The Effect of Market Orientation on Business Profitability', *Journal of Marketing*. 54(4), 20–35.

National Science Foundation (1998) *Science and Engineering Indicators*, http://www.nsf.gov/sbe/srs/seind98/frames.htm.

NEETF/Roper Starch Worldwide (2000) *The Ninth Annual National Report Card on Environmental Attitudes, Knowledge and Behaviours*. NEETF/Roper Starch.

New Scientist (2001) 'Clean me a river', 171(2303), 17.

Noble, C. H. and Mokwa, M. P. (1999) 'Implementing Marketing Strategies: Developing and Testing a Managerial Theory', *Journal of Marketing*. 63(4), 57–73.

Nonaka, I. (1991) 'The knowledge-creating company', *Harvard Business Review*, November–December, 96–104.

Nonaka, I. and Konno, N. (1993) 'Knowledge-based Organization', *Business Review*. November–December, 41(1), 59–73 (in Japanese).

Nonaka, I. and Takeuchi, H. (1995) *The knowledge-creating company*. Oxford University Press.

Nordstrom, K. A. (1991) *The Internationalisation Process of the Firm*. Doctoral Dissertation, Stockholm, Institute of International Business, Stockholm School of Business.

Northedge, R. (2001) 'Slow decline of high-street champion', *Sunday Business*. 30 September.

Norton, R. (1994) 'Strategies for the New Export Boom', *Fortune*. 22 August, 124–32.

O'Connor, A. (2000) 'A short, sharp read', *Financial Times*. 19 December.

O'Connor, J. and Galvin, E. (1997) *Marketing and Information Technology*. London: Pitman.

O'Connor, J. and Galvin, E. (1998) *Creating Value Through E-Commerce*. London: Financial Times Management.

Oliver, R. L. and Swan, J. E. (1989) 'Equity and Disconfirmation Perceptions as Influences on Merchant and Product Satisfaction', *Journal of Consumer Research*. 16, 372–83.

O'Reilly, C. (1989) 'Corporations, culture and commitment: motivation and social control in organizations', *California Management Review*. Summer, 9–25.

O'Reilly, C. A., Chatman, J. and Caldwell, D. F. (1991a) 'People and Organizational Culture: A Profile Comparison Approach to Assessing Person-Organization Fit', *Academy of Management Journal*. 34(3), 487–516.

O'Reilly, C. A., Chatman, J. and Caldwell, D. (1991b) 'People and Organizational Culture: A Q-sort Approach to Assessing Person-Organization Fit', *Academy of Management Journal*, 34, 487–516.

Organization for Economic Co-operation and Development (OECD) (1997) *Principles of Corporate Governance*. Paris: OECD. http://www.oecd.org.

OTC Bulletin (2001) 'Loss of RPM leaves a stalemate in its wake', *Advertising Ideas Supplement*, 31 October, 2–3.

Ottman, J. (1993) Green Marketing: Challenges and Opportunities for the New Marketing Age. Lincolnwood, IL: NTC Books.

Ouchi, W. G. (1980) 'Markets, Bureaucracies, and Clans', *Administrative Science Quarterly*. 25, 129–41.

Oyewole, P. (2001) 'Social Costs of Environmental Justice Associated with the Practice of Green Marketing', *Journal of Business Ethics*. 29, 239–51.

Palmer, R. and Lucas, M. (1994) Formulating Retail Strategy in *The Retailing of Financial Services* edited by McGoldrick, P. J. and Greenland, S. J. London: McGraw-Hill.

Patron, M. (1996) 'The Future of Marketing Databases', *Journal of Database Marketing*. 4(1), 6–10.

Pearce, J. and David, F. (1987) 'Corporate Mission Statements: The Bottom Line', *Academy of Management Executive*. 1(2).

Peattie, K. (1995) *Environmental Marketing Management*. London: Pitman.

Peattie, K. and Charter, M. (1997) 'Green Marketing', in McDonagh, P. and Prothero, A. (eds) *Green Management: A Reader*. London: Dryden Press, 388–412.

Peattie, K. and Peters, L. (1998) 'The Marketing Mix in the 3rd Age of Computing', *Marketing Intelligence and Planning*. 15(2/3), 142.

Pelham, A. M. and Wilson, D. T. (1996) 'A longitudinal study of the impact of market structure, firm structure, strategy, and market orientation culture on dimensions of small-firm performance', *Journal of the Academy of Marketing Science*, 24(1), 27–43.

Peters, L. (1998) 'The New Interactive Media: One-to-one, But Who to Whom?' *Marketing Intelligence & Planning*. 16(1), 22–30.

Pettigrew, A. M. and McNulty, T. (1995) 'Power and Influence In and Around the Boardroom', *Human Relations*, 48(8), 845–73.

Pfeffer, J. and Salancik, G. R. (1978) *The External Control of Organisations: A Resource Dependence View*. New York: Harper and Row.

Pharoah, A. (2002) 'Image in the balance', *Financial Times*. 16 September.

Piaseckie, W. B., Fletcher, K. A. and Mendelson, F. J. (1999) *Environmental Management and Business Management: Leadership Skills for the 21st Century*. John Wiley and Sons.

Piercy, N. (1989) 'Marketing Concepts and Actions: Implementing Marketing-led Strategic Change', *European Journal of Marketing*. 24(2), 24–42.

Porter, M. (1985) *Competitive Advantage*. NY: The Free Press.

Porter, M. E. (2001) 'Strategy and the Internet', *Harvard Business Review*. March.

Power, C., Driscoll, L. and Bomn, E. (1992) 'Smart Selling', *Business Week*. August, 3, 46–48.

Preston, L. E. and Donaldson, T. (1999) 'Stakeholder Management and Organisational Wealth', *Academy of Management Review*. 24(4), 619.

Pulendra, S., Speed, R. and Widing, R. E. (1998) 'The emergence and decline of market orientation', *American Marketing Association*. Winter, 49–59.

Quinn, R. (1988) *Beyond Rational Management*. San Francisco: Josey Bass.

Quinn, R. and Rohrbaugh, J. (1981) 'A competing values approach to organizational effectiveness', *Public Productivity Review*. 5, 122–40.

Quinn, R. and Rorburgh, J. (1983) 'A Special Model of Effectiveness Criteria: Toward a Competing Value Approach to Organisational Analysis', *Management Science*, 29 (3), 363–77.

Ranchhod, A. (1998) 'Advertising Into the Next Millennium', *International Journal of Advertising*. 17(4), 427–46.

Ranchhod, A. and Gurau, C. (1999) 'Looking Good: Public Relations Strategies for Biotechnology', *Nature Biotechnology*, Europroduct Focus, Summer.

Ranchhod, A. and Hackney, R. A. (1997) 'Marketing Through Information Technology: From Potential to Virtual Reality', UK. Academy of Marketing. 1, 781–79.

Rand Corporation (2000) *Consumer Power and Green Consumption*. http://www.rand.org/scitech/stpi/ourfuture/Consumer/sec6_consumption.html.

Reichheld, F. and Sasser, W. (1990) 'Zero Defections Comes to Services', *Harvard Business Review*. September–October, 105–11.

Reid, S. (1984) 'Market Expansion and Firm Internationalisation', in Kaynak, E. (ed) *International Marketing Management*. NY: Praeger.

Remenyi, D., Money, A. and Twite, A. (1995) *Effective Measurement and Management of IT Costs and Benefits*. London: Butterworth–Heinemann.

Richards, A. (1995) 'Does Charity Pay?' *Marketing*. 21 September, 24–25.

Robinson, R. (1986) 'Some New Competitive Factors in International Marketing', in Cavusgil, S. T. (ed) *Advances in International Marketing*. 1. Greenwich: JAI Press.

Robinson, S. J. Q., Hitchen, R. E. and Wade, D. P. (1978) 'The Directional Policy Matrix – Tools for Strategic Planning', *Long Range Planning*. June.

Rogers, E. M. (1995) *Diffusion of Innovations*, 4th edn. New York: The Free Press.

Rohner, K. (1998) *Marketing in the Cyber Age: the Why, the What, and the How*. Chichester, West Sussex: John Wiley and Sons.

Root, F. (1987) *Entry Strategies for International Markets*. Lexington, MA: Lexington Books.

Rosenberg, L. J. and Czepiel, J. A. (1984) 'A Marketing Approach to Customer Retention', *Journal of Consumer Marketing*, 1, 45–51.

Roux, E. (1979) 'The Export Behaviour of Small and Medium Size French Firms', in Mattsson, L. G. and Wiedersheim-Paul, F. (eds) *Recent Research on the Internationalisation of Business*, Uppsala, *Proceedings of the Annual Meeting of the European International Business Association*.

Rowe, A. J., Mason, R. O. and Dickel, K. E. (1986) *Strategic Management*. Reading, MA: Addison-Wesley.

Rowley, T. (1997) 'Moving Beyond Dyadic Ties: a Network Theory of Stakeholder Influences', *Academy of Management Review*. 22, 889–910.

Ruekert, R. W. (1992) 'Developing a Market Orientation: an Organisational Strategy Perspective', *International Journal of Marketing*. 9, 225–45.

Rust, R. T., Zeithaml, V. A. and Lemon, K. N. (2000) *Driving Customer Equity: How Customer Lifetime Value is Reshaping Corporate Strategy*. NY: The Free Press.

Sashittal, H. C. and Tankersley, C. (1997) 'The Strategic Market Planning – Implementation Interface in Small and Midsized Industrial Firms: an Exploratory Study', *Journal of Marketing*. Summer, 77–92.

Saxe, R. and Weitz, A. (1982) 'The SOCO Scale: a Measure of the Customer Orientation of Salespeople', *Journal of Marketing Research*, XIX (August), 343–51.

Schein, E. H. (1983) 'The role of the founder in creating organizational culture', *Organizational Dynamics*, 12, 13–28.

Schein, E. H. (1992) *Organizational Culture and Leadership*, Jossey-Bass, 2nd edn.

Schein, E. H. (1992a) 'Organisational Culture', *American Psychologist*. 45, 109–19.

Schein, E. H. (1993) 'On dialogue, culture and organizational learning', *Organizational Dynamics*, Autumn, 40–51.

Scherpereel, C., Koppen, V. and Heering, G. B. F. (2001) 'Selecting environmental performance indicators', *Greener Management International*, 33 (Spring), 97–114.

Schlegelmilch, B. B. and Sinkovic, R. R. (1998) 'Marketing into the Information Age: CAN Incoming Goods Plan for an Unpredictable Future?' *International Marketing Review*, 15(3), 162–70.

Senge, P. M. (1990) 'The leader's new work: building learning organizations', *Strategic Management Review*, Fall, 7–23

SETAC – Society of Environment Toxicology and Chemistry (1998) 'Evolution and development of the conceptual framework and methodology of life-cycle impact assessment', http://www.setac.org/files/addendum.pdf

Shani, D. and Chalasani, S. (1992) 'Exploiting Niches Using Relationship Marketing', *Journal of Services Marketing*, Autumn, 43–52.

Sheth, J. and Sisodia, R. S. (1995) 'Feeling the heat: Making marketing more productive', *Marketing Management*. 4(2), 8–23.

Sheth, J. N. and Sisodia, R. S. (1999) 'Revisiting marketing's lawlike generalisations', *Academy of Marketing Science Journal*. Winter, 27(1), 71–87.

Sheth, J. N., Sisodia, R. S. and Sharma, A. (2000) 'The Antecedents and Consequences of Customer-Centric Marketing', *Journal of the Academy of Marketing Science*. 28(1), 55–66.

Shrivastava, P. (1983) 'A typology of organizational learning systems', *Journal of Management Studies*. 20(1), 7–28.

Simkin, L. and Dibb, S. (1998) 'Prioritising Target Markets' *Marketing Intelligence & Planning*. 16(7), 407–17.

Simms, J. (2000) 'Quest for Online Youth Credibility', *Marketing*. August.

Simpson, P. (1998) 'County open air "genetic testing site"', *The Daily Echo (Southampton)*, 14 April.

Sinkula, J. M. (1994) 'Market information processing and organizational learning', *Journal of Marketing*. 58 (January), 35–45.

Slater, S. F. and Narver, J. C. (1995) 'Market orientation and the learning organization', *Journal of Marketing*, 59 (July), 63–74

Spencer-Cooke, A. (1998) 'The true asset of the social bottom line', *The Tomorrow Exchange* (interactive video conference programme) Stockholm: Tomorrow Publishing.

Spender, J. C. and Baumard, P. (1995) *Turning troubled firms around: Case evidence for a Penrosian view of strategic recovery*. Academy of Management Annual Meeting, Vancouver.

SPOLD (1995) 'Synthesis Report on the Social Value of LCA Workshop', SPOLD/IMSA (obtainable from Procter & Gamble Services Company, Temsalaan 100, 1853 Strombeek-Bever, Belgium, (Fax +32 2 568 4812). Spold terminated its activities at the end of 2001. Its history may be obtained on http://www.spold.org/whatis.html.

St. John, C. H. and Young, S. T. (1995) 'Functional Coordination Within the Global Firm', *International Business Review*. 4(3), 341–54.

Stauber, J. and Rampton, S. (1995) *Toxic Sludge is Good For You: Lies, Damn Lies and the Public Relations Industry*. Monore, ME: Common Courage Press.

Steger, U. (1998) 'A Mental Map of Managers: An Empirical Investigation into Managers' Perceptions of Stakeholder Issues', *Business and the Contemporary World*. X(4), 579–609.

Stiles, P. (2001) 'The Impact of the Board on Strategy: an Empirical Examination', *Journal of Management Studies*. 38(5), 627–50.

Stinchcombe, A. L. (1965) 'Social Structure in Organisations' in March, J. G. (ed.) *Handbook of Organisations*. Chicago: Rand McNally.

Szymanski, D. M., Troy, L. C. and Bharadwaj, S. G. (1995) 'Order of Entry and Business Performance: an Empirical Synthesis and Reexamination', *Journal of Marketing*. 59(4), 17–34.

Tanner, J. F. (1996) 'Reengineering Using the Theory of Constraints', *Industrial Marketing Management*. 25(4), 311–20.

Tedlow, R. (1993) 'The Fourth Phase of Marketing', in Tedlow, R. S. and Jones, G. (eds) *The Rise and Fall of Marketing*. London: Routledge.

Tellis, G. J. and Golder, P. N. (1996) 'First to Market, First to Fail? Real Causes of Enduring Market Leadership', *Sloan Management Review*. 37(2), 65–76.

Thearling, K. (1999) 'Increasing customer value by integrating data Mining and Campaign Management software', *Direct Marketing Magazine*. February.

Thorelli, H. (1990) 'Networks: the Gay 90s in International Marketing', in Thorelli, H. and Cavusgil, S.T. (eds) *International Marketing Strategy*. 3rd edn. NY: Pergamon Press.

Tomkins, R. (2000) 'Fallen icons: Coca-Cola and McDonald's seemed ready to take over the world. But global branding has lost its appeal', *Financial Times*. 1 February.

USA TODAY.com (2002) 'Eminem music sales impressive despite music sharing', *The Associated Press*. 31 May. http://usatoday.com/life/cyber/tech/2002/05/31/eminem.htm.

U.S. Bureau of the Census (1998) Current Population Reports, Series P23–194, *Population Profile of the United States: 1997*. Washington, DC: U.S. Government Printing Office.

Usunier, J-C. (1999) *Marketing Across Cultures*. London: Prentice Hall.

Van Raaij, W. F. (1982) *Consumer Classification Based on Behavioural Measures. Seminar on Classifying Consumers: a Need to Rethink*. Brugge, Belgium: European Society for Opinion and Marketing Research (ESOMAR).

Venkatesh, A., Sherry, J. F. Jr. and Firat, A. F. (1993) 'Postmodernism and the Marketing Imaginary', *International Journal of Research in Marketing*. 10, 215–23.

Venkatramen, N. and Ramanujam, V. (1986) 'Measurement of business performance in strategy research: a comparison of approaches', *Academy of Management Review*. 11(4), 801–14.

Wagner, S. A. (2001) *Understanding Green Consumer Behaviour*. London and New York,: Routledge.

Walker, O. C. and Ruekert, R. W. (1987) 'Marketing's role in the implementation of business strategies: a critical review and conceptual framework', *Journal of Marketing*. 51 (July), 15–33.

Wasik, J. F. (1996) *Green Marketing and Management: a Global Perspective*. Cambridge, MA: Blackwell.

Webster, F. E. (1997) 'The Future Role of Marketing in the Organisation', in Lehmann, D. R. and Jocz, K. E. (eds) *Reflections on the Futures of Marketing*. Cambridge, MA: Marketing Science Institute.

Weick, K. E. (1987) 'Organizational culture as a source of high reliability', *California Management Review*. XXIX(2), Winter, 112–27.

Weick, K. E. (1995) *Sensemaking in Organizations*. Newbury Park, CA: Sage.

Weiss, M. J. (1994) *Latitudes and Attitudes: an Atlas of American Tastes, Trends, Politics and Passions from Abilene, Texas, to Zanesville, Ohio*. Boston: Little Brown and Company.

Wells, W. D. (1975) 'Psychographics: a Critical Review', *Journal of Marketing Research*. 12 (May), 196–213.

Wensley, R. (1981) 'Strategic Marketing: Betas, Boxes, or Basics', *Journal of Marketing*. 45 (Summer), 173–82.

What the Papers Say (2002) 'Big Brother a regular shopping item on the housemates' shopping lists', http://www.wtps.co.uk/news?aspdnid=14797.

Wicks, A. C., Berman, S. L. and Jones, T. M. (1999) 'The structure of optimal trust: moral and strategic implications', *Academy of Management Review*. (24) 99–131.

Wilkie, W. (1990) *Consumer Behaviour*. 2nd edn. NY: John Wiley and Sons.

Wilkie, W. L. and Cohen, J. B. (1976) 'An Overview of Market Segmentation: Behavioural Concepts and Research Approaches', *Marketing Science Report*. Cambridge, MA. 77–105.

Wirthlin Worldwide (2000) *Environmental Update*. 10(8), http://www.wirthlin.com/pdf/TWR0011.pdf

Wong, V., Turner, W. and Stoneman, P. (1996) 'Marketing Strategies and Market Prospects for Environmentally-Friendly Consumer Products', *British Journal of Management*. 7(3), 263–81.

Worcester, R. (1997) 'Public Opinion and the Environment', in Jacobs, M. (ed) *Greening the Millennium? The New Politics of the Environment*. Oxford: Blackwell.

World Wildlife Fund (2002) http://www.wwf.org.

Worldwatch Institute (2000) *World Watch*, 13, March/April.

Wundermann, C. J. (2001) 'Unlocking the True Value of Customer Relationship Management', http://www.Tcare.cl/CAM/pdf/27.pdf.

Wyner, G. A. (2002) 'Tracking an expanding universe', *Marketing Research*. 14(1), 4–8.

Yang, Z. and Jun, M. (2002) 'Consumer perception of e-service quality: From internet purchaser and non-purchaser perspectives', *Journal of Business Strategies*. 19(1), 19–41.

Yasumuro, K. (1993) 'Conceptualising an Adaptable Marketing System', in Tedlow, R. S. and Jones, G. (eds) *The Rise and Fall of Marketing*. London: Routledge.

Yorke, D. A. (1993) 'The Modified Index: a Technique for the Identification and Targeting of Market Segmentations', *Marketing Intelligence and Planning*. 11(4), 20–24.

Ziff, R. (1971) 'Psychographics for Market Segmentation', *Journal of Advertising Research*. 11(2), 3–9.

Zuboff, S. (1988) *In the Age of the Smart Machine*. London: Heinemann Publishing.

Index

Note: illustrations (Figures) and tables are indicated by *italic page numbers*, case studies by **emboldened numbers**.